# MANAGEMENT ACCOUNTING

Series editor
Brian Coyle

*PASSWORD* MANAGEMENT ACCOUNTING

First edition January 1990

ISBN 1 871824 11 7

Published by
BPP Publishing Ltd
BPP House, Aldine Place,
142/144 Uxbridge Road, London W12 8AA

Printed by Dotesios Printers Ltd, Trowbridge

A CIP Catalogue reference for this book
is available from the British Library

Copyright © 1990 BPP Publishing Ltd

# CONTENTS

|  | Page |
|---|---|
| Preface. | v |
| How to use this book. | vi |

| SECTION 1: NOTES AND QUESTIONS | Page | SECTION 2: MARKING SCHEDULES AND COMMENTS | Page |
|---|---|---|---|
| 1. Overheads and cost behaviour. | 3 | .................... | 149 |
| 2. Budgets. | 19 | .................... | 161 |
| 3. Budgetary control and standard costing I. | 35 | .................... | 172 |
| 4. Standard costing II. | 50 | .................... | 181 |
| 5. Decision accounting. | 61 | .................... | 189 |
| 6. Investment appraisal. | 84 | .................... | 205 |
| 7. Uncertainty and decision making. | 99 | .................... | 218 |
| 8. Performance measurement and transfer pricing. | 113 | .................... | 231 |
| 9. Joint products and process costs. | 131 | .................... | 247 |

| | Page |
|---|---|
| DCF tables. | 262 |
| Logarithm tables. | 264 |

# PREFACE

*Password* is a series of multiple choice question books on business and accountancy topics. If you are studying for an examination, or would just like to test your knowledge on one of these topics, Password books have two special features which are designed to help you.

**1** They contain about 300 multiple choice questions, with answers provided later in the book. You can get an objective idea of your strengths and weaknesses, and whether your standard is as high as you would like it to be.

**2** We explain most solutions in some detail, to show why one answer is correct and the others are wrong. Our comments should help you to learn from any mistakes you have made, and to improve your understanding of the subject.

Objective testing is an increasingly popular method of examination. An answer is right or wrong, and there are no 'grey areas' or 'in-between answers' that are half-right or arguably correct. Multiple choice questions (MCQs) are the form of objective testing that is now most widely used. Professional bodies that have adopted MCQs for some examination papers include the Institute of Chartered Accountants in England and Wales, the Institute of Chartered Accountants of Scotland and the Chartered Institute of Management Accountants. The Chartered Association of Certified Accountants has recently taken a first step in the same direction.

MCQs offer much more than exam practice, though. They test your knowledge and understanding. And they help with learning.

- The brevity of the questions, and having to select a correct answer from four choices (A, B, C or D), makes them convenient to use. You can do some on your journey to or from work or college on the train or the bus.

- We know from experience that many people like MCQs, find them fun and enjoy the opportunity to mark their own answers exactly.

- Being short, MCQs are able collectively to cover every aspect of a topic area. They make you realise what you know and what you don't.

If you're looking for the fun and challenge of self-testing, or preparing for an examination - not just a multiple choice exam - Password is designed to help you. You can check your own standard, monitor your progress, spot your own weaknesses, and learn things that you hadn't picked up from your text-book or study manual. Most important, Password books allow you to find out for yourself how good you are at a topic, and how much better you want to be.

*Good luck!*

Brian Coyle
January 1990

*PASSWORD.* MULTIPLE CHOICE

# HOW TO USE THIS BOOK

## Aims of the book

This book is designed:

- to develop your knowledge of Management Accounting through repeated practice on questions covering all areas of the subject. There are nearly 300 questions in this book.

- To enable you to assess your standard of knowledge or ability of Management Accounting by providing an objective test with these questions

- to explain any errors you are making, by means of comments and solutions to the questions

- to help with your revision of the subject by means of short chapter notes and comments to some of the solutions

## The multiple choice approach

A multiple choice question is in two parts.

- The *stem* sets out the problem or task to be solved. It may be in the form of a question, or it may be an unfinished statement which has to be completed.

- The *options* are the possible responses from which you must choose the one you believe to be correct. There is only one correct option (called the *key*); the other, incorrect, options are called *distractors*.

There are various ways in which you may be asked to indicate your chosen response. If you meet with MCQs in an examination, you should obviously read the instructions carefully. In this book, you will find that the options are identified by the letters A, B, C, D. To indicate your choice, draw a circle round the letter you have chosen.

## The notes

In Section 1 of this book each chapter begins with brief notes which are designed to refresh your memory of the subject area and get you thinking along the right lines before you begin to tackle the questions.

The notes are *not* a substitute for a textbook: Password assumes that you are already broadly familiar with the topics covered in the chapter. Nor do they give you answers to all the questions.

- The notes are a *reminder* of the key points in each topic area. If your studies have left you feeling that you can't see the wood for the trees, the notes may help to bring the important issues into focus.

- They provide brief *guidance* on particularly knotty points or areas which often cause problems for students.

## The questions

The questions are arranged roughly in the order of the key areas highlighted by the notes. But it is difficult, and undesirable, to keep topics completely separate: there's a great deal of overlapping.

The general principle has been for questions *on each topic* to get progressively harder. The result of this is that within a single chapter the level of difficulty will rise, and then fall back to begin rising again. So if you have trouble with two or three questions, don't assume that you have to give up on the whole chapter: there may be easier questions ahead!

Try to work through a whole chapter before turning to the solutions. If you refer to the marking schedule after each question you will find it almost impossible to avoid seeing the answer to the next question, and the value of the book will be lessened.

However, the length of each chapter is variable. Some are quite short, but others are very long. We have taken the view that there is no point in dividing up longer chapters into two just for the sake of making chapters shorter, and so some chapters contain about 40 questions (for example on decision accounting). In these cases you might decide to tackle the questions in a chapter in several different sessions, over a period of time, and check your answers at the end of each session.

Finally, don't rush your answers. Distractors are exactly what their name suggests: they are meant to look plausible and distract you from the correct option. Unless you are absolutely certain you know the answer, look carefully at each option in turn before making your choice. You will need a calculator and a pen, and paper for rough workings would be helpful, although you could use the blank space on each page for any rough workings that you need to do.

## The marking schedules

The marking schedules indicate the correct answer to each question and the number of marks available. You should add up the marks on all the questions you got right and compare your total with the maximum marks available.

At the foot of each marking schedule there is a rating, which is intended to be helpful in indicating the amount of work you still need to do on each topic. You'll need to use your discretion in interpreting your rating, though. The book may be used by a very wide range of readers, from non-accountancy college students and students of professional, business and accountancy courses, to qualified accounts personnel with years of practical experience. A mark of 10 out of 35 might be worryingly low for an experienced management accountant, while representing a very creditable achievement for someone at an earlier stage of his studies.

## The comments

The answers to purely factual questions generally need no explanation, but for most questions there is a commentary or a numerical solution, usually set out in some detail.

These comments will usually describe why a particular option is correct and (more commonly) set out the calculations leading to the correct answer. Distractors are usually chosen to illustrate common misconceptions, or plausible, but incorrect, lines of calculation. The comments will often highlight what is wrong about particular distractors and this should help in clarifying your ideas about topics that you may have misunderstood.

## Conclusion

Password Management Accounting is designed as an aid both to learning and to revision. It is not primarily aimed at those who are already expert in the subject. So don't expect to score 100%. And don't despair if your marks seem relatively low. Choosing the wrong answer to a question is not a failure, if by studying the solution and comments you learn something you did not know before. This is particularly relevant if you are using the book at an early stage in your studies, rather than in the final stages of revision.

And if you *do* score 100%? There are 14 other Password titles to get through...

# SECTION 1
# NOTES AND QUESTIONS

# CHAPTER 1

# OVERHEADS AND COST BEHAVIOUR

> This chapter covers the following topics:
> - Overhead allocation, apportionment and absorption
> - Marginal costing and absorption costing
> - Activity based costing (ABC)
> - Cost behaviour patterns
> - Learning curve theory

## 1. Overhead allocation, apportionment and absorption

1.1 Overhead allocation, apportionment and absorption are stages in the analysis of costs in an absorption costing system.

You should know about absorption costing from earlier studies of costing. Here are the key points.

1.2 Overhead allocation is the charging of whole items of overhead to cost centres. This can only be done with overheads which are direct costs of the particular cost centre. Overhead allocation is needed in a marginal costing system as well as an absorption costing system, in order to record expenditures in the cost accounts.

1.3 Overhead apportionment is used when it is not possible to allocate overheads directly to cost centres. The overheads are divided between cost centres in a way which reflects the benefit received. For instance, rent may be apportioned according to the floor space occupied by each cost centre.

1.4 The apportionment of service department costs may recognise the work done by service departments for each other - reciprocal services. The costs can be apportioned by the repeated distribution method, or with the use of algebra. There is a question in this chapter which will let you test your ability to deal with reciprocal services.

1.5 Overhead absorption is the process by which overheads are charged to individual cost units. It takes place once the allocation and apportionment procedures have determined the total cost centre overhead. The basic formula for the calculation of an overhead absorption rate is:

$$\text{Overhead absorption rate} = \frac{\text{budgeted total cost centre overhead}}{\text{budgeted level of activity}}$$

# 1: OVERHEADS AND COST BEHAVIOUR

1.6 When a choice exists as to which absorption base to use, then a time-based method is preferred. Absorbing overhead according to the time taken to produce a cost unit is likely to be more equitable, since most overhead costs increase with time.

1.7 Overhead absorption rates are calculated in advance, to be used throughout a particular period. This can mean that they turn out to be either:

- too high, so that overhead is over-absorbed, or
- too low so that overhead is under-absorbed.

1.8 Absorption costing information has relatively little value as management information for decision making, but has traditionally been significant mainly because:

- stock values are commonly based on full cost
- profits are reported by the absorption costing method
- occasionally, selling prices are fixed at full cost plus a percentage profit margin.

## 2. Marginal costing and absorption costing

2.1 Marginal costing systems use variable or marginal costs to value stock. Fixed production overheads are treated as period costs and are written off as they are incurred.

2.2 Marginal costing statements highlight the contribution for a period, which is the difference between the sales revenue and the variable or marginal cost of sales.

2.3 Under- or over-absorption of fixed costs cannot arise with marginal costing.

2.4 Absorption costing uses the fully absorbed unit cost, including fixed production overheads, to value stocks. To comply with SSAP9, the absorption rate must be based on the normal level of activity.

2.5 The profit figures produced from marginal costing and absorption costing systems will be different *but only* if there is a difference between the value of opening stock and the value of closing stock in the period.

> - If stocks increase in value, absorption costing profit will be higher than marginal costing profit, because there is an increase in the amount of fixed overhead carried forward to future periods
>
> - If stocks decrease, absorption costing profit will be lower, because fixed overhead is being released from stock to be charged against sales for the period.

## 3. Activity based costing

3.1 A fairly recent development in costing systems is Activity Based Costing, which rejects both marginal costing and 'traditional' absorption costing as inadequate costing methods in the modern manufacturing environment of high technology, flexible manufacturing systems, Just In Time techniques and relatively low labour costs.

3.2 ABC takes the view that many 'traditional' fixed overhead costs for support services, such as materials handling and despatch costs, set up costs, engineering costs and product design costs, are more properly regarded as variable in the long term. They do not vary with the volume of output, but rather with the size of the product range and the complexity, flexibility and variety of production. 'Cost drivers' can be identified for these costs. These are activities which 'cause' or 'drive' the support costs. In costing, overheads should therefore be charged to these cost driver activities, and then allocated to product costs on the basis of the use made by each product of the various support activities.

## 4. Cost behaviour patterns

4.1 The term 'cost behaviour' is used in management accounting to describe the way in which costs vary in relation to the level of activity. A cost behaviour graph shows, for any individual cost item, how either the total cost of the item or the cost per unit changes as the level of activity increases. Your knowledge of some of these is tested in the questions that follow.

4.2 The most common cost behaviour patterns are fixed, variable, and semi-fixed or semi-variable.

The fixed and variable elements in a semi-variable cost can be separated using linear regression analysis. The most common techniques are:
- scattergraph technique
- high-low method
- least squares regression analysis.

4.3 The high-low method is the most commonly used in management accounting examinations and it uses historical cost data for the analysis.

- If necessary, the effects of price inflation must be removed by adjusting the costs to a common price level.

- Next, two historical costs are selected:

    (i) The total cost of the highest activity level in the data available. Suppose this is Cost £$C_1$ for activity $Q_1$ units.
    (ii) The total cost of the lowest activity level in the data available. Suppose this is Cost £$C_2$ for activity $Q_2$ units.

|  | Activity level | £ |
|---|---|---|
| Highest activity | $Q_1$ | $C_1$ |
| Lowest activity | $Q_2$ | $C_2$ |
| Difference | $Q_1 - Q_2$ | $C_1 - C_2$ |

Since both cost figures contain the same fixed cost base, the difference ($C_1 - C_2$) must be caused by a change in the total variable cost.

Variable cost per unit = $\dfrac{(C_1 - C_2)}{(Q_1 - Q_2)}$

# 1: OVERHEADS AND COST BEHAVIOUR

## 5. Learning curve theory

5.1 With certain labour-intensive tasks which involve a complex set of repetitive activities, the work force may improve in efficiency with experience. This speeding up of a task with repeated performance is known as the learning curve effect and it may be possible to quantify the reduction in the required direct labour time for the task.

5.2 The cumulative average time per unit is assumed to fall by a constant percentage every time total output doubles. For instance, if an 80% learning curve applies, the *cumulative* average time to produce a unit falls by 20% for each doubling of the total output.

| Number of units produced | Cumulative average time (hours) | | Total time required (hours) | Incremental time for additional units (hours) |
|---|---|---|---|---|
| 1 | 100 | (x1) | 100 | 100 |
| 2 (80%) | 80 | (x2) | 160 | 60 (for 2 extra units) |
| 4 (80%) | 64 | (x4) | 256 | 96 (for 4 extra units) |

5.3 The learning curve can be expressed in a formula:

$$y = ax^b$$

$y$ = cumulative average time per unit
$a$ = time for first unit
$x$ = cumulative number of units
$b$ = the learning index

The learning index is given by:

*Method 1*

$$b = \frac{\log(1 - \text{proportionate decrease})}{\log 2}$$

For an 80% learning curve,

$$b = \frac{\log 0.8}{\log 2} = \frac{\overline{1}.903}{0.3010} = \frac{-0.0969}{0.3010}$$

$$= -0.322$$

*Method 2*

$$b = - \frac{\log \text{ of reciprocal of learning rate}}{\log 2}$$

For an 80% learning curve

$$b = - \frac{\log(1 \div 0.8)}{\log 2} = - \frac{\log 1.25}{\log 2}$$

$$= - \frac{0.0969}{0.3010} = -0.322$$

5.4 Learning curve theory can be used:

- to calculate the incremental cost of producing extra units
- to calculate selling prices for repeat orders
- to quote a realistic yet competitive price when tendering for major contracts, eg in aircraft manufacturing or defence equipment manufacturing
- to improve production scheduling and manpower planning
- to set realistic times and budgeted costs for control purposes.

1: OVERHEADS AND COST BEHAVIOUR

# QUESTIONS

**1** The production overhead absorption rate for Department P has increased to £15 per direct labour hour this year. Last year the rate was £10 per direct labour hour. Which one of the following factors is *least* likely to have contributed to this increase?

- A  A reduction in the level of activity due to a recession
- B  An improvement in the productivity of direct labour
- C  An increase in the level of mechanisation
- D  An increase in the rate of pay for direct labour

*Circle your answer*

A   B   C   D

**2** Bow Neidel Limited has three production cost centres, 1, 2 and 3, and two service cost centres, P and Q. The expenses of service cost centre P are charged out on the basis of the number of personnel in each cost centre. The expenses of cost centre Q are charged out on the basis of the usage of its services by each cost centre. Data for next year are as follows:

|  | Production cost centre | | | Service cost centre | |
|---|---|---|---|---|---|
|  | 1 | 2 | 3 | P | Q |
| Budgeted overhead | £72,800 | £28,960 | £54,310 | £20,000 | £48,000 |
| % of personnel | 23 | 28 | 21 | 10 | 18 |
| Usage of cost centre Q (hours) | 8,000 | 12,000 | 38,000 | 2,000 | - |
| Direct labour hours | 20,000 | 28,000 | 19,000 | - | - |

Overhead absorption rates are to be based on direct labour hours, taking account of the reciprocal services between the two service cost centres. What will be the overhead absorption rate per direct labour hour for Cost Centre 1?

- A  £4.27
- B  £4.82
- C  £4.91
- D  £5.08

*Circle your answer*

A   B   C   D

**3** Pitt Head Limited produces a single product and currently uses absorption costing for its internal management accounting reports. The fixed production overhead absorption rate is £34 per unit. Opening stocks for the year were 100 units, and closing stocks were 180 units. Cole Meinschaft, the company's management accountant, is considering a switch to marginal costing as the stock valuation basis.

If marginal costing were used, the management accounting profit for the year, compared with the profit calculated by the absorption costing method, would then be:

# 1: OVERHEADS AND COST BEHAVIOUR

A £6,120 lower
B £3,400 lower
C £2,720 lower
D £3,400 higher

*Circle your answer*

A  B  C  D

## Data for questions 4 and 5

Scent Packing Limited uses absorption costing for its management accounts. Profit and loss accounts for the latest years are as follows:

|  | Year 2 | | Year 3 | |
|---|---:|---:|---:|---:|
|  | £ | £ | £ | £ |
| Sales revenue |  | 128,000 |  | 128,000 |
| Opening finished goods stock | 20,000 |  | 36,500 |  |
| Full cost of production | 100,000 |  | 88,000 |  |
|  | 120,000 |  | 124,500 |  |
| Closing finished goods stock | 36,500 | 83,500 | 36,300 | 88,200 |
|  |  | 44,500 |  | 39,800 |
| Production overhead under-absorbed |  | 10,000 |  | 6,000 |
|  |  | 34,500 |  | 33,800 |
| General overhead |  | 14,300 |  | 14,300 |
| Profit |  | 20,200 |  | 19,500 |

The unit cost rates used for stock valuation in year 2 were identical to those used in year 1. In year 3 the fixed production overhead absorption rate was increased, in an attempt to eliminate the under-absorbed overhead. Actual fixed production overhead incurred in both years 2 and 3 was £30,000.

Dee Audrey Rant, the company's management accountant, is currently considering changing to a marginal costing system.

**4** The reported profit in Year 2, using marginal costing for stock valuation purposes, would be:

A £6,900
B £10,200
C £16,900
D £21,200

*Circle your answer*

A  B  C  D

8

# 1: OVERHEADS AND COST BEHAVIOUR

**5** The reported profit in year 3, using marginal costing for stock valuation purposes, would be:

A £6,900
B £10,200
C £16,900
D £21,200

*Circle your answer*

A    B    C    D

## Graphs for questions 6 - 11

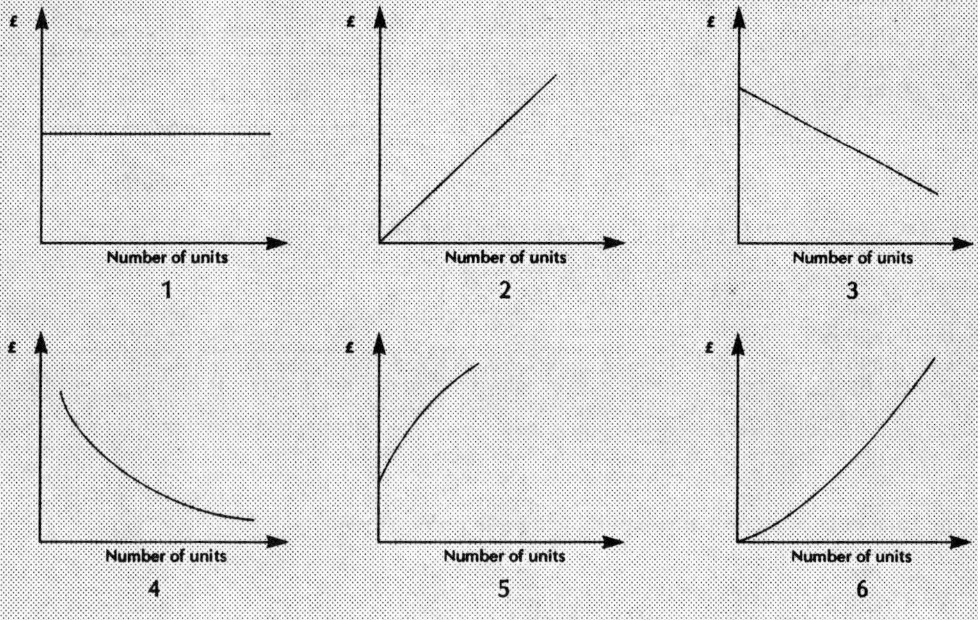

Which of the graphs best depicts each of the costs described in questions 6 to 11?

**6** A linear variable cost - when the vertical axis represents total cost incurred.

A Graph 1
B Graph 2
C Graph 5
D Graph 6

*Circle your answer*

A    B    C    D

# 1: OVERHEADS AND COST BEHAVIOUR

**7** A fixed cost - when the vertical axis represents total cost incurred.

- A   Graph 1
- B   Graph 3
- C   Graph 4
- D   Graph 5

*Circle your answer*

A   B   C   D

**8** A linear variable cost - when the vertical axis represents the cost per unit.

- A   Graph 1
- B   Graph 2
- C   Graph 3
- D   Graph 4

*Circle your answer*

A   B   C   D

**9** A fixed cost - when the vertical axis represents the cost per unit.

- A   Graph 1
- B   Graph 3
- C   Graph 4
- D   Graph 6

*Circle your answer*

A   B   C   D

**10** The total cost of a company experiencing a learning curve.

- A   Graph 2
- B   Graph 4
- C   Graph 5
- D   Graph 6

*Circle your answer*

A   B   C   D

**11** The total cost of wages paid on a piecework scheme, where the rates increase in small steps at progressively higher output levels.

- A   Graph 2
- B   Graph 3
- C   Graph 5
- D   Graph 6

*Circle your answer*

A   B   C   D

# 1: OVERHEADS AND COST BEHAVIOUR

**12** Cost forecasts are often based on data obtained from a linear regression analysis of past cost behaviour. Which of the following conditions should apply for such an analysis to be valid?

*Condition*
1. The level of activity must be the only factor affecting costs
2. There must be an underlying linear relationship between cost and activity
3. A narrow range of activity levels must be used
4. Past data must be a reliable indicator of future events

A  Conditions 1 and 4 only
B  Conditions 1, 2 and 4 only
C  Conditions 2, 3 and 4 only
D  Conditions 1, 2, 3 and 4

*Circle your answer*

| A | B | C | D |

**13** The following distribution costs have been recorded during the last five years by Jagger Naughton Ltd.

| Year | Volume (units) | Total cost £ | Average price index |
|---|---|---|---|
| 1 | 65,000 | 145,000 | 100 |
| 2 | 80,000 | 179,200 | 112 |
| 3 | 90,000 | 209,100 | 123 |
| 4 | 60,000 | 201,600 | 144 |
| 5 | 75,000 | 248,000 | 160 |

What will be the likely distribution cost in Year 6 when the expected activity level is 85,000 units and the average price index will be 180?

A  £165,000
B  £207,850
C  £297,000
D  £316,200

*Circle your answer*

| A | B | C | D |

## Data for questions 14 - 16

Some companies which regard product quality as a critical issue for their continued success have introduced 'quality cost' measurement schemes to support their efforts to achieve acceptable quality standards. Where quality costs are measured, they can be classified into four main groups.

*Group*
1  Costs of failure during production
2  Failure after production

*Group*
3  Costs of quality control
4  Cost of quality promotion and failure avoidance

# 1: OVERHEADS AND COST BEHAVIOUR

**14** Into which of these groups would the costs of quality standard setting and preparing quality reports belong?

A  Group 1
B  Group 2
C  Group 3
D  Group 4

*Circle your answer*

A    B    C    D

**15** Into which of these groups would the costs of operators' test equipment belong?

A  Group 1
B  Group 2
C  Group 3
D  Group 4

*Circle your answer*

A    B    C    D

**16** Into which of these groups would the costs of warranty work belong?

A  Group 1
B  Group 2
C  Group 3
D  Group 4

*Circle your answer*

A    B    C    D

## Data for questions 17 - 19

Burr Straw Termain Ltd uses a standard absorption costing system. Production overhead is absorbed into production at a standard rate per standard machine hour. The following data relate to the latest six periods:

| Period | Standard machine hours for actual production | Budgeted overhead for actual production £ | Total overhead absorbed £ |
|---|---|---|---|
| 1 | 4,270 | 9,198 | 8,967 |
| 2 | 4,930 | 10,122 | 10,353 |
| 3 | 4,650 | 9,730 | 9,765 |
| 4 | 4,180 | 9,072 | 8,778 |
| 5 | 4,730 | 9,842 | 9,933 |
| 6 | 4,860 | 10,024 | 10,206 |
|   | 27,620 | 57,988 | 58,002 |

# 1: OVERHEADS AND COST BEHAVIOUR

**17** The standard variable overhead absorption rate per standard machine hour is:

- A £1.20
- B £1.40
- C £1.80
- D £2.10

*Circle your answer*

A   B   C   D

**18** The budgeted fixed overhead per period is:

- A £294
- B £1,764
- C £2,100
- D £3,220

*Circle your answer*

A   B   C   D

**19** The activity level used for absorbing fixed overheads is:

- A 4,500 standard machine hours
- B 4,600 standard machine hours
- C 4,700 standard machine hours
- D 4,800 standard machine hours

*Circle your answer*

A   B   C   D

**20** In activity based costing (ABC), a cost driver is

- A an overhead cost that is incurred as a direct consequence of an activity
- B any direct cost element in a product's cost
- C any activity or product item for which costs are incurred
- D a resource-consuming activity that incurs overhead costs

*Circle your answer*

A   B   C   D

**21** Which of the following statements about the principles of activity-based costing (ABC) is *incorrect?*

*Statement*
1. Short term variable overhead costs should be traced to products using volume-related cost drivers, such as machine hours or direct labour hours worked.
2. Long-term variable production overhead costs are driven partly by the complexity and

13

## 1: OVERHEADS AND COST BEHAVIOUR

diversity of production work, as well as by volume of output.
3. Transactions undertaken by support department personnel are the appropriate cost drivers for long term variable overhead costs.
4. A cost centre should be established for each cost driver, such as the cost of set-ups. Overheads should be charged to these cost centres and then allocated to product costs on the basis of the number of transactions for each cost driver.

A  Statement 1 is incorrect
B  Statement 2 is incorrect
C  Statement 3 is incorrect
D  Statement 4 is incorrect

*Circle your answer*

A     B     C     D

## Data for questions 22 - 24

The following data relate to costs, output volume and cost drivers of Heighway Rubbery Ltd for June 19X1.

|  | Product P | Product Q | Product R | Total |
|---|---|---|---|---|
| 1. Production and sales | 3,000 units | 2,000 units | 1,500 units | |
| 2. Direct production costs | £ per unit | £ per unit | £ per unit | |
| Direct materials | 12 | 11 | 8 | £70,000 |
| Direct labour | 3 | 6 | 2 | £24,000 |
|  | 15 | 17 | 10 | £94,000 |
| 3. Labour hours per unit | $\frac{1}{2}$ | 1 | $\frac{1}{3}$ | |
| 4. Machine hours per unit | 2 | 1 | 2 | |
| 5. Number of production runs | 8 | 2 | 10 | 20 |
| 6. Number of deliveries to customers | 3 | 2 | 10 | 15 |
| 7. Number of production orders | 30 | 5 | 15 | 50 |
| 8. Number of deliveries of materials into store | 17 | 3 | 20 | 40 |

9. Production overhead costs

| | £ |
|---|---|
| Machining | 71,500 |
| Set-up costs | 10,500 |
| Materials handling (receiving) | 35,000 |
| Packing costs (despatch) | 22,500 |
| Engineering | 25,500 |
| | 165,000 |

Indirect production overheads that are not driven by production volume are:

| Item | Cost driver |
|---|---|
| Set-up costs | Production runs |
| Materials handling | Deliveries of materials |
| Packing | Deliveries to customers |
| Engineering | Production orders |

There were no opening stocks at the beginning of June.

# 1: OVERHEADS AND COST BEHAVIOUR

**22** What would be the full production cost per unit of product R if overheads were absorbed on the basis of direct labour hours?

A £13.75
B £23.75
C £30.00
D £51.25

*Circle your answer*

A    B    C    D

**23** What would be the full production cost per unit of product R if materials handling overhead were absorbed on the basis of direct material cost and all other overheads were absorbed on a machine hours basis?

A £17.94
B £25.82
C £37.64
D £40.00

*Circle your answer*

A    B    C    D

**24** What would be the full production cost per unit of product R using activity-based costing and the cost drivers described above, with overheads that are driven by production volume allocated on a machine hour basis?

A £21.80
B £40.27
C £51.17
D £53.27

*Circle your answer*

A    B    C    D

**25** Grey Matter Limited is considering the application of a learning curve in Department Y. Which of the following factors are likely to influence them *against* taking account of the learning curve in preparing price quotations?

*Factor*
1. Labour operations involve a complex set of repetitive activities
2. Labour is not a significant proportion of total cost
3. There is a high rate of labour turnover in Department Y
4. There may be a long time delay between successive orders

A Factors 1 and 4 only
B Factors 2 and 3 only
C Factors 3 and 4 only
D Factors 2, 3 and 4 only

*Circle your answer*

A    B    C    D

**26** Robin Jobbing Ltd is about to commence a job for a customer which involves making 4 units of a product. It is expected that a 90% learning curve will apply to the labour operations. Data for the product are as follows:

15

# 1: OVERHEADS AND COST BEHAVIOUR

Time taken to produce the first unit       100 hours at £6 per hour
Direct materials cost                      £500 per unit
Fixed cost per customer order, irrespective of size    £8,000

The average unit cost of producing the 4 units will be

A  £2,932
B  £2,986
C  £3,040
D  £3,364

Circle your answer

| A | B | C | D |

## Data for questions 27 and 28

Luffy Mee Limited is preparing a price quotation to tender for a contract, taking account of an 80% learning curve which is normal for its industry. The following data relate to a potential initial order of 200 units:

|  |  | Per unit £ | Per unit £ | Per unit £ |
|---|---|---|---|---|
| Direct materials |  |  |  | 150 |
| Direct labour | - department 1 | 20 |  |  |
|  | - department 2 | 180 | 200 |  |
| Variable overhead | - 10% of labour |  | 20 |  |
| Fixed overhead | - department 1 | 60 |  |  |
|  | - department 2 | 90 | 150 | 370 |
|  |  |  |  | 520 |
| Profit and general overhead - 10% of production cost |  |  |  | 52 |
| Selling price |  |  |  | 572 |

The managing director of Luffy Mee is Jay Louserock. He wants this contract to be treated as part of routine business, so that the contract must absorb an appropriate amount of fixed overhead and include a standard profit margin on budgeted full costs.

Department 1 is highly automated and its output is little influenced by operator efficiency. In contrast, output in department 2 is almost exclusively influenced by operator skills.

An 80% learning curve can be represented as follows:

| Output | Cumulative average time for elements subject to the learning effect % | Output | Cumulative average time for elements subject to the learning effect % |
|---|---|---|---|
| 1.0 | 100.0 | 1.6 | 86.1 |
| 1.1 | 96.9 | 1.7 | 84.4 |
| 1.2 | 93.3 | 1.8 | 83.0 |
| 1.3 | 91.7 | 1.9 | 81.5 |
| 1.4 | 89.5 | 2.0 | 80.0 |
| 1.5 | 87.6 |  |  |

# 1: OVERHEADS AND COST BEHAVIOUR

**27** The prospective customer is considering increasing the initial order to 300 units. If the order were increased to 300 units, what should be the Luffy Mee tender price per unit for this order?

A £454.16
B £501.07
C £532.72
D £536.29

*Circle your answer*

A    B    C    D

**28** Suppose the customer now decides that he cannot guarantee an order for 300 units. Instead he places a firm order for 200 units at £572 each, with a possibility of a second order for 100 units within a month. Assuming that the learning effect would still apply, what would be the appropriate price per unit to charge for the second order?

A £454.16
B £501.07
C £532.72
D £536.29

*Circle your answer*

A    B    C    D

**29** Ohm Works Ltd is currently quoting for a contract which is to be produced in Department P. Relevant data is as follows:

|  | Department P |
|---|---|
| Direct labour rate | £4 per hour |
| Production overhead - fixed and variable | £7 per hour |
| Estimated time for first 75 units of contract | 10 hours per unit |
| Capacity available per period, normal time | 3,000 direct labour hours |
| Current workload per period (excluding this contract) | 1,800 direct labour hours |
| Expected rate of learning curve | 70% |
| Overtime rate | Time and a half |
| Direct material cost of this contract | £30 per unit produced |

The company wishes this quotation to be treated as part of routine business, so that the contract must absorb an appropriate amount of fixed overhead. The overhead rate of £7 per hour includes no allowance for overtime premium.

In arriving at selling prices, the company adds 20% to total production cost. Any overtime premium that is incurred will be charged as a direct cost to the contract.

The original estimates were prepared for 75 units, but it now seems likely that the customer will increase the initial order to 300 units. The order is to be completed in a single period.

What price should be quoted for an order of 300 units?

A £100.68
B £102.84
C £114.26
D £128.40

*Circle your answer*

A    B    C    D

# 1: OVERHEADS AND COST BEHAVIOUR

**30** Plague Round Limited wishes to establish a standard time per unit of production for the forthcoming period. The standard will be used for cost control and for price quotations. The time taken for the first unit of production was 220 hours, and labour time on the product is subject to a 90% learning effect. The learning curve has been shown to follow the general form:

$$y = ax^b$$

where  y = average labour hours per unit
a = number of labour hours for first unit
x = cumulative number of units
b = the learning index

The cumulative production at the start of the period will be 190 units, and budgeted production during the period is 25 units.

What should be the standard time allowance per unit for the forthcoming period? (*Note.* You will need to use logarithms to answer this question).

A  83.2 hours
B  91.7 hours
C  97.3 hours
D  99.1 hours

*Circle your answer*

A   B   C   D

**31** Sumeroli Day Limited is aware that there is a learning effect for the production of one of its new products, but is unsure about the degree of learning. The following data related to this product:

Time taken to produce the first unit  = 28 direct labour hours
Production to date  = 15 units
Cumulative time taken to date  = 104 direct labour hours

What is the percentage learning effect? (*Note.* You will need to use logarithms to answer this question).

A  70%
B  75%
C  80%
D  90%

*Circle your answer*

A   B   C   D

# CHAPTER 2

# BUDGETS

> This chapter covers the following topics:
>
> - Preparation of functional budgets
> - Cash budgets
> - Fixed and flexible budgets
> - Zero base budgets

## 1. Preparation of functional budgets

1.1 A budget is a quantified plan of action that management will attempt to achieve in a given period of time - the budget period. Budgetary planning ensures that the organisation sets out in the right direction, with all of its activities co-ordinated. Budgetary control ensures that the organisation continues in the right direction:

- by the continual comparison of the actual results with the budget and the taking of control action if necessary

- or by comparing current (revised) forecasts with the original budget, and taking control action if possible.

1.2 Each functional budget has an effect on other budgets. No part of an organisation works in total isolation, therefore it is vital that the budgets are co-ordinated with each other. One of the best ways to achieve this co-ordination is through regular meetings of a budget committee. This committee consists of members of all parts of the organisation which are involved in the budgetary process.

1.3 The budgeting process will start with the identification of the principal budget factor, which is the factor that limits the organisation's activities. This is often sales demand, and once the sales budget has been prepared, the other budgets can be co-ordinated with it.

1.4 Remember that the production budget is not necessarily the same as the sales budget. The production planning process must take account of changes in budgeted stock levels for finished goods and work in progress.

## 2. Cash budgets

2.1 Cash budgets show the cash effect of all the decisions taken in the planning process. Decisions concerning stock levels, credit policies, fixed asset purchases, and so on will all affect cash. The cash budget will show any resulting surpluses and deficits so that management can decide whether the decisions need to be changed, or whether the cash effect is acceptable. They can also plan more effectively to cover any deficits or to invest any forecast surpluses, if they are forewarned about them.

2.2 A common error in preparing cash budgets in examinations is to include depreciation in the figures. Depreciation is not a cash flow and it must be excluded from cash budgets.

## 3. Fixed and flexible budgets

3.1 Fixed budgets are established for a single level of activity and they remain unchanged if the activity level fluctuates. Comparisons of actual results against a fixed budget can become meaningless if there are large fluctuations in activity. For instance, if activity increases above the level contained in the budget, it is not possible to tell from a fixed budget whether adverse variances are caused by the activity change, or by genuine over-spending.

3.2 Flexible budgets are designed to flex if the level of activity changes from that contained in the original budget, so that the flexed budget represents a more realistic target for the actual activity level achieved.

3.3 A pre-requisite of flexible budgeting is a knowledge of cost behaviour. If activity increases, a higher allowance will be given for variable costs, but the allowance for fixed costs will not change. The only time that increased fixed costs will be shown is when activity passes the level at which there is a step in the fixed costs.

3.4 The expected expenditure for each cost item at any level of activity is given by:

| Budget cost allowance = Budgeted fixed cost + ( Number of units produced × Standard variable cost per unit ) |
| --- |

## 4. Zero base budgets

4.1 Zero base budgets are designed to eliminate budgetary slack - unnecessary expenditure built into the budgets. They are most effective in areas of work where cost control through productivity measurements or standard costs is not feasible, eg for administrative work and other overhead costs. One of the main causes of budgetary slack is incremental budgeting, whereby last year's budget is used as the starting point for next year.

4.2 Zero base budgets start each budget from scratch. In outline, the zero base process is as follows.

- Each budget centre manager is required to prepare a 'decision package' for activities for which he or she has responsibility. The decision package will describe the activity and the benefit to be received from each different level of expenditure, to allow the manager to carry out incremental cost and incremental benefit analysis for each successive increase in activity level.

- Marginal activities for which the incremental cost exceeds the incremental benefit should be dropped from the budget.

- All of the different decision packages are collected together and are ranked using some form of cost-benefit analysis. The ranking will depend on management's judgement of the relative importance of each increment in activity level, taking into consideration the cost involved.

- The available resources are allocated in the budget according to the ranking of the different expenditure levels in the decision packages.

## 2: BUDGETS

# QUESTIONS

**1** Southsea Bauble Limited operates in a market which is affected by dramatic inflation and currency rate fluctuations. As a result the company is experiencing difficulty in establishing effective budgetary planning and control procedures. The main problem is that the budget managers have difficulty in forecasting costs and revenues with any degree of accuracy for more than three months ahead. As a result they doubt the usefulness of their annual budgets for planning and control purposes. Which of the following budgetary procedures would be most applicable to this company's situation?

A  Fixed budgets
B  Flexible budgets
C  Rolling budgets
D  Zero base budgets

*Circle your answer*

A    B    C    D

### Data for questions 2 and 3

Gould and Silver plc purchases a basic commodity and then refines it for resale. Budgeted sales of the refined product are as follows:

|  | March | April | May | June |
|---|---|---|---|---|
| Sales in kg | 9,000 | 9,000 | 8,000 | 7,000 |

Other relevant data:

(i)   The basic raw material cost is £3 per kg purchased.
(ii)  Material losses are 10% of finished output.
(iii) Material suppliers are paid 20% in the month of purchase and 80% in the month following purchase.
(iv)  The target month-end raw material stock level is 5,000 kg plus 25% of the raw materials required for next month's budgeted production.
(v)   The target month-end stock level for finished goods is 6,000 kg plus 25% of next month's budgeted sales.

**2** What are the budgeted raw material purchases for April?

A  8,500 kg
B  9,350 kg
C  9,444.25 kg
D  9,831.25 kg

*Circle your answer*

A    B    C    D

## 2: BUDGETS

**3** What are the budgeted payments in April to suppliers of raw material?

    A  £26,550
    B  £27,305
    C  £27,990
    D  £29,205

*Circle your answer*

| A | B | C | D |

**4** Which of the following factors affect cash flow, but are *not* included in the profit and loss account?

*Factor*
1. Funds from the issue of share capital
2. Revaluation of a fixed asset
3. Decrease in the level of trade debtors
4. Repayment of a bank loan

    A  Factors 1 and 4 only
    B  Factors 2 and 4 only
    C  Factors 1, 2 and 3 only
    D  Factors 1, 3 and 4 only

*Circle your answer*

| A | B | C | D |

### Data for questions 5 - 7

Haver Drift Limited is currently preparing its cash budget for the next quarter. The accountant has produced the following forecasts:

|  | January £ | February £ | March £ |
|---|---|---|---|
| Sales | 75,000 | 80,000 | 65,000 |
|  |  |  |  |
| Cost of production | 56,920 | 62,180 | 49,120 |
| Stock adjustment | 2,530 | 1,680 | (500) |
| Cost of sales | 59,450 | 63,860 | 48,620 |
| Selling and distribution costs | 5,875 | 6,000 | 5,625 |
| Administration costs | 4,900 | 5,100 | 5,000 |
|  | 70,225 | 74,960 | 59,245 |
|  |  |  |  |
| Profit | 4,775 | 5,040 | 5,755 |

*Notes*

(i) Monthly fixed production overhead amounts to £15,000 and it is treated as a period cost. £3,000 of this represents depreciation on production machinery. All fixed production overhead is paid in the month it is incurred.

23

## 2: BUDGETS

(ii) Material costs account for 30% of the variable production cost. The material required for each month's production is purchased in the preceding month. Suppliers are paid 50% in the month of purchase and 50% in the following month.

(iii) The remaining variable production costs are paid as they are incurred.

(iv) 20% of the fixed selling and distribution costs represents depreciation of delivery vehicles. The remaining cost is paid as it is incurred.

(v) Administration costs include monthly depreciation of £500. The remainder is paid as it is incurred.

(vi) 20% of customers pay immediately and receive a 3% prompt payment discount. The remainder settle in the month following the sale.

(vii) The cash balance at the end of January will be £4,820.

**5** What are the budgeted payments to material suppliers in February?

A £12,915
B £12,372
C £14,222
D £16,695

*Circle your answer*

A    B    C    D

**6** What is the budgeted cash payment for selling and distribution costs in March?

A £4,500
B £4,800
C £4,825
D £6,000

*Circle your answer*

A    B    C    D

**7** What is the budgeted cash balance at the end of February?

A £9,019
B £11,519
C £13,319
D £13,799

*Circle your answer*

A    B    C    D

## 2: BUDGETS

### Data for questions 8 - 10

Ben Clone Limited is currently planning the schedule of payments to material suppliers. All suppliers grant one month's credit and up to 25% of purchases attract a 4% discount if paid for immediately on purchase.

Company policy is to take as much of the discount as possible, as long as this action does not directly result in the month-end cash balance falling below £2,500.

For purchases on which Ben Clone Ltd is not able to take discount, the company pays in the month after purchase, using overdraft facilities if necessary. No discount will be taken on the £5,800 purchases made in August. Relevant budgeted data is as follows:

|  | September £ | October £ | November £ |
|---|---|---|---|
| Material purchases | 5,900 | 6,200 | 6,000 |
| Net cash inflow/(outflow), excluding payments to material suppliers | 12,420 | 281 | (2,490) |
| Opening cash balance | 2,400 | | |

**8** What are the budgeted payments to material suppliers in September?

A £5,841
B £6,984
C £7,216
D £7,275

*Circle your answer*

A   B   C   D

**9** What are the budgeted payments to material suppliers in October?

A £5,385
B £5,425
C £5,444
D £5,695

*Circle your answer*

A   B   C   D

## 2: BUDGETS

**10** What is the budgeted overdraft at the end of November?

A £5,080
B £5,190
C £5,230
D £5,260

*Circle your answer*

A   B   C   D

### Data for questions 11 and 12

Extracts from the budgeted balance sheet for Owen Money plc as at the end of year 2 are as follows:

Trade debtors            £612,500
Trade creditors          £160,000

You are informed that:

(i) debtors are allowed two months to pay;
(ii) sales in November were 75% of sales in December;
(iii) creditors allow 1½ months' credit;
(iv) purchases in November were double the level of purchases in December. Purchases are made evenly throughout the month.

**11** What are the budgeted receipts from debtors in January, Year 3?

A £262,500
B £284,200
C £306,250
D £350,000

*Circle your answer*

A   B   C   D

**12** What are the budgeted payments to suppliers in January, Year 3?

A £80,000
B £100,000
C £120,000
D £140,000

*Circle your answer*

A   B   C   D

## 2: BUDGETS

### Data for questions 13 and 14

Tryal Ottmore Limited is about to commence production of a new product. Because of doubt about the long term prospects, the company wishes to keep the permanent labour force employed for this product as low as possible. A trade union agreement states that overtime hours must not exceed 15% of the basic paid hours in any 4-week period, and overtime is paid at time and a half.

The basic week is 40 hours and the budgeted wage rate is £4 per hour. All non-productive hours are paid at the basic rate. Other wages costs amount to £16 per week for each employee. Expected output levels are 0.7 standard hours of output for each hour of attendance; the balance of time is lost through production delays and inefficiencies.

Paid absence for sickness and holidays is expected to vary in each period. Standard hours of production and expected paid absence for the first six months are budgeted as follows:

| Period | Standard hours of production | Paid absence - % of paid hours, including overtime hours |
|--------|------------------------------|----------------------------------------------------------|
| 1 | 10,090.5 | 7 |
| 2 | 9,765.0 | 7 |
| 3 | 9,569.7 | 7 |
| 4 | 9,937.2 | 9 |
| 5 | 9,809.8 | 9 |
| 6 | 9,576.0 | 10 |

**13** What is the *minimum* number of employees that should be included in the manpower budget?

A 82
B 83
C 84
D 85

*Circle your answer*

A  B  C  **D**

**14** What labour cost will be shown in the manpower budget for the first six periods?

A £385,200
B £398,240
C £412,980
D £417,840

*Circle your answer*

A  B  C  **D**

27

## 2: BUDGETS

**15** What is a flexible budget?

A   A budget which is prepared using an adaptive process, taking into consideration the different aspiration levels of the budget managers responsible for its achievement

B   A budget which is continually extended and updated to allow for changes in costs and revenues which have rendered the original budget out of date

C   A budget which is designed to enable variable and fixed costs to be identified separately, so that the budget can be changed if there are fluctuations in output, turnover or other activity-related factors.

D   A budget which is prepared through careful co-ordination of all the subsidiary functional budgets, each function adapting to the requirements of other functions affected by its activities.

*Circle your answer*

A   B   C   D

**16** Extracts from flexible budgets prepared by Custer Lyons Limited are as follows:

| | | |
|---|---:|---:|
| Sales units | 5,000 | 7,000 |
| Production units | 6,000 | 7,500 |
| | | |
| *Budget cost allowance* | £'000 | £'000 |
| Direct materials | 60 | 75 |
| Production direct labour | 51 | 60 |
| Production overheads | 49 | 55 |
| Administration costs | 20 | 20 |
| Selling and distribution costs | <u>28.5</u> | <u>37.5</u> |
| Total cost allowance | <u>208.5</u> | <u>247.5</u> |

The variable element of selling and distribution costs is a function of sales units. All other variable costs are a function of production units.

What is the total budget cost allowance for the latest period, when sales and production were both equal to 6,200 units?

A   £210,300
B   £215,400
C   £217,900
D   £220,400

*Circle your answer*

A   B   C   D

28

# 2: BUDGETS

## Data for questions 17 and 18

A local college is introducing a system of flexible budgetary control and the financial accountant is attempting to establish a suitable index of activity for the registrar's department. Four possible indices have been suggested. These indices, together with the inflation index and the total costs of the registrar's department for the last six periods, are as follows:

| Period | Registrar department costs £ | Index of inflation | Index No 1 Number of full-time students | Index No 2 Total number of students | Index No 3 Student registrations processed | Index No 4 Grant applications processed |
|---|---|---|---|---|---|---|
| 1 | 11,440 | 100 | 1,250 | 1,400 | 120 | 78 |
| 2 | 11,676 | 101 | 1,380 | 1,340 | 130 | 85 |
| 3 | 11,975 | 102 | 1,410 | 1,610 | 145 | 96 |
| 4 | 11,474 | 103 | 1,200 | 1,420 | 95 | 90 |
| 5 | 12,072 | 104 | 975 | 1,000 | 134 | 101 |
| 6 | 11,722 | 105 | 900 | 1,030 | 97 | 112 |

**17** Which of the indices is the best measure of activity of the registrar's department?

   A   Index No 1
   B   Index No 2
   C   Index No 3
   D   Index No 4

*Circle your answer*

   A   B   C   D

**18** In period 9, the inflation index will be 108. The other indices will show:

   Index No 1 = 970          Index No 3 = 100
   Index No 2 = 1,025        Index No 4 = 110

What is the correct budget cost allowance for period 9?

   A   £11,200
   B   £12,096
   C   £12,312
   D   £12,440

*Circle your answer*

   A   B   C   D

## 2: BUDGETS

### Data for questions 19 and 20

Payne and Dable Limited are currently preparing their budgets for Year 4. Latest estimates for Year 3 are as follows:

Annual sales = £8.4 million; company fixed costs = £150,000 per month.
The variable cost and revenue structure is:

|  | % | % |
|---|---|---|
| Sales |  | 100 |
| Materials | 40 |  |
| Other variable costs | 20 |  |
| Total variable cost - used for stock valuation purposes |  | 60 |
| Contribution |  | 40 |

For Year 4, selling prices are to be increased by 5%, and sales volume by 10%. All sales and production will occur evenly throughout the year. Fixed costs will increase by 8%, but the unit variable costs are expected to remain unaltered. Working capital requirements in Year 4 are expected to be:

(i) raw material stock: sufficient for 1 month's production;
(ii) finished goods stock: sufficient for 2 months' sales;
(iii) work in progress stock and cash balance: negligible
(iv) debtors: 2 months
(v) creditors for raw material: 2 months
(vi) other creditors: negligible.

**19** What is the budgeted annual profit for Year 4?

A £1,920
B £2,088
C £2,172
D £2,214

*Circle your answer*

A    B    C    D

**20** What is the budgeted balance sheet value of working capital in Year 4?

A £2,226,000
B £2,233,000
C £2,254,000
D £2,261,000

*Circle your answer*

A    B    C    D

## 2: BUDGETS

**21** Nilbottom plc is using zero base budgeting to allocate available resources in next years' budget. Three operations are currently being evaluated: office cleaning, staff canteen and storekeeping. For each of these operations, four activity levels are under consideration. The incremental costs of each of these, together with their priority weightings, are shown in the following table:

| Level of activity | Office cleaning Incremental cost £'000 | Weighting | Staff canteen Incremental cost £'000 | Weighting | Storekeeping Incremental cost £'000 | Weighting |
|---|---|---|---|---|---|---|
| 1 | 24 | 1.0 | 37 | 0.9 | 28 | 0.9 |
| 2 | 22 | 0.7 | 11 | 0.8 | 16 | 0.8 |
| 3 | 7 | 0.6 | 13 | 0.3 | 15 | 0.7 |
| 4 | 8 | 0.4 | 8 | 0.3 | 12 | 0.3 |

The priority weightings are used to calculate a total score for each increment: priority score = incremental cost x priority weighting. Available funds will be allocated according to the ranking obtained from these priority scores. The whole of each increment of cost must be incurred for each activity level; fractional increases are not possible. The budget funds available for these operations is £165,000.

What level of expenditure should be allocated to the staff canteen?

A  £37,000
B  £48,000
C  £61,000
D  £69,000

*Circle your answer*

A   B   C   D

## Data for questions 22 and 23

Pitt Ottaway Limited operates with two departments, each producing a saleable product. Department P produces product P; department Q produces product Q. Production planning is complicated because each department uses finished output from the other department in the manufacturing process. The management accountant has used a computer program to perform an input-output analysis. The program has calculated a matrix of work needed in each department, as follows:

|  | Column P | Column Q |
|---|---|---|
| Row P | 1.0526 | 0.26316 |
| Row Q | 0.2105 | 1.05263 |

Sales demand for the next period will be 2,850 units of P and 5,700 units of Q. Finished goods stock will be kept at a constant level.

## 2: BUDGETS

**22** How many units must department P produce in order to achieve sufficient production to meet the sales demand?

- A 4,200 units
- B 4,500 units
- C 6,600 units
- D 6,750 units

*Circle your answer*

A B C D

**23** How many units must department Q produce in order to achieve sufficient production to meet the sales demand?

- A 5,900 units
- B 6,300 units
- C 6,600 units
- D 6,750 units

*Circle your answer*

A B C D

**24** Modlyn Limited uses a variety of management accounting models in both routine and ad hoc decision making. Four of these models are described below.

*Model*

1. An economic order quantity model, which uses a single forecast of each variable to obtain the optimum order quantity.

2. A cost-volume-profit model which attaches probabilities to a range of forecasts of sales volumes, costs and revenues, to produce a figure for the expected value of profit.

3. A PERT network analysis model which uses optimistic, pessimistic and most likely values for activity times, with their associated probabilities.

4. A goal programming model for budgetary planning, which uses single estimates of costs, revenues and volumes to achieve a satisfactory profit target.

Which of these is a stochastic model?

- A Models 1 and 4 only
- B Models 1, 2 and 4 only
- C Models 2 and 3 only
- D Models 2 and 4 only

*Circle your answer*

A B C D

**25** Foresails Cast plc uses exponential smoothing to prepare forecasts of sales demand, with a smoothing constant, $\alpha$, equal to 0.2. For period 4, the forecast of demand was 4,800 units, but actual demand was 4,950 units. What will be the forecast of demand for period 5?

A  4,830 units
B  4,980 units
C  5,100 units
D  5,910 units

*Circle your answer*

A   B   C   D

## Data for questions 26 and 27

Twindex plc is preparing forecasts of the material and labour production costs for Year 9. The forecasts are to be based on the estimated actual results for Year 8, adjusted by cost indices for performance and price:

Year 8 estimated actual cost of production:
- direct material      £175,000
- direct labour        £78,000

Year 9 production volume will be 8% higher than in Year 8. Indices of the cost effect of changes in performance and price levels are:

|  | Performance level cost index | | Price level index | |
|---|---|---|---|---|
|  | Material usage | Labour efficiency | Material price | Labour rate |
| Year 8 | 100 | 100 | 100 | 100 |
| Year 9 | 98 | 101 | 110 | 105 |

The indices show the cost effect of changes in performance and price levels, but do not reflect changes caused by fluctuations in the level of activity.

The direct labour cost for Year 8 includes a fixed element of £28,000 which is not affected by changes in the efficiency of labour. Direct material cost is wholly variable.

**26** What is the forecast material cost of production for Year 9?

A  £188,650
B  £200,435
C  £203,742
D  £212,143

*Circle your answer*

A   B   C   D

## 2: BUDGETS

**27** What is the forecast labour cost of production for Year 9?

    A   £86,667
    B   £86,961
    C   £89,019
    D   £89,337

*Circle your answer*

A     B     C     D

**28** What is the term used to describe 'a systematic inter-disciplinary examination of factors affecting the cost of a product or service, in order to devise means of achieving the specified purpose most economically at the required standard of quality and reliability'?

    A   Quality costing
    B   Work study
    C   Cost benefit analysis (CBA)
    D   Value analysis

*Circle your answer*

A     B     C     D

**29** With Just In Time techniques of manufacturing, there are certain identifiable 'cost improvers' for which targets should be set so as to reduce costs. Which of the following items are cost improvers in JIT systems?

*Item*
1. Work in progress reduction targets
2. Set up time reduction targets
3. Quality improvement targets
4. Purchasing quality targets
5. Lead time reduction targets

    A   Items 1, 3 and 4 only
    B   Items 1, 3, 4 and 5 only
    C   Items 2, 3, 4 and 5 only
    D   Items 3, 4 and 5 only

*Circle your answer*

A     B     C     D

# CHAPTER 3

# BUDGETARY CONTROL AND STANDARD COSTING I

> This chapter covers the following topics:
>
> - Budgetary control
> - Deciding whether to investigate a variance
> - Cost variances
> - Fixed production overhead variances

## 1. Budgetary control

1.1 Budgetary control refers to the system of controlling an organisation's operations by means of budgeting and

- regular comparisons of actual and budgeted results; or
- regular comparisons of budgeted results against current (revised) forecasts.

1.2 Behavioural issues in budgeting control can be itemised as follows.

- Clear targets for individual managers. Targets should ideally be realistic, but challenging.

- Holding managers accountable and responsible for their results.

- Targets/results should be within the ability/authority of the responsible manager to influence.

- Co-ordination and communication of budgeted targets.

- Regular feedback of actual results.

- Possibly, a system of rewards (pay etc) based on achievements and results.

- In some circumstances, a participative approach to budgeting, as a means of motivating managers.

## 2. Deciding whether to investigate a variance

2.1 Variances are differences between actual results and standard costs/budgeted results. Only variances that exceed a certain limit will be worth investigating. Approaches to deciding when variances should be investigated are:

- a rule-of-thumb approach - eg if a cost variance exceeds, say, 5% of standard cost

- a statistical approach, which involves deciding a control limit for each variance by statistical methods

- a cost-benefit approach, which involves comparing the expected value of the costs of investigating/correcting a variance with the expected value of any benefits from taking control action

- a multi-period approach, monitoring cumulative variances over several reporting periods, not just a single period, and establishing control limits for the cumulative sum of variances over this multi-period time span.

2.2

*Cost-benefit approach*

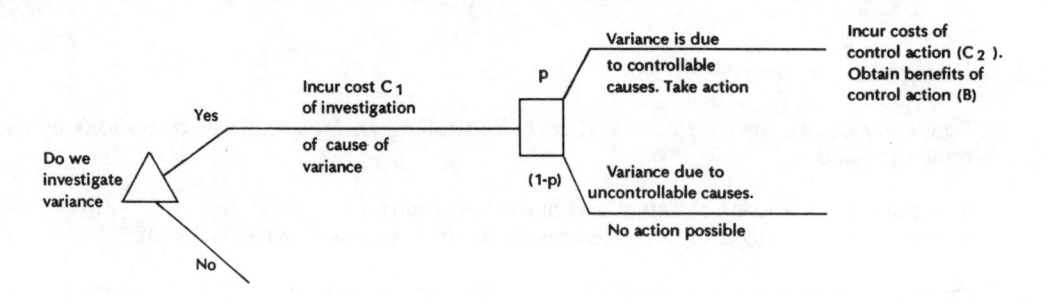

```
                                                          Variance is due          Incur costs of
                                                          to controllable          control action (C₂).
                                         p                causes. Take action      Obtain benefits of
                        Incur cost C₁                                              control action (B)
            Yes         of investigation
Do we                   of cause of
investigate             variance
variance                               (1-p)   Variance due to
                                               uncontrollable causes.
            No                                 No action possible
```

Investigation of a variance is justified if

$p(B - C_2) - C_1 > 0$

This is the same as

$p(B - C_1 - C_2) > (1 - p) C_1$

## 3. Cost variances

3.1 You ought to be able to calculate cost variances, including mix and yield variances for materials. Several questions in this chapter test your ability in this area. If you are not yet sure about your variances, go back to your study text and learn them before tackling this chapter.

3.2 A few comments are given on the next page about fixed production overhead variances in a standard absorption costing system.

## 4. Fixed production overhead variances

4.1 The total fixed production overhead variance represents the amount of under- or over-asorbed fixed overhead. A favourable variance indicates over-absorption; an adverse variance results from under-absorption.

4.2 The expenditure variance calculates the potential under- or over-absorption which results from the fixed overhead expenditure being higher or lower than the original budget:

> Fixed overhead expenditure variance = Budgeted fixed overhead expenditure - Actual expenditure

4.3 If the total fixed overhead variance = £X and the fixed overhead expenditure variance = £Y, the difference £(X - Y) represents the potential under- or over-absorption arising because the volume of production was lower or higher than budgeted:

> Fixed overhead total volume variance = [Actual production - Budgeted production] x Standard fixed overhead per unit

4.4 This total volume variance can be sub-analysed to indicate the reasons why the volume of production was not as budgeted:

- either the efficiency level was not as standard (the efficiency variance)

- or the utilisation of capacity was different to the level incorporated in the standard cost calculations (the capacity variance). This capacity variance, confusingly, is also called a *volume variance*.

> Fixed overhead efficiency variance = [Standard hours for actual production - Actual hours] x Standard fixed overhead rate per hour

Notice the similarity between this variance and the direct labour and variable overhead efficiency variances.

> Fixed overhead capacity or volume variance = [Actual hours worked - Original budgeted labour hours] x Standard fixed o/head rate per hour

# 3: BUDGETARY CONTROL AND STANDARD COSTING I

# QUESTIONS

**1** Which of the following is likely to be a consequence of switching from labour intensive to automated production systems in manufacturing industries?

A   Ideal and attainable standards should now be the same.

B   Any reported variances are likely to be due to uncontrollable causes.

C   The significance of any direct labour cost variances will be reduced.

D   It will not be possible to establish standard costing systems properly

*Circle your answer*

A   B   C   D

**2** Luke Hine and Sinker plc uses a variety of computer models in its budgetary planning and control process. Three of these models are described below:

*Models*

1. An exponential smoothing model is used to prepare a forecast of sales volumes each month. If these forecasts indicate that budgeted sales levels will not be achieved, the marketing department is required to take appropriate control action.

2. A stock control model is used to determine minimum and maximum levels for each stock item. The model produces an exception report whenever the actual stock level reaches minimum or maximum, so that control action can be taken if necessary.

3. A target is set for month-end cash balances. A spreadsheet model is used to forecast the net cash flow and the resulting cash balances for each month. Control action is taken if necessary to achieve the desired cash balances.

Which of these is a feedforward control model?

A   Models 1 and 2 only
B   Models 1 and 3 only
C   Models 2 and 3 only
D   Models 1, 2 and 3

*Circle your answer*

A   B   C   D

## 3

What is an attainable standard?

A  A standard which is established for use in the short term, relating to currently attainable conditions

B  A standard established for use over a long period, which is used as the basis for developing a current standard

C  A standard which can be attained under ideal conditions, and which gives no allowance for waste, machine breakdowns and other inefficiencies

D  A standard which represents reasonably achievable future performance, giving some allowance for normal waste, machine breakdowns and other inefficiencies

*Circle your answer*

A    B    C    D

## 4

Hugh Manrey Sauce plc (HMS) has established a budget allowance of £18,000 per month for personnel costs. The decision of whether or not to investigate variances is based on a test of statistical significance. Past records show that personnel costs have a standard deviation of £1,700 and a 0.05 significance level is used. HMS plc's accountant assumes that costs display a normal distribution around the budget allowance.

What is the upper control limit for personnel costs per month?

A  £18,085
B  £18,900
C  £21,332
D  £22,386

*Circle your answer*

A    B    C    D

## 5

The following information relates to the standard price of one hundred kilograms of good grade material X:

| | |
|---|---|
| Gross purchase price | £500 |
| Freight inwards | £20 |
| Receiving and handling | £20 |
| Trade discount receivable | £30 |

The following information relates to the standard quantity of material X going into one unit of product P:

| | |
|---|---|
| Weight of materials in final product | 5.5 kg |
| Allowance for wastage and spoilage | 0.3 kg |
| Allowance for rejects | 0.2 kg |

What is the standard cost of material X per unit of product P?

A  £25.5
B  £27.0
C  £30.6
D  £34.2

*Circle your answer*

A    B    C    D

## Data for questions 6 - 9

Fowell O'Durr plc manufactures an industrial insect repellent Wingblitz. Standard data for budgeted monthly production of 1,000 litres is as follows:

*Material*

|  | £ |
|---|---|
| Chemical W - 700 litres | 1,400 |
| Chemical P - 400 litres | 600 |
|  | 2,000 |

Material stocks are valued at standard price, and stocks for the month of June were as follows:

|  | Chemical W litres | Chemical P litres |
|---|---|---|
| 1 June | 650 | 380 |
| 30 June | 680 | 295 |

During June, 670 litres of Chemical W were purchased for £1,474 and 320 litres of Chemical P at a price of £1.60 per litre. 900 litres of repellent were produced in June.

**6** What is the total direct materials price variance for June?

A  £162 Adverse
B  £163 Adverse
C  £166 Adverse
D  £180 Adverse

*Circle your answer*

A    B    C    D

**7** What is the total direct materials usage variance for June?

A  £20 Adverse
B  £87.50 Adverse
C  £112.50 Favourable
D  £180 Favourable

*Circle your answer*

A    B    C    D

## 3: BUDGETARY CONTROL AND STANDARD COSTING I

**8** What is the direct materials mix variance for June?

A  £12.50 Favourable
B  £15 Favourable
C  £20 Adverse
D  £180 Favourable

*Circle your answer*

| A | B | C | D |

**9** What is the direct materials yield variance for June?

A  Nil
B  £90 Adverse
C  £100 Adverse
D  £200 Adverse

*Circle your answer*

| A | B | C | D |

**10** Corton Quickly Ltd's figures for March relating to material purchases and usage were:

|  | £ |
|---|---|
| Budgeted cost of materials (4,000 kg at £10.50) | 42,000 |
| Actual cost of materials used | 32,480 |
| Adverse material usage variance | 3,150 |

Output for the month was 80% of budget.

The actual cost of materials per kilogram was

A  £9.28
B  £10.15
C  £10.50
D  £11.20

*Circle your answer*

| A | B | C | D |

**11** N Sime Ltd, a UK company, purchases a chemical from a US distributor and is required to pay for deliveries in US dollars. The company calculates separate variances in the following order: exchange rate variance, then materials price variance followed by materials quantity variance. You are given the following data.

Chemical standards:

|  | Input price £/litre | Exchange rate $/£ |
|---|---|---|
|  | 4.8 | 1.60 |

Actual results:

| Input quantity | Total cost | Exchange rate |
|---|---|---|
| 80,000 litres | £420,000 | $1.50 to £1 |

What is the adverse material price variance?

41

A  £9,750
B  £26,250
C  £36,000
D  £38,400

*Circle your answer*

A    B    C    D

**12** Wharton Nose Limited produces nostrels, the standard cost card of which is as follows:

|  | gms |  | pence |
|---|---|---|---|
| Ingredient X | 25 | @ 2p/gm | 50 |
| Ingredient Y | 75 | @ 1p/gm | 75 |
| Ingredient Z | 50 | @ 4p/gm | 200 |
|  | 150 |  | 325 |
| Normal loss | 50 |  | - |
| Output | 100 gms |  | 325 |

At the end of the most recent accounting period, the following summary was obtained relating to the production of nostrels.

|  | gms purchased | £ | gms consumed |
|---|---|---|---|
| X | 5,000 | 110 | 4,000 |
| Y | 16,000 | 160 | 14,000 |
| Z | 15,000 | 510 | 12,000 |

19,000 gms of nostrels were produced.

Which of the following mix and yield variance summaries is correct?

|  | Mix variance £ | Yield variance £ |
|---|---|---|
| A | 36 Adv | 32.5 Adv |
| B | 50 Fav | 32.5 Adv |
| C | 50 Adv | 32.5 Adv |
| D | 80 Adv | 162.5 Adv |

*Circle your answer*

A    B    C    D

## Data for questions 13 - 16

The following standard cost data relates to the assembly department of Wark Kingman Limited:

| Standard wage rate per hour | - Grade 1 £3 |
|---|---|
|  | - Grade 2 £5 |
| Standard input mix of direct labour | - Grade 1 60% |
|  | - Grade 2 40% |
| Standard output efficiency | - 80%, ie 0.8 standard hours of output is expected in each labour hour |

*Continued...*

Data for October in the assembly department is as follows:

| | |
|---|---|
| Standard hours produced | 7,200 |
| Wages | - Grade 1 £26,970 |
| | - Grade 2 £15,696 |
| Labour hours worked | - Grade 1 8,700 |
| | - Grade 2 3,270 |

**13** What is the direct labour rate variance for October?

  A  £144 Favourable
  B  £180 Adverse
  C  £216 Adverse
  D  £720 Favourable

*Circle your answer*

A   B   C   D

**14** What is the direct labour efficiency variance for October?

  A  £8,250 Adverse
  B  £9,029 Adverse
  C  £18,126 Adverse
  D  £23,598 Adverse

*Circle your answer*

A   B   C   D

**15** What is the direct labour mix variance for October?

  A  £2,820 Favourable
  B  £3,036 Favourable
  C  £13,084 Adverse
  D  £14,061 Adverse

*Circle your answer*

A   B   C   D

**16** What is the total direct labour productivity variance for October?

  A  £4,055 Favourable
  B  £9,537 Adverse
  C  £11,286 Adverse
  D  £20,946 Adverse

*Circle your answer*

A   B   C   D

## 3: BUDGETARY CONTROL AND STANDARD COSTING I

**17** A company's figures for November relating to expenditure on direct labour were as follows.

                                £

Budgeted costs                          192,000 for 8,000 units of output
Actual costs                              227,000 for 9,000 units of output
Direct labour efficiency variance     4,000 Favourable

What was the actual hourly rate of pay, expressed as a percentage of the budgeted rate of pay (to 2 decimal places)?

A   93.80%
B   103.18%
C   106.94%
D   107.08%

Circle your answer

A   B   C   D

**18** The following variances are extracted from the monthly management accounts of Slav Laber Limited.

*Department 1*

                                      £

Direct labour total variance            920 Favourable
Direct labour rate variance           3,200 Adverse

Consider the following statements:

*Statement*

1. Direct labour achieved levels of efficiency which were higher than standard, and were accordingly paid bonuses at higher rates than budgeted.

2. The original standard labour rate was unrealistically low because it failed to take account of rapid wage inflation.

3. The production manager elected to use more skilled labour at a higher hourly rate of pay than budgeted.

Which of these statements are consistent with the variances shown?

A   Statements 1 and 2 only
B   Statements 1 and 3 only
C   Statements 2 and 3 only
D   Statements 1, 2 and 3

Circle your answer

A   B   C   D

# 3: BUDGETARY CONTROL AND STANDARD COSTING I

## Data for questions 19 - 24

The management accountant of Ed Dover Eels plc is reviewing actual and standard labour and overhead costs for the assembly department last month. The company manufactures a single product, and relevant data is as follows:

*Standard costs*

|  | £ per unit |
|---|---|
| Direct labour, 1 hour at £7 per hour | 7 |
| Variable production overhead | 3 |
| Fixed production overhead | 4 |

The fixed production overhead absorption rate is based on budgeted monthly production of 2,000 units. Overheads are assumed to be related to direct labour hours of active working.

*Actual results*

| Production | 1,800 units |
|---|---|
|  | £ |
| Direct wages paid - 1,600 hours | 12,000 |
| Variable production overhead | 6,000 |
| Fixed production overhead | 8,200 |

A machine breakdown resulted in 200 hours of idle time during the month

**19** What is the idle time variance?

- A  £1,400 Adverse
- B  £1,500 Adverse
- C  £2,000 Adverse
- D  £2,800 Adverse

*Circle your answer*

A   B   C   D

**20** What is the variable overhead efficiency variance?

- A  £600 Favourable
- B  £600 Adverse
- C  £1,200 Favourable
- D  £1,200 Adverse

*Circle your answer*

A   B   C   D

## 3: BUDGETARY CONTROL AND STANDARD COSTING I

**21** What is the variable overhead expenditure variance?

A Nil
B £600 Adverse
C £1,200 Adverse
D £1,800 Adverse

*Circle your answer*

A  B  C  D

**22** What is the fixed overhead expenditure variance?

A £200 Adverse
B £1,000 Adverse
C £1,800 Adverse
D £2,600 Adverse

*Circle your answer*

A  B  C  D

**23** What is the fixed overhead capacity variance (also referred to as the fixed overhead volume variance)?

A £200 Adverse
B £800 Adverse
C £1,600 Adverse
D £2,400 Adverse

*Circle your answer*

A  B  C  D

**24** What is the fixed overhead efficiency variance?

A £800 Adverse
B £800 Favourable
C £1,600 Adverse
D £1,600 Favourable

*Circle your answer*

A  B  C  D

**25** Muesli Coll Limited, a manufacturer of musical instruments, absorbs fixed production overhead at a predetermined rate based on budgeted output. Extracts from the variance analysis for April are as follows:

Fixed production overhead variances:
Expenditure                £6,000 Favourable
Efficiency                 £8,000 Adverse
Capacity/volume            £7,000 Favourable

Consider the following statements concerning production in April:

*Statement*

1. The fixed production overhead was over-absorbed by £5,000.
2. Production output was higher than budget.
3. Labour hours worked were higher than budget.
4. Labour hours worked were more than the standard allowance for the actual output.

Which of these statements are consistent with the reported variances?

A  Statements 1 and 4 only
B  Statements 2 and 3 only
C  Statements 1, 2 and 3 only
D  Statements 1, 3 and 4 only

*Circle your answer*

| A | B | C | D |

**26** The diagram below shows the recovery rate for a company which uses a two-way analysis of fixed overhead manufacturing variances.

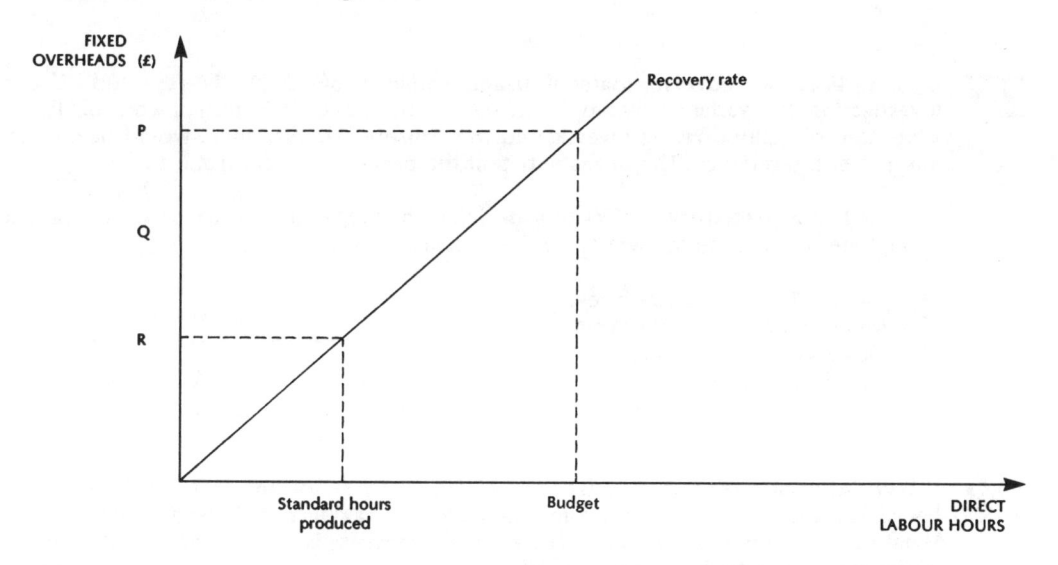

Which of the following identifies the fixed overhead expenditure and production volume variances?

|   | Fixed overhead expenditure variance | Production total volume variance |
|---|---|---|
| A | PR | QR |
| B | PQ | PR |
| C | PR | PQ |
| D | PQ | QR |

*Circle your answer*

| A | B | C | D |

47

## Data for questions 27 - 28

Gon Gnomes Ltd's management use a simple decision model for deciding whether or not to investigate a material usage variance. The model is shown in the table below.

|  | State of process | |
|---|---|---|
| Decision | In control $X_1$ | Out of control $X_2$ |
| Do not investigate | 0 | 0 |
| Investigate | -C | B-C |

where  C  is the cost of investigating the causes of the variance
       B  are the benefits from taking control action, if the process is found on investigation to be out of control.

**27** In July 19X1, an adverse material usage variance of £3,400 is reported. The cost of investigating the variance would be £2,000. If the process is out of control, the benefits from control action, having investigated the cause of the variance, would be $3\frac{1}{2}$ times the amount of the variance. The probability that the process is in control is 0.8.

What is the expected value (EV) of a decision to investigate the cause of the variance, and should the decision be to investigate the variance or not?

A   Minus £1,320.   Do not investigate
B   Minus £760.     Do not investigate
C   Plus £380.      Investigate
D   Plus £1,580.    Investigate

*Circle your answer*

A   B   C   D

**28** If there is an adverse usage variance of £5,000, the cost of investigating the variance would be £3,600 and the benefits from investigating and taking control action would be £10,000. What must be the minimum probability that the process is *out* of control for an investigation of the variance to be judged worthwhile?

A   0.28
B   0.36
C   0.64
D   0.86

*Circle your answer*

A   B   C   D

## 3: BUDGETARY CONTROL AND STANDARD COSTING I

**29** The management of Ron Gaggain Ltd is deciding whether or not to investigate an adverse variance which would have an expected present value of cost of £5,250 if not corrected now. The following information is available:

| | |
|---|---:|
| Probability that the variance cannot be corrected | 0.70 |
| Probability that the variance can be corrected | 0.30 |
| Cost to investigate the variance | £800 |
| Cost to correct the process if the variance can be corrected | £1,500 |

If the cost to correct the process were incorrectly predicted and should be £2,800, what is the expected present value of the prediction error?

A £390
B £575
C £910
D £1,300

*Circle your answer*

A    B    C    D

**30** The following data are available to a company's management:

| | £ |
|---|---:|
| Cost of investigating whether an adverse variance can be eliminated: | |
|     Variable cost | 1,100 |
|     Fixed cost (allocated on a time basis) | 900 |
| | 2,000 |
| Correction cost if the variance can be eliminated | 700 |

It has been estimated that the present value of the cost of not correcting an adverse variance which can be eliminated is four times the size of the observed variance.

If a variance of £1,000 is observed, what is the minimum probability that the variance can be eliminated which would justify an investigation (to 3 decimal places)?

A 0.333
B 0.403
C 0.606
D 0.607

*Circle your answer*

A    B    C    D

# CHAPTER 4

# STANDARD COSTING II

> This chapter covers the following topics:
> - Sales variances
> - Planning and operational variances
> - Standard marginal costing

## 1. Sales variances

1.1 The sales price variance measures the increase or decrease in revenue (and profit) as a consequence of the actual sales price being higher or lower than standard:

$$\text{Sales price} = \left[ \text{Actual sales price} - \text{Standard sales price} \right] \times \text{Number of units sold}$$

1.2 In an absorption costing system, the sales volume variance measures the increase or decrease in standard profit resulting from the sales volume of each product being higher or lower than budgeted:

$$\text{Sales volume variance} = \left[ \text{Actual sales volume of each product} - \text{Budget of sales volume of each product} \right] \times \text{Standard profit margin per unit for each product}$$

The important thing to notice here is that it is the change in standard *profit* which is measured, not the change in sales *revenue*. Students of management accounting frequently calculate this variance incorrectly.

1.3 When two or more products are sold in a standard mix, it is possible to analyse the sales volume variance further into its sub-components of sales quantity variance and sales mix variance.

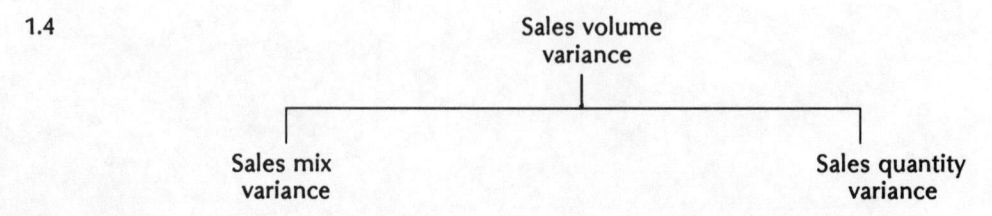

1.4

```
              Sales volume
                variance
              /           \
      Sales mix          Sales quantity
      variance             variance
```

1.5 The sales mix variance measures the change in standard profit resulting from the mix of sales being different from budget. There are two different ways of calculating the variance.

- *Method 1:* Standard mix based on budgeted sales quantities in units.
- *Method 2:* Standard mix based on budgeted sales in revenue terms.

1.6 For each product in the mix in units (method 1) or at standard selling price (method 2), we calculate:

- the standard mix
- the actual sales

1.7 The difference between actual sales mix and standard sales mix for each product item in the mix is converted into a profit margin variance at:

- the standard profit per unit for the product (method 1) or
- the standard profit/sales ratio for the product (method 2).

The sum of all the profit margin variances for the individual products gives the total sales mix variance.

1.8 The sales quantity variance measures the increase or decrease in standard profit resulting from the *total* sales quantity being higher or lower than budget, on the assumption that products are sold in the standard/budgeted proportions.

$$\text{Sales quantity variance} = \left[ \text{Actual total sales volume} - \text{Budget total sales volume} \right] \times \text{Weighted average profit margin}$$

- When the sales mix variance is calculated on a units basis, the weighted average profit margin is the weighted average standard profit margin per unit for all the products in the budget

- When the sales mix variance is calculated on a standard sales revenue basis, the weighted average profit margin is the weighted average standard profit/sales ratio for all the products in the budget.

## 2. Planning and operational variances

2.1 Problems with traditional variance analysis are that

- the standard cost can soon become out-of-date and unrealistic
- there can be planning errors in setting the original standard.

The calculation of planning variances attempts to overcome these problems by updating the standard costs so that they represent, with hindsight, more realistic targets and control measures.

2.2 You should be aware of the terms:

- 'ex ante'   - meaning original budget or standard
- 'ex post'   - meaning a budget or standard that is seen in retrospect to be more appropriate.

2.3 Operational variances are calculated by comparing actual results with the *ex post* standard or budget, and variances are calculated in the normal way, using this standard or budget.

2.4 Planning variances are the difference between:

- the ex post budget or standard for the number of units produced/sold
- and the ex ante budget or standard for the number of units produced/sold.

2.5 Planning variances are usually outside the control of management, but operational variances are calculated on a more realistic 'opportunity cost' basis.

## 3. Standard marginal costing

3.1 Most of the variances in a standard marginal costing system will be identical to those in a standard absorption costing system. There are only two differences in the way that variances are calculated.

> - Since fixed overheads are not absorbed into production costs, there will be no fixed overhead volume or efficiency variance. There will, however, be the same fixed overhead *expenditure* variance as with absorption costing.
>
> - The sales volume variance will be valued at standard contribution margin, instead of standard profit margin. Similarly, any sales mix and sales quantity variances will be valued at contribution margin instead of profit margin.

# 4: STANDARD COSTING II

# QUESTIONS

## Data for questions 1 - 5

Sultan Pepper Limited manufactures and sells three products, and the management accountant is currently reviewing the sales variances for the latest month. Relevant data are as follows:

| Product | Red | White | Blue |
|---|---|---|---|
| *Standard data* | | | |
| Selling price per unit | £25 | £42 | £36 |
| Profit margin per unit | £7 | £15 | £9 |
| Budgeted monthly sales (units) | 2,000 | 5,000 | 3,000 |
| *Actual results for last month* | | | |
| Sales revenue | £64,220 | £191,840 | £167,000 |
| Sales units | 2,600 | 4,400 | 5,000 |

**1** What is the sales price variance?

A £6,740 Adverse
B £12,760 Adverse
C £55,060 Favourable
D £61,800 Favourable

*Circle your answer*

A    B    C    D

**2** What is the sales volume variance?

A £13,200 Favourable
B £23,200 Favourable
C £55,060 Favourable
D £61,800 Favourable

*Circle your answer*

A    B    C    D

**3** What is the sales mix variance, using the units method of calculation?

A £6,740 Favourable
B £10,000 Adverse
C £11,800 Adverse
D £13,200 Favourable

*Circle your answer*

A    B    C    D

53

# 4: STANDARD COSTING II

**4** What is the sales quantity variance, using the units method of calculation?

A £13,200 Favourable
B £23,200 Favourable
C £50,400 Adverse
D £73,600 Favourable

*Circle your answer*

A    B    C    D

**5** What is the sales mix variance, using the revenue method of calculation?

A £3,444(A)
B £5,110(A)
C £6,280(A)
D £19,480(F)

*Circle your answer*

A    B    C    D

## Data for questions 6 - 8

Bacon and Higgs Limited set a monthly direct labour budget for their single product as follows:

| | |
|---|---|
| Budgeted production | 270 units |
| Direct labour hours | 810 |
| Wages cost | £4,050 |

During the year it was realised that due to certain planning errors, the original standard cost was unrealistic and was not useful for cost control.

Accordingly, the standard was revised for variance analysis purposes to:

   4 direct labour hours at £4.50 per hour = £18 per unit produced

Actual results for August were:

| | |
|---|---|
| Production | 300 units |
| Direct labour hours | 1,140 |
| Wages cost | £5,586 |

**6** What is the total planning variance for August?

A £228 Favourable
B £810 Adverse
C £900 Adverse
D £1,350 Adverse

*Circle your answer*

A    B    C    D

## 4: STANDARD COSTING II

**7** What is the operational labour rate variance for August?

- A  £114 Favourable
- B  £186 Adverse
- C  £456 Adverse
- D  £1,086 Adverse

*Circle your answer*

A   B   C   D

**8** What is the operational labour efficiency variance for August?

- A  £270 Favourable
- B  £270 Adverse
- C  £300 Favourable
- D  £2,505 Adverse

*Circle your answer*

A   B   C   D

### Data for questions 9 - 12

Lowke Hilary plc can use one of two types of material in its product; Laird or Greece. These materials are perfect substitutes for each other. In this period's budget, the company planned to use Greece instead of Laird, because they forecast that it would be the cheaper of the two. The standard direct material cost was set as:

6 kilograms of Greece at £8 per kg = £48 per unit produced

Unfortunately, competitors also decided to use Greece and the consequent high demand superimposed on unexpected general price inflation resulted in the following prevailing market prices:

|        | £ per kg |
|--------|----------|
| Greece | 12       |
| Laird  | 11       |

During the period the amount of Greece actually purchased and used to produce 730 units of finished product was 4,350 kilograms at a total cost of £52,000.

Lowke Hilary plc is aware that there are two parts to their planning error:
(1) the variance caused by the setting of an unrealistically low standard price
(2) the variance caused by specifying the incorrect material.

**9** What is the planning variance caused by the setting of an unrealistically low standard price?

- A  £4,150 Adverse
- B  £4,350 Adverse
- C  £13,050 Adverse
- D  £13,140 Adverse

*Circle your answer*

A   B   C   D

# 4: STANDARD COSTING II

**10** What is the planning variance caused by specifying the more expensive material?

A £4,350 Adverse
B £4,380 Adverse
C £13,050 Adverse
D £17,520 Adverse

*Circle your answer*

A  B  C  D

**11** What is the operational material price variance?

A £200 Favourable
B £560 Favourable
C £4,150 Adverse
D £17,200 Adverse

*Circle your answer*

A  B  C  D

**12** What is the operational material usage variance?

A £120 Favourable
B £240 Favourable
C £330 Favourable
D £360 Favourable

*Circle your answer*

A  B  C  D

**13** In order to indicate to managers the trend and materiality of variances, Vin O'Garbottle Limited express them as percentages as in the following examples:

|  | July | August | Sept | Oct | Nov |
|---|---|---|---|---|---|
| Material usage variance as a percentage of standard total production cost | 3% (F) | 2% (A) | 6% (A) | 10% (A) | 12% (A) |
| Material price variance as a percentage of standard cost of material used | 1% (A) | 2% (A) | 7% (F) | 8% (F) | 9% (F) |

A denotes an adverse variance; F denotes a favourable variance

Which of the following statements is or are consistent with the results shown?

*Statement*

1. In September the buyer located a new supplier who charged a much lower price than the previous supplier. The material was however found to be of low quality, leading to a high level of wastage.

2. The general trend is that all direct material variances are becoming more significant and are likely to be worthy of management attention.

3. A change in the bonus payment scheme has improved the productivity of labour, who are now processing material much more effectively.

A  Statements 1 and 2 only
B  Statements 1 and 3 only
C  Statements 2 and 3 only
D  Statement 2 only

*Circle your answer*

A   B   C   D

## Data for questions 14 - 17

Boyle Degg Limited manufacture a single product. An extract from a variance control report together with relevant standard cost data is shown below:

| | |
|---|---|
| Standard selling price per unit | = £70 |
| Standard direct material cost | = 5 kg per unit x £2 per kg = £10 per unit |
| Budgeted total material cost of sales | = £2,300 per month |
| Budgeted profit margin | = £6,900 per month |

*Actual results for February*

| | |
|---|---|
| Sales revenue | = £15,200 |
| Total direct material cost | = £2,400 |
| Direct material price variance | = £800 Adverse |
| Direct material usage variance | = £400 Favourable |

There was no change in stock levels during the month.

**14** What was the actual production for February?

A  180 units
B  200 units
C  240 units
D  280 units

*Circle your answer*

A   B   C   D

**15** What was the actual average price paid for direct material during February?

A  £1.50 per kg
B  £2.00 per kg
C  £2.40 per kg
D  £3.00 per kg

*Circle your answer*

A   B   C   D

## 4: STANDARD COSTING II

**16** What was the sales price variance for February?

A £1,200 Favourable
B £1,600 Adverse
C £2,600 Favourable
D £4,400 Adverse

*Circle your answer*

A    B    C    D

**17** What was the sales volume variance for February?

A £900 Adverse
B £1,500 Favourable
C £2,100 Adverse
D £3,500 Adverse

*Circle your answer*

A    B    C    D

**18** A certain company that operates in a competitive market can sell all it produces at a sales price of £60 per unit. Its accountant has estimated that average monthly costs of sales would be, in £, 10 + 0.25Q per unit, where Q is the volume of output and sales. It budgets its output accordingly so as to maximise profits. At the end of the month, it finds that its average costs of sales should have been estimated as 16 + 0.2Q. What is the opportunity cost variance?

A £20 (A)
B £80 (A)
C £220 (A)
D £240 (A)

*Circle your answer*

A    B    C    D

### Data for questions 19 - 25

The standard cost and selling price structure for the single product that is made by M N Tall Limited is as follows:

|                           | £ per unit |
|---------------------------|-----------|
| Selling price             | 82        |
| Variable cost             | (47)      |
| Fixed production overhead | (29)      |
| Standard profit margin    | 6         |

The budgeted level of production and sales is 3,200 units per month.

*Extract from the actual results for March*

Fixed production overhead total volume variance
(capacity/volume variance + efficiency variance)    £8,700 Favourable
Fixed production overhead expenditure variance    £2,200 Adverse

There was no change in stock levels during the period.

M N Tall Limited is considering using standard marginal costing as the basis for variance reporting in future.

# 4: STANDARD COSTING II

**19** What was the actual expenditure on fixed production overhead during March?

A £86,300
B £90,600
C £95,000
D £99,300

*Circle your answer*

A   B   C   D

**20** What sales volume variance would be shown in a marginal costing statement for March?

A £1,800 Favourable
B £10,500 Favourable
C £14,100 Favourable
D £24,600 Favourable

*Circle your answer*

A   B   C   D

**21** What variance for fixed production overhead would be shown in a marginal costing statement for March?

A No variance would be shown
B Expenditure variance: £2,200 adverse
C Total variance: £6,500 favourable
D Volume variance: £8,700 favourable

*Circle your answer*

A   B   C   D

## Data for questions 22 - 25

Mr Dann Kress Limited uses a standard marginal costing system. Actual and budgeted results for year 4 are shown below:

|  | Actual £ | Budget £ |
|---|---|---|
| Sales revenue | 204,120 | 180,000 |
| Variable cost | 136,700 | 120,000 |
| Contribution | 67,420 | 60,000 |
| Fixed overhead | 38,000 | 40,000 |
| Profit | 29,420 | 20,000 |

The management accountant has established that during Year 4 the average unit sales price was 8% higher than standard.

## 4: STANDARD COSTING II

**22** By how much did actual sales volume exceed budgeted sales volume, as a percentage of the budgeted sales quantities?

A 4.328%
B 5.000%
C 13.400%
D 13.917%

*Circle your answer*

A  B  C  D

**23** What is the total sales price variance for Year 4?

A £14,400 Favourable
B £15,120 Favourable
C £16,330 Favourable
D £24,120 Favourable

*Circle your answer*

A  B  C  D

**24** What is the total sales volume variance for Year 4?

A £1,000 Favourable
B £3,000 Favourable
C £7,420 Favourable
D £9,420 Favourable

*Circle your answer*

A  B  C  D

**25** What is the total variable cost variance for Year 4?

A £620 Adverse
B £7,100 Adverse
C £10,700 Adverse
D £16,700 Adverse

*Circle your answer*

A  B  C  D

# CHAPTER 5

# DECISION ACCOUNTING

> This chapter covers the following topics:
> - Incremental costs and revenues in decision making
> - Relevant costs and opportunity costs
> - Allocation of scarce resources
> - Pricing decisions
> - Stock control

## 1. Incremental costs and revenues in decision making

1.1 Decision accounting is the provision of accounting information to assist with decision-making by management. The assumption for short-run decisions is that a decision should not be taken unless the incremental revenues/benefits exceed the incremental costs that would be incurred.

- Incremental revenues are the extra revenues earned as a direct result of a particular course of action. Incremental benefits consist of incremental revenues and any savings in costs that would occur as a direct result of the course of action.

- Incremental costs are the extra costs incurred as a result of an action being taken. They are often the marginal or variable costs, but incremental fixed costs can also occur.

- Identifiable fixed costs are sometimes called *attributable fixed costs,* and they are the fixed costs which are directly caused by a product, which would be saved if the product were discontinued.

1.2 When using incremental analysis, the management accountant must include all incremental costs and revenues; however, costs and revenues which remain the same whatever the decision can be omitted from the analysis.

1.3 Examples of decision making which should use incremental cost analysis are:

- *Whether or not to discontinue making a product.* From a management accounting point of view, a product should be discontinued if the savings in variable costs and attributable fixed costs exceed the loss of revenue that would result. However, any "one-off" costs of discontinuation, such as redundancy costs or de-commissioning costs, would introduce a need for DCF analysis.

- *Make or buy decisions.* From a management accounting viewpoint, a company should manufacture its own requirements if the incremental costs of doing so are less than the price quoted by an outside supplier. Non-financial factors are often very important in make or buy decisions, including such considerations as the quality and reliability of supply. This is an important issue in Just In Time manufacturing systems. Similarly, developing technology and the importance of product design mean that many manufacturers no longer have enough resources to make their own components, but must buy in.

## 2. Relevant costs and opportunity costs

2.1 Relevant costs are costs which will be incurred *in the future* as a result of a decision taken now. Relevant costs are *cash flows*. Non-cash costs, such as depreciation and *absorbed* overheads cannot be relevant costs. Overheads are only relevant costs if they consist of extra cash costs that would be incurred as a direct consequence of taking a particular course of action.

2.2 Costs which have already been incurred are not relevant to future decisions and must be excluded from a relevant cost analysis. Such costs are called sunk costs, past costs or historical costs.

2.3 An opportunity cost is the net benefit forgone by not accepting the best available alternative. An opportunity cost is a relevant cost in decision making.

- An opportunity cost can be represented by a contribution or revenue forgone, or by a cost saving forgone as a result of a particular course of action.

- When a resource is in scarce supply and could be used for other purposes, the opportunity cost of using it in one way is the benefit forgone from not using it in the best alternative way.

2.4
> A useful decision rule for identifying the relevant cost of a scarce resource is that the total relevant cost consists of:
>
> (1) the contribution/incremental profit forgone from the next-best opportunity for the scarce resource, *plus*
>
> (2) the variable cost of the scarce resource.

For example, suppose that a special contract is to use 1,000 hours of labour which is in short supply. The labour rate is £3 per hour, and the labour would have to be diverted from other work which is currently earning a contribution of £2 per hour, after covering labour costs and variable overhead costs of £0.50 per hour.

The relevant cost is:

|  |  | £ |
|---|---|---|
| Variable cost of direct labour | (1,000 x £3) = | 3,000 |
| Variable overhead cost | (1,000 x £0.50) = | 500 |
| Opportunity cost: contribution forgone | (1,000 x £2) = | 2,000 |
|  |  | 5,500 |

## 3. Allocation of scarce resources

3.1 When there are scarce resources which put a limit on an organisation's activities, the role of decision accounting is to identify how the scarce resources should be used so as to maximise profits.

3.2 When only *one resource* is in short supply, the task of the management accountant is to identify this limiting factor and then to apply the decision rule:

> Decision Rule: Maximise the contribution per unit of limiting factor

This often involves ranking items in order of contribution per unit of limiting factor in order to determine the profit-maximising output.

3.3 Whenever there are scarce resources there will be opportunity costs. The shadow price (or dual price) of a scarce resource is the marginal contribution towards fixed costs and profit that can be earned by each unit of the resource that is available.

3.4 > When there is *more than one scarce resource* it is no longer possible to use the simple decision rule given in paragraph 3.2. Instead, the technique of *linear programming* can be used to determine the contribution-maximising use of the resources.

- When there are just two 'unknowns' in the problem, for instance in determining the optimum production levels for two products, then graphical analysis can be used.

- When there are more than two variables, or a large number of constraints which makes graphical analysis difficult, then the *Simplex technique* can be used. This technique is a step-by-step process that tests a number of feasible solutions in turn, each in the form of a table or tableau of figures. You should be capable of interpreting the final tableau produced by the Simplex technique.

3.5 The technique is best illustrated by considering the following optimal tableau. This tableau has been produced for two products, x and y, which earn a contribution of £20 and £16 respectively.

| Variable in solution | x | y | a | b | c | Solution column |
|---|---|---|---|---|---|---|
| x | 1 | 0 | 0 | -0.2857 | 0.4286 | 400 |
| a | 0 | 0 | 1 | 0.5714 | -1.8571 | 100 |
| y | 0 | 1 | 0 | 0.4286 | -0.1429 | 450 |
| Solution row | 0 | 0 | 0 | 1.1428 | 6.2858 | 15,200 |

Materials, labour hours, and machine hours are all in short supply.

# 5: DECISION ACCOUNTING

a = quantity of unused materials
b = number of unused labour hours
c = number of unused machine hours

} a, b and c are known as *slack variables*.

3.6 The table can be interpreted as follows:

- Optimum production is 400 units of product x and 450 units of product y, earning a total contribution of £15,200.

- There will be 100 units of unused materials.

- The figures in the b and c columns of the solution row indicate that the shadow prices (opportunity costs) of a labour hour and a machine hour are £1.1428 and £6.2858 respectively. These resources have an opportunity cost because there is no spare capacity shown in the optimum solution.

3.7 The shadow prices can be used by the management accountant to determine whether it is worth taking action to obtain more of the particular resource. The shadow price indicates the maximum price which should be paid for an additional unit of resource above its variable cost.

For example, if one extra machine hour (slack variable c) is made available, contribution could be increased by £6.2858, by increasing output of product x by 0.4286 units, reducing output of product y by 0.1429 units, and this would use up a further 1.8571 units of materials.

3.8 Linear programming solutions can be set out in different ways, but the basic principles of interpretation are much the same whichever method of presentation is used.

## 4. Pricing decisions

4.1 Although cost should not be the sole determinant of selling price, the management accountant is often called upon to provide cost data for selling price decisions. The pricing method which determines selling prices by adding a percentage mark-up to costs is called *cost plus* pricing.

4.2 Those responsible for selling price decisions should be aware of the effect that any price changes will have on the demand for a good. The change in demand will depend to some extent on the *price elasticity of demand* for the good.

$$\text{Price elasticity of demand} = \frac{\text{percentage change in quantity demanded}}{\text{percentage change in price}}$$

4.3 If management knows whether demand for its goods and services is elastic or inelastic then they can readily assess the effect on total *revenue* of a price change.

Remember that maximising *revenue* is not the same as maximising *profits*. Profits depend also on relative costs structures.

4.4 | Profits are maximised at the output level where marginal costs are equal to marginal revenue.

If the management accountant knows the equation of the marginal cost and marginal revenue functions, it would be possible to determine the profit-maximising selling price. The marginal cost and marginal revenue functions can be derived by differentiating the total cost and total revenue functions respectively. There are two questions in this chapter to test your ability to perform this type of analysis.

## 5. Stock control

5.1 The Economic Order Quantity (EOQ) is the quantity of stock which should be ordered from suppliers to minimise the total costs associated with stock:

$$\text{Economic Order Quantity} = \sqrt{\frac{2cd}{h}}$$

where  $c$ = incremental cost of placing an order
 $d$ = annual demand
 $h$ = incremental cost of holding one item in stock for one year

5.2 The basic Economic Quantity model can also be used for items which are produced internally. In this case the cost of setting up machines for a production run is used in the formula instead of the cost of placing an order. The quantity derived from the calculation is often called the *Economic Batch Quantity*.

5.3 The EOQ model makes many simplifying assumptions. Two of the most important are:

- stock is used at an even rate throughout the year
- stock level falls to exactly zero and further supplies are received immediately this happens.

The important implications of these assumptions is that, when applying the model, the management accountant can assume that average stocks are equal to exactly half of the order quantity. Unless you are clearly told otherwise, try to remember this assumption when you are answering questions on stock control.

5.4 The belief that use of the EOQ will minimise stock costs has been challenged in recent years by the use of Just In Time manufacturing techniques, and flexible manufacturing systems (FMS). JIT techniques try to keep stock levels to a minimum - ideally at a zero level - by being able to rely on:

(a) prompt deliveries of parts and materials from suppliers;
(b) short production runs; and
(c) prompt completion of finished goods to customers' orders.

# 5: DECISION ACCOUNTING

# QUESTIONS

## Data for questions 1 and 2

Gavin Waysign plc manufactures a product which has a selling price of £14 and variable costs of £6 per unit, and incurs annual fixed costs of £24,400. Annual sales demand is 8,000 units.

A new production method is currently under consideration that would increase fixed costs by 30%, but would reduce variable costs to £5 per unit. The superior quality of the finished product would enable sales to be increased to 8,500 units per annum at a price of £15 each.

**1** If the change in production method were to take place, the breakeven output level would be:

A  610 units lower
B  122 units higher
C  372 units higher
D  915 units higher

*Circle your answer*

A   B   C   D

**2** At what level of sales would the annual profit be the same with both production methods?

A  3,660 units
B  4,280 units
C  4,960 units
D  6,140 units

*Circle your answer*

A   B   C   D

**3** Rod Humber-Green, management accountant of Terrific Lights Limited, has prepared the following budget for next year:

|  | £ | £ |
|---|---|---|
| Sales |  | 480,000 |
| Direct materials | 140,000 |  |
| Direct labour | 110,000 |  |
| Variable overhead | 50,000 | 300,000 |
| Contribution |  | 180,000 |
| Fixed cost |  | 130,000 |
| Profit |  | 50,000 |

The sales and production volume can be increased by 15% if an extra shift is added, but the company will have to reduce the sales price on all units by 3% to sell the extra volume. The extra shift will use the same grade of labour, but Rod will have to pay time and a half to the workers on this shift. Increased material purchases will mean that a bulk discount of 2% will be available on all purchases. Additional fixed overheads of £2,000 will be incurred.

What will be the budgeted profit if Rod decides to use the extra shift?

A £51,400
B £52,150
C £53,410
D £60,060

Circle your answer

A    B    C    D

**4** Dubble Park Ltd generates a 12% contribution on its weekly sales of £280,000. The company's management have decided to run a special offer on a new product, Z, which has not been sold before, in collaboration with the large Kashenkari chain of supermarkets. It is hoped that the special offer on Z will both bring the new product to consumers' attention, and increase weekly sales of the company's other products by 5%. Product Z will have a variable unit cost of £2.20 to make and £0.15 to distribute. Weekly sales of Z, at a special offer price of £1.90 per unit, are expected to be 3,000 units.

The effect of the special offer will be to increase the company's weekly profit by:

A £330
B £780
C £1,612.5
D £1,680

Circle your answer

A    B    C    D

**5** Outer Gass holds no stocks. Its budget for a recent week was as follows:

| | | |
|---|---:|---:|
| Units to be produced and sold (standard items) | | 20,000 |
| | | £ |
| Sales | | 145,000 |
| Less: materials | 32,000 | |
| direct labour (at £5 per hour) | 50,000 | |
| overhead that varies with labour hours worked | 5,000 | |
| fixed overhead | 40,000 | |
| | | (127,000) |
| Budgeted net profit | | 18,000 |

No production was possible during that week because of a strike. Of the lost production:

1. 11,000 units have since been produced and sold but production was in overtime hours, the overtime premium being 50% of normal pay;

2. 9,000 units were lost, as customers went to competitors of Outer Gass for their supplies.

# 5: DECISION ACCOUNTING

Ignoring the time value of money, the strike had an adverse effect on the company's profit of

A £39,850
B £41,225
C £42,100
D £53,750

*Circle your answer*

A   B   C   D

## Data for questions 6 and 7

Five Mail Jam plc manufactures four products, W, X, Y and Z, on specialised machines. Of the 21 machines available, 9 are suitable for all four products, but 12 are suitable only for products X and Z.

Each machine has a capacity of 46 weeks per year, and can only be used for making a given product for whole weeks and not for fractions of a week.

Information on the four products is as follows:

| Product | Contribution per unit £ | Units produced per machine per week |
|---|---|---|
| W | 115 | 22 |
| X | 80 | 8 |
| Y | 160 | 14 |
| Z | 125 | 16 |

There is unlimited demand for all four products, and market requirements dictate that a minimum of 500 units of each product should be produced and sold each year. Fixed costs are £1.2 million per annum.

**6** What is the maximum annual profit that Five Mail Jam plc could earn?

A £752,350
B £855,300
C £855,590
D £856,660

*Circle your answer*

A   B   C   D

**7** What is the shadow price of one week's capacity on a machine which is suitable for making all four products?

A £640
B £2,000
C £2,240
D £2,530

*Circle your answer*

A   B   C   D

# 5: DECISION ACCOUNTING

**8** Rhonda Bout Limited uses three components, P, Q and R, in its main product. The budget for next year indicates a requirement for 3,000 of each component. The components are all manufactured on the same machine, for which only 50,000 machine hours are available next year. The variable cost of internal manufacture of each component, together with the machine hours used, are shown in the table below. The table also shows the prices quoted by a sub-contractor for supplying the components.

| Component | Machine hours per unit | Variable cost £ per unit | Sub-contractor price, £/unit |
|---|---|---|---|
| P | 9 | 45 | 65 |
| Q | 5 | 70 | 78 |
| R | 12 | 56 | 80 |

What is the minimum total cost at which Rhonda Bout can obtain the full requirement of components?

A £562,992
B £563,016
C £565,900
D £575,016

*Circle your answer*

A  B  C  D

## Data for questions 9 - 11

Multiple Pileup (Carpets) plc manufactures and sells three standard types of carpet: Square, Round and Oblong. Budgeted costs and revenues for the products for next year are as follows.

|  | Square £000 | Round £000 | Oblong £000 | Total £000 |
|---|---|---|---|---|
| Sales | 220 | 260 | 380 | |
| **Production costs:** | | | | |
| Materials | 16 | 14 | 24 | |
| Labour | 48 | 60 | 108 | |
| Variable production overhead | 20 | 42 | 40 | |
| Fixed production overhead | 55 | 48 | 102 | |
|  | 139 | 164 | 274 | |

|  | Square £000 | Round £000 | Oblong £000 | Total £000 |
|---|---|---|---|---|
| Delivery costs | 18 | 32 | 40 | |
| Selling costs | 15 | 24 | 40 | |
| General overhead | 22 | 26 | 38 | |
|  | 55 | 82 | 118 | |
| Profit | 26 | 14 | (12) | 28 |

You are given the following information concerning cost behaviour.

• Material costs and variable production overhead are wholly variable.

*Continued...*

# 5: DECISION ACCOUNTING

- Labour cost is a combination of variable labour cost and a 20% surcharge which is added to the variable labour cost to recover the fixed cost of indirect labour. Indirect labour would not be saved if the manufacture of any product were discontinued.

- Fixed production overhead consists of some directly attributable fixed costs, which are allocated to their appropriate product, plus an apportionment of general fixed production overhead. This apportionment is at the rate of 50% of variable production overhead.

- Delivery costs consist of some directly attributable fixed costs, which are allocated to their appropriate product, plus an apportionment of general delivery costs. This apportionment is based on 50% of material cost.

- Selling costs consist of a 5% sales commission, plus apportioned general fixed costs.

- General overhead is a fixed cost which is apportioned according to sales value.

**9** The directors are considering ceasing the production and sale of Oblong. Assuming that this would not affect the sales of other products, what total annual profit or loss for the company will result?

A £69,000 loss
B £116,000 loss
C £40,000 profit
D £97,000 profit

*Circle your answer*

A    B    C    D

**10** It is possible to increase the sales of Round by 8%, if the sales commission is increased to 7% of sales revenue for this product only. Assuming that plans for Square and Oblong are not changed from the original budget, what annual profit would result?

A £32,624
B £33,664
C £38,920
D £39,780

*Circle your answer*

A    B    C    D

**11** Independent of the option in question 10, it is possible to invest £10,000 in an advertising campaign. The effect of this would be to increase the sales of Round by 25% and reduce the sales of Square by 15%. The sales of Oblong would be unaffected. Ignoring the option in question 10, what annual profit would result?

A £28,550
B £33,300
C £38,150
D £43,300

*Circle your answer*

A    B    C    D

# 5: DECISION ACCOUNTING

## Data for questions 12 and 13

Leftern Nonely Ltd has two machines which it uses to make the same product. Each machine has an annual output capacity of 40,000 units, but each has different characteristics resulting in the following total annual costs at different production levels, which must be in lots of 10,000 units.

| Annual production level | Annual total costs | |
|---|---|---|
| | Machine X | Machine Y |
| units | £000 | £000 |
| Nil* | 33 | 19 |
| 10,000 | 55 | 36 |
| 20,000 | 79 | 62 |
| 30,000 | 104 | 100 |
| 40,000 | 140 | 138 |

*This figure includes (1) direct material costs and (2) direct labour and direct expenses costs, which would be usable in other parts of the company if the machine were not used.

There is no option to dispose of either machine. The product sells for £3 per unit.

**12** If Leftern Nonely Ltd wished to manufacture 40,000 units per year, what would be the least-cost method of making them?

|   | On machine X | On machine Y |
|---|---|---|
| A | Nil units | 40,000 units |
| B | 10,000 units | 30,000 units |
| C | 20,000 units | 20,000 units |
| D | 30,000 units | 10,000 units |

Circle your answer

A    B    C    D

**13** What is the profit-maximising or loss-minimising volume of production and sales for the product?

A  50,000 units
B  60,000 units
C  70,000 units
D  80,000 units

Circle your answer

A    B    C    D

71

## 5: DECISION ACCOUNTING

**14** Lovell Crossing Limited is in the process of preparing a quotation for a special job for a customer. The job will require the following materials:

| Material | Units Required | Units already in stock | Book value of stock units £/unit | Net realisable value £/unit | Replacement price £/unit |
|---|---|---|---|---|---|
| P | 400 | - | - | - | 40 |
| Q | 230 | 100 | 62 | 50 | 64 |
| R | 350 | 200 | 48 | 23 | 59 |
| S | 170 | 140 | 33 | 12 | 49 |
| T | 120 | 120 | 40 | - | 68 |

Material Q is used regularly by the company. Materials R, S and T are in stock as the result of previous over-buying. No other use can be found for R, but the 140 units of material S could be used in another job as a substitute for 225 units of material V, which are about to be purchased at a price of £10 per unit. Material T has no other use, and Lovell Crossing Ltd has been informed that it will cost £160 to dispose of the material currently in stock.

What is the relevant cost of the materials for this special job for the customer?

A  £37,410
B  £38,880
C  £47,530
D  £47,730

Circle your answer

A     B     C     D

**15** The following budgeted information is available for a division of a company that manufactures small motors.

|  | £ |
|---|---|
| Variable costs | 48,000 |
| Fixed costs | 52,000 |
| Total cost | 100,000 |
| | |
| Production in units | 8,000 motors |
| Machine hours available/needed for production | 5,000 hours |

The motors are needed elsewhere in the company, and up to 4,000 units could be purchased from an outside supplier at a cost of £2 each above the variable cost of producing the motors internally. The machine hours released could then be used on the following production.

| Product | Unit contribution £ | Maximum demand in the period units | Machine hours per unit |
|---|---|---|---|
| L | 10 | 250 | 5 |
| M | 30 | 125 | 10 |
| N | 4 | 1,250 | 1 |

# 5: DECISION ACCOUNTING

Profit will be greatest if the division:

A  manufactures 4,000 motors, 125 units of M and 1,250 units of N

B  manufactures 4,000 motors, 250 units of L and 125 units of M

C  manufactures 6,000 motors, and 1,250 units of N

D  manufactures 8,000 motors

*Circle your answer*

| A | B | C | D |

**16** Parkun Tuckett is considering the purchase of a photocopier. Each alternative provides the same quality of copy, although there are considerable differences in cost as detailed below.

| Model | PHC1 | Model PHC2 | PHC3 |
|---|---|---|---|
| Variable cost (per 100 copies) | £15 | £18 | £20 |
| Annual fixed cost | £20,500 | £16,000 | £12,500 |

The annual fixed costs would all be incremental costs.

Management is uncertain about the expected number of copies, n hundred, to be taken next year. Which one of the following decision rules would be appropriate?

A  If n < 1,500     buy PHC2
    If n > 1,500     buy PHC1

B  If n < 1,500     buy PHC3
    If 1,500 < n < 1,600     buy PHC2
    If n > 1,600     buy PHC1

C  If n < 1,750     buy PHC3
    If n > 1,750     buy PHC2

D  If n < 1,600     buy PHC3
    If n > 1,600     buy PHC1

*Circle your answer*

| A | B | C | D |

**17** Roy Dwirks Ltd, a company selling product Z for £10 per unit, has estimated the market capacity to be 200,000 units per year divided evenly between Sales Area S and Sales Area N. The company has estimated that the market penetration it can achieve for its product will depend on the size of its direct sales force, as follows.

## 5: DECISION ACCOUNTING

| Number of salesmen used per area | Market penetration expected % |
|---|---|
| 1 | 50 |
| 2 | 60 |
| 3 | 66 |
| 4 | 70 |
| 5 | 72 |

Salesmen can be employed at an incremental cost of £23,500 per year each. Variable costs of sales of product Z would be:

|  | Area S | Area N |
|---|---|---|
| Up to 65,000 units pa | £5 per unit | £6 per unit |
| Over 65,000 units pa | £6 per unit, for units above 65,000 | £7 per unit, for units above 65,000 |

Roy Dwirks Limited can employ up to 6 salesmen. What is the profit-maximising sales force?

|   | Area S | Area N |
|---|---|---|
| A | 2 salesmen | 2 salesmen |
| B | 3 salesmen | 2 salesmen |
| C | 3 salesmen | 3 salesmen |
| D | 4 salesmen | 2 salesmen |

*Circle your answer*

A   B   C   D

## Data for questions 18 and 19

Marta Wise Limited have been asked to quote a price for a special contract which will take one week to complete. An extract from the costing information is as follows.

Labour requirements:

| Grade of labour | Hours required | Basic wage rate per hour |
|---|---|---|
| Skilled | 27 | £7 |
| Semi-skilled | 14 | £4 |
| Unskilled | 20 | £2 |

A shortage of skilled labour means that the relevant staff would have to be moved from other work which is currently earning a contribution of £8 per hour, net of wages cost.

Semi-skilled labour are currently being paid semi-skilled rates to do unskilled work. If they are moved from this work for the contract, unskilled labour would be taken on to replace them.

Unskilled labour hours are charged to contracts at the basic wage rate plus 50% to cover production overheads, of which 60% are variable.

The contract will utilise a specialised machine which is currently being hired out at £175 per week. Depreciation on this machine is £120 per week.

*Continued...*

# 5: DECISION ACCOUNTING

> £280 has already been spent preparing specialised drawings for this contract. If it does not go ahead, the drawings can be sold for £250. Drawings costs are allocated to the relevant contracts as administration overhead.
>
> In addition to the drawings cost, fixed administration overhead of £150 is to be apportioned to this contract.

**18** Using an opportunity cost approach, what is the relevant cost of labour for this contract?

A £284
B £312
C £473
D £501

*Circle your answer*

A   B   C   D

**19** What is the minimum price for this contract, which would only just cover net relevant costs?

A £910
B £926
C £1,121
D £1,190

*Circle your answer*

A   B   C   D

**20** Orpen Rhodes plc has set a target 20% annual rate of return on investment for all products. The fixed assets employed on one of their products, the Banger, amount to £160,000; working capital investment for the Banger is £52,500. Total costs to be incurred on the Banger for next year are forecast at £250,000. Orpen Rhodes plc uses cost plus pricing.

What is the required percentage mark up on cost for Bangers?

A 4.2%
B 12.8%
C 17.0%
D 20.0%

*Circle your answer*

A   B   C   D

**21** The demand for a product at the current price has a price elasticity greater than one. Which of the following statements must be correct?

*Statement*
1  A reduction in price will increase total revenue.
2  A reduction in price by z% will result in a percentage increase in sales demand which is greater than z%.
3  An increase in price will increase total profit.

75

A   Only Statements 1 and 2 must be correct
B   Only Statements 1 and 3 must be correct
C   Only Statements 2 and 3 must be correct
D   Statements 1, 2 and 3 must all be correct

Circle your answer

A   B   C   D

**22** Graphic Signals Limited has derived the following functions for the total cost (TC) and price (P) of their product:

$$TC = 48{,}000 + 75Q + 0.3Q^2$$
$$P = 89 - 0.7Q$$

where Q is quantity demanded.
What is the price per unit which will maximise profit?

A   £10.77
B   £84.10
C   £104.20
D   £126.17

Circle your answer

A   B   C   D

**23** A profit maximising firm has the following annual total cost (TC) and demand functions for its single product, where x represents the number of units produced and sold.

$$TC = 10{,}000 + 100x$$
Demand function: $P = (280 - 0.3x)$

There is sufficient capacity to increase annual production by 40 units.

The firm is considering whether to spend £18,000 per annum to modernise its equipment so reducing variable costs to £70 per unit.

What effect would the decision to modernise the equipment have on annual profits and would surplus capacity remain?

|   | Annual profits | Surplus capacity |
|---|---|---|
| A | Increase | Yes |
| B | Increase | No |
| C | Decrease | Yes |
| D | Decrease | No |

Circle your answer

A   B   C   D

**24** Derek Track, the managing director of Moddy Paths Limited has recently experimented with a substantial price reduction for the company's single product. As expected, the quantity demanded rose significantly.

Price charged per unit                      £145      £120
Quantity demanded per month (units)         5,000     11,250

Continued...

The marketing director believes that the demand function for the product is linear, and that further price reductions are needed to maximise profit. The variable cost of the product is £27 per unit.

Assuming that the marketing director is correct, what unit price should be charged in order to maximise monthly profit?

A £83
B £84
C £95
D £96

*Circle your answer*

A    B    C    D

**25** Which of the following statements correctly describes ABC Inventory Analysis?

*Statement*

A   A method of analysing material stocks according to the rate of turnover. Group A contains those items where turnover is fastest, and Group C consists of dormant and slow-moving items. Management can ensure that turnover rates are on target, and the analysis helps to highlight the stock items which are in danger of becoming obsolete.

B   A method of analysing material stocks according to their unit value. Group A contains stock items with highest unit value, Group C contains the cheapest items. This analysis helps managers to concentrate their control action on the most costly stock items.

C   A method of analysing material stocks according to the annual usage quantity. Group A contains the items which are used most during the year, Group C contains the least used items. This analysis helps managers to concentrate their control action on the items which are most important to the production programme.

D   A method of analysing material stocks according to the annual usage value. Group A contains those items which account for the greatest proportion of annual material usage cost, and Group C contains the items representing the least annual usage value. This analysis helps management to concentrate their control action on the items which represent the greatest proportion of total material cost.

A Statement A
B Statement B
C Statement C
D Statement D

*Circle your answer*

A    B    C    D

**26** Information for a particular stock item is as follows:

Cost of placing an order     = £5 per order
Annual demand     = 42,000 units
Cost of holding a stock unit for one month     = £0.50

What is the economic order quantity, to the nearest 5 units?

## 5: DECISION ACCOUNTING

A  265 units
B  315 units
C  675 units
D  915 units

*Circle your answer*

A   B   C   D

**27** Roden Arrows Limited currently places orders for a particular stock item at quarterly intervals. Information concerning this item is as follows:

Cost of placing an order = £10
Annual demand = 20,000 units
Purchase price per unit = £0.50

The cost of storing the stock item amounts to 20% of the stock value per annum.

What annual cost saving would result if Roden Arrows used the economic order quantity for order sizes, instead of their current policy?

A  £80
B  £90
C  £150
D  £240

*Circle your answer*

A   B   C   D

**28** Speared Lummet plc is deciding on its stock ordering policy for an important component, the MPH. Relevant data is as follows.

Annual requirement = 300,000 units
Cost of placing an order = £2
Cost of holding one unit of MPH in
  stock for one year = £1.20

The supplier quotes a basic price of £0.05 per unit for orders below 1,200 units. Thereafter, the following discount structure applies:

On orders of 1,200 - 1,599 units   -  5% discount on all units ordered
On orders of 1,600 - 1,999 units   -  7.5% discount on all units ordered
On orders of 2,000 units and above -  8% discount on all units ordered

What quantity should Speared Lummet plc order each time, in order to minimise total costs?

A  1,000 units
B  1,200 units
C  1,600 units
D  2,000 units

*Circle your answer*

A   B   C   D

# 5: DECISION ACCOUNTING

## Data for questions 29 and 30

Friel Lane Hemway Ltd buys and re-sells a product which has variable monthly demand. Its selling price is £50 per unit. Data for the past quarter were as follows.

| Month | Orders received 000 units | Purchases 000 units |
|---|---|---|
| 1 | 15,000 | 12,000 |
| 2 | 14,000 | 11,000 |
| 3 | 11,000 | 15,000 |

At the beginning of month 1, there was opening stock of 2,000 units.

1. There is an arrangement with the supplier for a standing monthly order of 12,000 units at a price of £30 each. This order can only be changed by giving three months' notice in advance.

2. If the monthly order is reduced below 12,000 units, the company must pay a penalty of £7 per unit for each unit by which the revised order falls below 12,000 units.

3. If the monthly purchase order exceeds 12,000 units per month, the purchase price for the extra units (above 12,000) is £42 per unit.

4. Stockholding costs are £2 per month, for any units in stock at the beginning of the month.

5. If the company is out of stock and cannot deliver to the customer in the month of order, the customer receives a discount on the selling price of 10% for each month of the delay.

6. Stock carried forward is valued at £30 per unit.

7. Fixed costs are £500,000 per quarter for the product.

**29** What was the company's profit for the product in the quarter?

- A £228,000
- B £243,000
- C £271,000
- D £288,000

*Circle your answer*

A  B  C  D

## 5: DECISION ACCOUNTING

**30** What would have been the effect on profit for the quarter if a decision had been taken to purchase a minimum of 12,000 units per month and a maximum of 14,000 per month, so that purchases in months 2 and 3 had been adjusted accordingly, and opening stock in month 1 had still been 2,000 units?

A  Profit would have been £7,000 higher
B  Profit would have been £12,000 higher
C  Profit would have been £17,000 higher
D  Profit would have been £24,000 higher

*Circle your answer*

A   B   C   D

### Data for questions 31 - 36

Doug Uptheroyd Limited manufactures two products, p and q, which earn a contribution of £8 and £14 per unit respectively. The company expects to have a limited availability of certain resources during the forthcoming year and the management accountant has used a linear programming computer package to assist in determining the optimal production plan. The contribution-maximising tableau produced by this package is as follows:

| Variables in the solution | p | q | j | k | l | m | Solution column |
|---|---|---|---|---|---|---|---|
| p | 1 | 0 | 1 | -2 | 0 | 0 | 1,000 |
| q | 0 | 1 | -0.5 | 1.5 | 0 | 0 | x |
| l | 0 | 0 | -0.375 | 0.625 | 1 | 0 | 125 |
| m | 0 | 0 | -1 | 2 | 0 | 1 | 200 |
| Solution row | 0 | 0 | y | 5 | 0 | 0 | 29,000 |

In this tableau:  
j  is the number of unused skilled labour hours
k  is the number of unused machine hours
l  is the number of unused tonnes of material
m  is the amount of unsatisfied demand for product p

x and y relate to the questions which follow.

**31** How many units of product q should be produced, as indicated by x in the tableau?

A  1,500 units
B  1,750 units
C  21,000 units
D  27,675 units

*Circle your answer*

A   B   C   D

## 5: DECISION ACCOUNTING

**32** Which of the following statements concerning the next period are correct?

*Statement*
1. There will be some machine hours unused.
2. All of the available material will be utilised.
3. The demand for product p will not be fully satisfied.

- A  Statement 1 only is correct
- B  Statements 1 and 2 only are correct
- C  Statements 2 and 3 only are correct
- D  Statement 3 only is correct

Circle your answer

A    B    C    D

**33** An equipment hire company can provide more machine capacity. The variable cost per machine hour for production within the company is £4 per hour. What is the breakeven price that Doug Uptheroyd can pay for one extra machine hour, in order to achieve the same level of profit?

- A  £1.5
- B  £5.0
- C  £5.5
- D  £9.0

Circle your answer

A    B    C    D

**34** For how many extra machine hours would the breakeven price in the previous question be valid?

- A  200 hours
- B  500 hours
- C  1,000 hours
- D  2,000 hours

Circle your answer

A    B    C    D

**35** What is the shadow price per skilled labour hour, as indicated by y in the tableau?

- A  nil
- B  £0.875
- C  £1.00
- D  £3.00

Circle your answer

A    B    C    D

**36** If one more machine hour is made available, what would be the change in the recommended production volume of q?

- A  Reduce production by 1.5 units
- B  No change in production
- C  Increase production by 1 unit
- D  Increase production by 1.5 units

Circle your answer

A    B    C    D

## 5: DECISION ACCOUNTING

### Data for questions 37 - 40

Zeikel Path Ltd produces three products P, Q and R, each of which uses the same three materials, M1, M2 and M3. These materials are all expected to be in short supply next month, with maximum availability restricted to 6,000 kg of M1, 6,125 kg of M2 and 3,200 kg of M3. Products P, Q and R earn contributions per unit of £20, £14 and £16 respectively, but production and sales of product P cannot exceed 1,000 units in any month.

Ben Tweel, the management accountant of the company, has used a linear programming model to establish a contribution-maximising production and sales budget for next month. (The company carries no stocks of materials or finished goods). The output from the model is as follows.

Objective function value 36,800.00

| Variable | Value |
|---|---|
| P | 1,000.00 |
| Q | 400.00 |
| R | 700.00 |

| Row | Slack or surplus | Dual prices |
|---|---|---|
| M1 | 0.00 | 2.00 |
| M2 | 425.00 | 0.00 |
| M3 | 0.00 | 4.00 |
| Demand P | 0.00 | 12.00 |

Ranges in which the basis is unchanged
Obj coefficient ranges

| Variable | Current coefficient | Allowable increase | Allowable decrease |
|---|---|---|---|
| P | 20.00 | Infinity | 12.0000 |
| Q | 14.00 | 2.0000 | 2.0000 |
| R | 16.00 | 2.6667 | 2.0000 |

Right hand side ranges

| Row | Current RHS | Allowable increase | Allowable decrease |
|---|---|---|---|
| M1 | 6,000.00 | 400.00 | 106.25 |
| M2 | 6,125.00 | Infinity | 425.00 |
| M3 | 3,200.00 | 50.00 | 200.00 |
| Demand P | 1,000.00 | 170.00 | 1,000.00 |

Use these figures to answer questions 37-40.

**37** If the contribution-maximising budget is chosen, for which materials will the maximum quantities available be fully utilised?

A  Material M1 only
B  Material M2 only
C  Material M3 only
D  Materials M1 and M3 only

Circle your answer

A   B   C   D

# 5: DECISION ACCOUNTING

**38** What would the contribution per unit of product P need to fall below before there would be a change in the budgeted quantities of P, Q and R in the model's optimal solution?

A  Below £8 per unit
B  Below £12 per unit
C  Below £17.33 per unit
D  Below £18 per unit

*Circle your answer*

A   B   C   D

**39** What would the contribution per unit of product R need to rise above before there would be a change in the budgeted quantities of P, Q and R in the model's optimal solution?

A  Above £16 per unit
B  Above £18 per unit
C  Above £18.67 per unit
D  Above £22 per unit

*Circle your answer*

A   B   C   D

**40** Suppose that the availability of material M1 might be above or below 6,000 kg for the month. The dual price of M1 in the model's solution is £2 per kg, but this dual price only applies if the available quantity of M1 is:

A  within the range 5,575 kg - 6,400 kg
B  within the range 5,600 kg - 6,106.25 kg
C  within the range 5,893.75 kg - 6,400 kg
D  6,000 kg exactly

*Circle your answer*

A   B   C   D

# CHAPTER 6

# INVESTMENT APPRAISAL

> This chapter covers the following topics:
> - Evaluating proposed investments
> - Accounting rate of return
> - Payback method
> - Discounted cash flow
> - Taxation in investment appraisal
> - Inflation in investment appraisal
> - Evaluating risk in investment appraisal

## 1. Evaluating proposed investments

1.1 The financial evaluation of proposed capital investments should consider both return and risk. There are several techniques for the evaluation of returns.

## 2. Accounting rate of return (ARR)

2.1 There are several different ways of calculating the ARR. One method is:

$$\text{ARR} = \frac{\text{Estimated average annual profits}}{\text{Estimated average investment}} \times 100\%$$

2.2 Using ARR as an investment criterion, if a proposed investment has an estimated ARR in excess of the organisation's target ARR, the decision would be to go ahead with the project.

2.3 The major criticisms of the ARR method are that

- it does not take account of the *timing* of cash flows and the time value of money
- it considers profits, not cash flows.

Investment appraisal should be a form of decision accounting, using incremental costs and opportunity costs etc, which are cash flow items.

# 6: INVESTMENT APPRAISAL

## 3. Payback method

3.1 The payback period is the time taken for the cash inflows from a project to repay the cash outflows. Notice that *cash flows* are used in calculating the payback period. This means excluding accounting items such as depreciation from the calculations.

3.2 Companies may use payback as an initial screening device for investment projects. If a project passes the first 'hurdle' of a desirable payback period, then more sophisticated investment appraisal techniques may be used.

3.3 As an alternative to using estimated cash flows to determine the payback period, cash flows from a project might be discounted to a present value, and a *discounted* payback period calculated. The discounted payback period will be longer than the non-discounted payback period.

3.4 Advantages claimed for use of payback are that

- it assists liquidity,
- it reduces risk, since short term forecasts are likely to be more accurate than long term forecasts.

3.5 A major disadvantage of the payback method is that it takes no account of the *overall* profitability of a project.

## 4. Discounted cash flow

4.1 The concept of the time value of money recognises that earlier cash flows are most important to a company. The sooner a company recovers cash from an investment project, the sooner the returns can be re-invested.

4.2 Discounted cash flow (DCF) is an investment appraisal technique which takes into account both the time value of money and also the total profitability over a project's life. DCF is therefore superior to both ARR and payback as a method of investment appraisal.

4.3 As with the payback method, DCF looks at the *cash flows* of a project, not accounting profits, because cash flows represent relevant costs and benefits in decision accounting. The timing of cash flows is taken into account by discounting them. The effect of discounting is to give a bigger value to cash flows that occur earlier - eg £1 earned after 1 year will be worth more than £1 earned after 2 years, which in turn will be worth more than £1 earned after 5 years, and so on.

4.4 The discounting formula to calculate the present value of a future sum of money at the end of n time periods is

$$\text{Present value} = \text{Future sum} \times \frac{1}{(1 + r)^n}$$

# 6: INVESTMENT APPRAISAL

where r is the cost of capital, expressed as a proportion. Present value tables show the value of $\frac{1}{(1+r)^n}$ for different values of r and n.

4.5 Present value can be defined as the cash equivalent now of a sum of money receivable or payable at a stated future date, discounted at a specified rate of return.

4.6 > Net Present Value, NPV, is the value obtained by discounting all cash flows of a capital project by a chosen target rate of return or 'cost of capital'. The NPV is the Present Value of cash inflows minus the Present Value of cash outflows.

A project will be financially viable if it has a positive NPV when the estimated cash inflows and outflows are discounted at the organisation's (or project's) cost of capital.

4.7 When a project produces constant cash flows for several years it is quicker to calculate the net present value by adding together the discount factors for the individual years. These total factors are described as 'annuity factors', or 'cumulative present value factors'.

Annuity tables give the present value of £1 per annum for n years, from years 1 to n, at a cost of capital of r, for different values of r and n.

4.8 > The *Internal Rate of Return (IRR)* of a project, also known as the *DCF Yield*, is the exact DCF rate of return which the project is expected to achieve - ie the rate at which the NPV = zero.

A project would be financially viable if its estimated DCF yield exceeded the company's cost of capital, or the project's target DCF yield.

4.9 The IRR is usually calculated by trial and error, interpolating between the NPVs obtained from two trial discount rates. For example:

> Net Present Value at 20% = £3,457
> Net Present Value at 25% = (£968)

The IRR can be estimated by interpolation as: $20\% + [\frac{3,457}{(3,457 + 968)} \times 5\%]$

$$= 23.9\%$$

This interpolation assumes that the NPV falls from £3,457 at 20% to (£968) at 25% at an even rate. This is not actually the case, and so there will be some inaccuracy in the estimated IRR; therefore the two test discount factors must be as close together as possible to avoid major computational inaccuracies.

## 5. Taxation in investment appraisal

5.1 Taxation has four main effects on an investment appraisal:

- profits and losses on projects may be subject to corporation tax and payments of taxation are cash outflows
- capital expenditure may attract capital allowances, and savings in taxation payments are cash savings/inflows
- taxation may affect the *timing* of cash flows
- taxation may affect the cost of capital (this is outside the scope of this book).

5.2 If profits are subject to taxation you should assume that the tax is paid in the year following that in which the profit is earned, unless the question states otherwise.

5.3 Capital allowance rules are often changed, and you should read examination questions carefully to ascertain how to calculate any allowances. Many examiners simplify the tax rules to speed up the cash flow computations. Check the question carefully and do not assume that standard tax rules apply. There is a question in this chapter to help you to test your ability to deal with capital allowances and other tax computations.

## 6. Inflation in investment appraisal

6.1
- If future cash flows are expressed in money values (ie inflated values) these cash flows must be discounted at the money rate of interest. This is usually the simplest method of calculation, because the cost of capital is generally expressed as a money cost of capital.

- If future cash flows are expressed in real values (ie discounted for the effects of inflation) these cash flows must be discounted again at the real rate of interest

- Both of these methods will result in the same NPV for a project

6.2 The link between the money rate of return (money cost of capital) and the real rate of return (real cost of capital) is expressed by the formula:

$$(1 + \text{money rate}) = (1 + \text{real rate}) \times (1 + \text{inflation rate})$$

However, this relationship is more difficult to assess in practice because of difficulties with the accurate measurement of inflation.

## 7. Evaluating risk in investment appraisal

7.1 Investments are not undertaken simply because their estimated returns exceed the organisation's targets. Estimated returns over a long-term project must be subject to considerable uncertainty, and this 'business risk' must be evaluated. Excessively risky projects should not be undertaken, if the prospective returns are not big enough to justify the risk.

7.2 Methods of evaluating risk include the following techniques.

- Applying a maximum payback period for the project

- Including an allowance for business risk in the company's cost of capital

- Sensitivity analysis - eg What if revenues from the project were 10% below expectation? What if labour costs were 15% higher etc? Alternatively, by what percentage would revenues have to fall short of expectation (or costs to exceed estimates) before the project ceased to be viable?

- Measuring the standard deviation of the NPV of the project, and relating this to the estimated size of the NPV

- Simulation modelling using a forecast model for the project and making variations in estimates of costs, benefits, timing of events etc.

> By assessing risk in one of these ways, it should be possible to make a judgement about whether the project's estimated returns are sufficient to make the project a desirable undertaking, given the level of risk involved.

# 6: INVESTMENT APPRAISAL

# QUESTIONS

In all questions in this chapter you should ignore the effects of inflation and taxation, unless otherwise stated.

## Data for questions 1 - 5

Verriott Curry plc is considering investing in a printing machine for a capital cost of £300,000. The machine will have a useful life of four years. Annual running costs will amount to £276,000, including straight line depreciation of £70,000 per annum. The estimated disposal value of the machine at the end of year 4 is its net book value.

The printing capacity of the machine will be 6 million copies per annum for each of the first two years, and 5 million copies per annum for each of the second two years. The company expects to be able to sell whatever the machine produces. Average contribution will be £60 per 1,000 copies.

**1** What is the payback period for the machine, assuming that all cash flows occur evenly?

A  0.83 years
B  1.92 years
C  1.95 years
D  2.09 years

*Circle your answer*

A    B    C    D

**2** What is the average Accounting Rate of Return, based on the initial investment?

A  18.0%
B  19.7%
C  65.3%
D  72.0%

*Circle your answer*

A    B    C    D

**3** What is the average Accounting Rate of Return, based on the average net book value?

A  33.8%
B  35.0%
C  36.0%
D  36.9%

*Circle your answer*

A    B    C    D

89

## 6: INVESTMENT APPRAISAL

**4** What is the Net Present Value of the project, at the company's cost of capital of 20%?

A £33,720
B £37,300
C £43,320
D £146,880

*Circle your answer*

A    B    C    D

**5** What is the approximate Internal Rate of Return (DCF Yield) of the project?

A 21.5%
B 27.9%
C 28.5%
D 32.1%

*Circle your answer*

A    B    C    D

**6** Saddler Flamm Limited have forecast the following cash flows for a project:

| Year | Cash flow £ |
|------|-------------|
| 0    | (280,000)   |
| 1    | 149,000     |
| 2    | 128,000     |
| 3    | 84,000      |
| 4    | 70,000      |

Using two decimal places in all discount factors, what is the Net Present Value of this project at a cost of capital of 16.5%?

A £29,270
B £32,195
C £33,580
D £35,120

*Circle your answer*

A    B    C    D

## Data for questions 7 - 9

Quayle Legges Ltd takes on a 5 year lease of a building for which it pays £27,200 as a lump sum payment. Quayle Legges then sub-lets the building for 5 years at a fixed annual rent, with the rent payable annually in arrears.

## 6: INVESTMENT APPRAISAL

**7** If the rent is set at a level that will earn a DCF yield of 17% for Quayle Legges, what will be the annual rental charge, to the nearest £100?

A £3,100
B £4,600
C £7,600
D £8,500

Circle your answer

A　B　C　D

**8** What would be the Net Terminal Value of the investment, to the nearest £100, if the annual rental had been £9,000 per annum and the company's cost of capital had been 16%?

A £4,800
B £6,200
C £14,500
D £14,700

Circle your answer

A　B　C　D

**9** Suppose that, instead of charging a fixed annual rent for the sub-lease of the building, Quayle Legges decides to charge a fixed rent for the first two years, and then to raise the annual rent by 10% in the third year. This rental charge would then be raised by a further 10% in year 5.

What would be the rental charge in year 1, to the nearest £100, that would give the company a DCF yield of 17% on its investment?

A £5,000
B £7,000
C £8,000
D £8,100

Circle your answer

A　B　C　D

### Data for questions 10 and 11

Barbara Q Dribbs Limited has funds of £130,000 available for investments in the forthcoming period, at a cost of capital of 20%. Capital will be freely available in the future, after the end of the forthcoming period. Details of six projects under consideration are as follows:

| Project | Investment required | Net Present Value at 20% |
|---|---|---|
| | £000 | £000 |
| P | 40 | 16.5 |
| Q | 50 | 17.0 |
| R | 30 | 18.8 |
| S | 45 | 14.0 |
| T | 15 | 7.4 |
| U | 20 | 10.8 |

The projects are completely independent of each other, and investment in one does not preclude investment in any other.

# 6: INVESTMENT APPRAISAL

**10** Assume that investment in fractions of projects is possible, and that the Net Present Value (NPV) would be reduced pro rata if a fractional investment is undertaken. What is the maximum NPV that Barbara Q Dribbs can earn from investment in these projects?

A £49,200
B £55,400
C £62,000
D £70,500

*Circle your answer*

A  B  C  D

**11** Barbara Q Dribbs now discovers that funds in the forthcoming period are actually restricted to £95,000. The directors decide to consider projects P, Q and R only. They wish to invest only in whole projects, but surplus funds can be invested to earn 25% per annum in perpetuity. Which of the following investment plans will produce the highest Net Present Value at a 20% cost of capital?

A Projects P and Q
B Projects P and R
C Projects Q and R
D Investing all the funds at 25%

*Circle your answer*

A  B  C  D

**12** Waldorf Solids Limited is currently deciding on the correct replacement period for its fleet of distribution vehicles. Relevant data is as follows:

| | £ |
|---|---|
| Purchase price per vehicle | 9,600 |
| Trade in value: | £ |
| after 2 years | 2,400 |
| after 3 years | 1,600 |
| after 4 years | 1,220 |
| after 5 years | 380 |

Operating costs, excluding depreciation:

| | £ |
|---|---|
| Year 1 | 1,890 |
| Year 2 | 3,180 |
| Year 3 | 3,230 |
| Year 4 | 3,480 |
| Year 5 | 4,620 |

The company's cost of capital is 15%.

What is the most economic replacement cycle for the vehicles?

A 2 years
B 3 years
C 4 years
D 5 years

*Circle your answer*

A  B  C  D

# 6: INVESTMENT APPRAISAL

**13** Ann Churvy-Hegg is considering the purchase of a mobile snack van for £12,000. The van will have a useful life of 6 years, but it will take some time for sales to build to maximum capacity. Ann estimates the sales pattern, plus food and running costs, to be as follows:

| Years | Costs, excluding depreciation £ | Sales demand as a % of maximum |
|---|---|---|
| 1 | 2,600 | 30% |
| 2 | 5,400 | 45% |
| 3 | 17,800 | 60% |
| 4 | 21,000 | 75% |
| 5 | 24,000 | 100% |
| 6 | 24,000 | 100% |

What must be the maximum annual sales capacity, to the nearest £100, in order to earn a DCF yield of 16% over the life of the van?

A   £15,000
B   £17,000
C   £22,000
D   £27,000

*Circle your answer*

A   B   C   D

**14** Fissench Ships Limited intends to invest in a machine to save on manual work in one of its departments. The directors had originally decided on a 20kg capacity machine, but they are now reviewing the possibility of a 25kg capacity machine. They are willing to make the additional investment in the bigger capacity machine if the incremental yield is sufficiently high. Both machines have a 10 year life.

Relevant data is as follows:

| Machine capacity | 20kg £000 | 25kg £000 |
|---|---|---|
| Purchase cost | 35 | 52 |
| Annual cost savings, excluding depreciation | 17 | 22 |

What is the approximate incremental DCF yield on the investment in an additional 5kg of capacity? Use DCF tables to 2 decimal places.

A   1.0%
B   6.9%
C   27.2%
D   29.4%

*Circle your answer*

A   B   C   D

## Data for questions 15 and 16

Duckworth Cherries plc are about to invest £400,000 in machinery and other capital equipment for a new product venture. Cash flows for the first 3 years are estimated as follows:

*Continued...*

## 6: INVESTMENT APPRAISAL

| Year | Net Cash Inflow £000 | Unskilled Labour Costs (included in net cash inflow) £000 |
|---|---|---|
| 1 | 210 | 52 |
| 2 | 240 | 61 |
| 3 | 320 | 68 |

Duckworth requires a 17% return for projects of this type. The above cash flows do *not* include expenditure on an advertising campaign, which will be incurred in equal annual amounts at the beginning of years 1, 2 and 3.

**15** Ignoring any residual values of the capital equipment, what is the maximum annual amount that can be spent on advertising, to the nearest £000?

A £57,000
B £59,000
C £61,000
D £69,000

*Circle your answer*

A   B   C   D

**16** The directors decide to incur the advertising expenditure recommended by you in your answer to the previous question, but they now discover that material costs will amount to £35,000 per annum, instead of the £28,000 annual cost contained in the original forecasts.

However, some savings can be made by investing in machinery to save on unskilled labour costs. Each machine costs £1,500 to buy and each machine will reduce unskilled labour costs by 2%.

How many machines must be purchased at the beginning of the project, in order to still achieve a 17% return?

A 4 machines
B 14 machines
C 18 machines
D 26 machines

*Circle your answer*

A   B   C   D

**17** Terry Massalata Limited is considering an investment which will earn a contribution of £40,000 each year for 25 years. The cost of capital for Terry Massalata Limited is 16%. What is the present value of the total contribution, to the nearest £000?

You should use the following information to calculate your discount factors.

Present value of £1 p.a. at 16%, for n years

| n = | Cumulative PV |
|---|---|
| 1 | 0.86 |
| 5 | 3.27 |
| 10 | 4.83 |
| 15 | 5.58 |

The PV factor at 16% of £1  at the end of year 5 = £0.48
at the end of year 10 = £0.23
and at the end of year 15 = £0.11

A £244,000
B £316,000
C £372,000
D £416,000

Circle your answer

A   B   C   D

**18** Blanquettes of Torquay is considering the purchase of an item of machinery costing £86,000. It would have a life of 4 years, after which it would be sold for £15,000. The machinery would earn a contribution of £41,000 per annum.

Annual writing down allowances of 25% will be available, and an allowance could be claimed against taxable profits of the current accounting year soon to come to an end.

The rate of corporation tax is 35%; the after tax cost of capital is 8%. Assume that tax payments occur in the year following the transactions.

What is the Net Present Value of the investment, to the nearest £100?

A £26,500
B £36,300
C £37,600
D £75,600

Circle your answer

A   B   C   D

**19** A company is appraising an investment which will save electricity costs. Electricity prices are expected to rise at a rate of 15% per annum in future, although the general inflation rate will be 10% per annum. The cost of capital for the company is 20%. What is the appropriate discount rate to apply to the forecast actual money cash flows for electricity?

A 20.0%
B 22.0%
C 26.5%
D 32.0%

Circle your answer

A   B   C   D

**20** Tree Cole Tarts plc is appraising an investment of £700,000 in plant, which will last four years and have no residual value. Fixed operating costs (excluding depreciation) will be £200,000 in the first year, increasing by 5% per annum because of inflation. The contribution in the first year is forecast at £620,000, increasing by 7% per annum due to inflation. The company's money cost of capital is 14%.

## 6: INVESTMENT APPRAISAL

What is the Net Present Value of the investment, to the nearest £1,000?

A £614,000
B £639,000
C £652,000
D £658,000

*Circle your answer*

A  B  C  D

**21** Victoria Plumb Ltd wishes to pay a consultant the following amounts:

| At the end of year | 1 | 2 | 3 |
|---|---|---|---|
| Amount to be paid | £12,000 | £14,500 | £16,200 |

However, the consultant prefers to receive a constant amount each year. The company's cost of capital is 15%. What annual amount should the company offer to pay, to the nearest £100? Use discount factors to 2 decimal places.

A £10,700
B £14,100
C £14,200
D £14,800

*Circle your answer*

A  B  C  D

**22** Cilla Bubb Ltd is considering investing £18,000 at a cost of capital of 18%, into a project which will earn £3,600 per annum in perpetuity. What is the net present value of the investment?

A £2,000
B £20,000
C £46,800
D £82,000

*Circle your answer*

A  B  C  D

**23** Cost Benefit Analysis (CBA) is a technique that can be used for evaluating projects such as the siting of new airports and building of new roads. Which of the following statements about CBA are correct?

*Statement*
1. Cost benefit analysis (CBA) attempts to include the social costs and benefits of a project in the project evaluation, by converting them into monetary values.

2. Social costs are valued at what the sufferers would regard as sufficient compensation to induce them to accept the cost willingly.

3. CBA also considers the 'distributional justice' of social costs and benefits, which is how social costs should be shared out between different sections of the community.

4. By providing a technique for evaluating social costs and benefits, CBA replaces the need for subjective judgement in public expenditure projects.

A  Statement 1 only is correct
B  Statement 1 and 2 only are correct
C  Statement 1, 2 and 3 only are correct
D  Statement 1, 2 and 4 only are correct

*Circle your answer*

A    B    C    D

## Data for questions 24 - 25

Pam Cakes, management accountant of Mixon Batter Ltd, has estimated that the cash flows for project XYZ would be as follows.

| Year | Investment £ | Running costs (all fixed) £ | Savings £ |
|---|---|---|---|
| 0 | (120,000) | | |
| 1 | | (80,000) | 150,000 |
| 2 | | (100,000) | 160,000 |
| 3 | | (120,000) | 170,000 |
| 4 | | (150,000) | 180,000 |

The project has a positive NPV of £22,900 when discounted at the company's cost of capital, which is 20% per annum.

**24** Suppose that on reviewing the cost estimates, Pam Cakes decides that running costs will in fact be 20% higher each year than originally estimated, although savings will be higher too. By what minimum percentage must annual savings be higher than originally estimated for the project to remain viable?

A  7.7%
B  8.4%
C  13.2%
D  13.5%

*Circle your answer*

A    B    C    D

**25** Suppose instead of the revised estimates in the previous question, Pam Cakes decides that savings will be 10% lower than originally estimated, although costs will not be as high either. By what minimum percentage must running costs be lower than originally estimated for the project to remain viable?

A  4.0%
B  5.5%
C  6.9%
D  15.2%

*Circle your answer*

A    B    C    D

## 6: INVESTMENT APPRAISAL

### Data for questions 26 - 28

Fiona Schnitzel, the accountant of Pomper Nichols Ltd, has estimated the cash flows from a proposed project as follows.

| | | |
|---|---|---|
| Life of project | 4 years | |
| Initial investment | £300,000 | |

| | First year | Annual rate of increase (compound) |
|---|---|---|
| Sales revenues | £300,000 | 3% pa |
| Direct materials | £80,000 | 5% pa |
| Direct labour and other direct expenses | £100,000 | 6% pa |

Cost of capital 18%.

Within any one year, direct costs vary with sales revenue.

**26** What is the NPV of the project?

A + £12,521
B + £19,858
C + £20,500
D + £36,836

*Circle your answer*

A  B  C  D

**27** Assuming unit sales prices, sales revenue growth of 3% per annum and all cost estimates to be correct, by what percentage (to the nearest decimal point, based on DCF tables in this book) could sales volume fall short of the expected amount in year 1 before the project ceased to be viable?

A 2.4%
B 6.2%
C 6.7%
D 10.9%

*Circle your answer*

A  B  C  D

**28** Assuming sales revenue estimates, the initial cost of the investment, year 1 cost estimates and the annual growth estimate for direct materials all to be correct, what is the maximum annual percentage growth rate in labour costs that could occur before the project ceased to be viable?

A 11%
B 12%
C 13%
D 14%

*Circle your answer*

A  B  C  D

# CHAPTER 7

# UNCERTAINTY AND DECISION MAKING

> This chapter covers the following topics:
> - Expected value
> - Sensitivity analysis and simulation models
> - Using standard deviation to measure risk

## 1. Expected value

1.1 Expected value (EV) takes account of uncertainty in a decision which can result in more than one possible outcome to which probabilities can be assigned.

> Example:
> 
> | Outcome £ | Probability | Outcome x Probability £ |
> |---|---|---|
> | 4,000 | 0.2 | 800 |
> | 7,000 | 0.4 | 2,800 |
> | 8,000 | 0.4 | 3,200 |
> | | Expected value | 6,800 |

1.2 The expected value of a decision is the weighted average result of the outcomes that will arise if the decision is repeated several times, or the outcomes will occur several times over. It is a valid basis for making a decision when the outcome *will* be repeated several times.

1.3 A decision for a *once-only event might* be taken by selecting the option with the highest EV of benefits or the lowest EV of costs, but it is arguable whether choosing the option with the best weighted average outcome is a valid basis for selection when the outcome is only going to happen once.

1.4 Expected values can also be used to assess the value of information (perfect or imperfect information) and how much it would be worth paying for more information before a decision is taken.

| | £ |
|---|---|
| EV of outcome if information is obtained | X |
| EV of outcome if decision is taken without the information | Y |
| Value of the information - maximum worth paying to obtain it | X - Y |

# 7: UNCERTAINTY AND DECISION MAKING

## 2. Sensitivity analysis and simulation models

2.1 Sensitivity analysis is a way of assessing the risk in a decision by varying the values of the key variables or forecasts (eg sales volume, exchange rates, unit costs) and showing the resultant effect on the outcome. A series of "what if" analyses can be carried out to see the effect of errors in the forecasts. For instance, it may be shown that a 5% change in the forecast sales volume has a negligible effect on the outcome, but that a 5% change in fixed costs has a dramatic effect. This would indicate that the decision is sensitive to changes in fixed costs. Management attention can be focused to ensure that the forecast for fixed costs is correct and that they are properly controlled once the decision is taken.

2.2 Computerised simulation models can also be used to assess the effect of uncertainty on decisions. The decision is simulated by recomputing the outcomes many times over using different values each time for the forecast variables. Scientific sampling procedures can be used to ensure that due weight is given to outcomes having higher probability ratings.

2.3 Sensitivity analysis and 'Monte Carlo' simulation models help with the assessment of risk, but do not indicate the optimal decision. The balance between risk and return in any choice or decision is one for management judgement.

## 3. Using standard deviation to measure risk

3.1 One way of measuring risk given probabilities of various outcomes is to calculate the standard deviation of the EV of the outcome. This indicates the scale of the possible spread of actual outcome values around the expected (average) value. If the possible outcomes are assumed to be normally distributed around the expected value, a statistical analysis of possible outcomes might be made, using normal distribution tables.

---

Example:

| Outcome £'000 $x$ | Probability $p$ | $x - \bar{x}$ (see note *) | $p(x - \bar{x})^2$ |
|---|---|---|---|
| 90 | 0.20 | - 32 | 204.8 |
| 120 | 0.40 | - 2 | 1.6 |
| 140 | 0.40 | 18 | 129.6 |
| | | | 336.0 |

Standard deviation = $\sqrt{336.0}$ = 18.330 (in £000) = £18,330

Note:* $\bar{x}$ = Expected value = (90 x 0.20) + (120 x 0.4) + (140 x 0.40) = 122 (in £000)

---

3.2 A useful comparison of the expected value of a decision against the measured risk is the ratio of one to the other, known as the *coefficient of variation*. The higher the coefficient of variation, the more risky the outcome.

# 7: UNCERTAINTY AND DECISION MAKING

# QUESTIONS

### Data for questions 1 - 3

Lebber Noone Seeders plc is launching a new product next year. Forecasts of sales are as follows:

| Annual sales £000 | Probability |
|---|---|
| 2,000 | 0.10 |
| 2,200 | 0.15 |
| 2,400 | 0.35 |
| 2,600 | |
| 2,800 | |

These are predicted to be the only possible outcomes, and the probability of sales of £2.6 million is exactly equal to the probability of sales of £2.8 million. The contribution to sales ratio (C/S ratio) for the product will be 25%. Fixed costs will be be £48,000 per month.

**1** What is the expected value of annual profit?

A £24,000
B £36,500
C £441,500
D £564,500

*Circle your answer*

A   B   C   D

**2** What is the probability of the product at least breaking even next year?

A 0.50
B 0.60
C 0.80
D 1.00

*Circle your answer*

A   B   C   D

**3** What is the probability of the product earning an annual profit of at least £100,000?

A 0.20
B 0.30
C 0.40
D 0.75

*Circle your answer*

A   B   C   D

# 7: UNCERTAINTY AND DECISION MAKING

**4**  Secombe Moore Limited forecast that the expected maintenance hours to be worked and their associated costs for next month are as follows:

| Maintenance hours | Probability | Cost £ |
|---|---|---|
| 54,000 | 0.4 | 14,250 |
| 60,000 | 0.5 | 15,000 |
| 66,000 | 0.1 | 15,900 |

The expected value of maintenance hours for next month is 58,200 hours. What are the expected value of maintenance costs for next month?

A £14,730
B £14,775
C £14,790
D £14,828

*Circle your answer*

A    B    **C**    D

## Data for questions 5 and 6

June Hipper Limited has four mutually exclusive investment opportunities, each one yielding different profits depending on the state of the market. There are four possible market states which could arise. The probability of each of these stages, together with the incremental profits with each project, are shown in the following pay-off table:

|  | Market state | | | |
|---|---|---|---|---|
|  | I | II | III | IV |
| Probability | 0.3 | 0.2 | 0.4 | 0.1 |
| *Investment opportunity* | £000 | £000 | £000 | £000 |
| North | 38 | 47 | 42 | 44 |
| South | 40 | 70 | 52 | 62 |
| East | 60 | 35 | 48 | 38 |
| West | 46 | 60 | 56 | 58 |

**5**  Using the highest expected value of profits as the selection criterion, which one of these four mutually exclusive projects should be undertaken?

A North
B South
C East
D West

*Circle your answer*

A    B    C    **D**

## 7: UNCERTAINTY AND DECISION MAKING

**6** What would be the value of perfect information about the state of the market?

A £600
B £4,100
C £6,600
D £16,000

*Circle your answer*

A   B   C   D

**7** Gordon Hedge Ltd is bidding for a contract which is due to be started within a few days. The contract will use up its stock of material XY which will otherwise be held for one month. In one month's time, there is a 0.6 probability that it will be used. If it is not used then, the material will be sold. Estimates are as follows:

|  | £ |
|---|---|
| Replacement cost of stock in one month's time | 15,000 |
| Sales value in one month's time | 12,000 |
| Stock holding costs for one month | 900 |

What is the expected relevant cost of material XY for use when evaluating the viability of the contract?

A £9,000
B £12,900
C £13,800
D £14,700

*Circle your answer*

A   B   C   D

**8** If Ortum Colours Ltd extends credit to a customer without first carrying out a credit check on the customer, there is a 15% probability that the customer will default, and the debt will have to be written off. The cost of carrying out a credit check on a customer is £180.

The company sells a variety of products, but for everything that it sells, the cost structure and profit margin are as follows.

|  | % |
|---|---|
| Variable cost | 60 |
| Fixed cost | 10 |
|  | 70 |
| Profit | 30 |
| Sales price | 100 |

What is the minimum order size per customer that would justify carrying out a credit check, assuming that the decision is based on expected values?

A £255 sales value
B £1,200 sales value
C £2,000 sales value
D £3,000 sales value

*Circle your answer*

A   B   C   D

103

# 7: UNCERTAINTY AND DECISION MAKING

## Data for questions 9 - 11

Roy O'Loke is about to embark on a new venture - selling strawberries from a roadside barrow. He has found a supplier who will provide him with strawberries at a basic price of £1 per kg, with discounts as follows:

| Purchases per day | Discount | (on full purchase quantity) |
|---|---|---|
| 100kg | - | |
| 200kg | 2% | |
| 300kg | 5% | |
| 400kg or more | 8% | |

Purchases can only be made in batches of 100kg, and Roy has to purchase the same quantity of strawberries every day of the season. He has to specify this daily requirement at the beginning of the season. Sales will be made at £1.50 per kg, and any stock unsold at the end of a day can be sold for pulp at £0.20 per kg.

---

**9** Roy decides that, on average, he can expect to sell 250kg per day. Viewing the market in this way, what is the maximum average daily profit that he can achieve?

- A £80
- B £100
- C £104
- D £132.50

*Circle your answer*

A    B    C    D

---

**10** Roy now decides to take a more sophisticated view of the market. He knows that his sales will depend on the weather, and produces the following sales and weather estimates:

| Weather | Daily sales quantity kg | Probability of weather conditions occurring |
|---|---|---|
| Sunny | 400 | 0.40 |
| Fine | 250 | 0.35 |
| Rainy | 100 | 0.25 |

On the basis of these weather estimates and sales estimates what level of daily purchases will give Roy the largest profit margin over a whole season?

- A 100kg
- B 200kg
- C 300kg
- D 400kg

*Circle your answer*

A    B    C    D

# 7: UNCERTAINTY AND DECISION MAKING

**11** Assume that the supplier is now willing to allow Roy to order varying amounts on a daily basis in batches of 100kg. Taking account of the probabilities for sales and weather conditions in the previous question, what is the maximum daily amount that Roy should pay for 100% correct weather prediction?

   A  £63.05
   B  £64.45
   C  £70.20
   D  £141.70

*Circle your answer*

A    B    C    D

## Data for questions 12 - 14

Wall Knott plc has the chance to pursue a short term venture that will utilise some spare resources. Possible sales volumes are as follows:

| Sales volume '000 units | Probability |
|---|---|
| 2 | 0.3 |
| 5 | 0.6 |
| 10 | 0.1 |

The sales price will be £65 per unit and promotion costs will amount to £50,000. This is a new product and no finished stocks are currently held. 5kg of material will be required per unit produced. 20,000kg of material are in stock at a book value of £6 per kg. The material is obsolete and could be sold off for £7 per kg. The current replacement price is £9 per kg.

Two hours of labour at £3 per hour are required per unit. If the venture is not undertaken, there are expected to be 10,000 hours of paid idle time.

Variable overhead is incurred at a rate of £5 per active labour hour. Fixed overhead will not be affected by the venture.

**12** What is the expected value of incremental profit from the venture?

   A  £27,000
   B  £36,000
   C  £51,000
   D  £77,000

*Circle your answer*

A    B    C    D

105

## 7: UNCERTAINTY AND DECISION MAKING

**13** What is the probability of at least breaking even on the venture?

A  0.10
B  0.30
C  0.70
D  1.00

Circle your answer

A    B    C    D

**14** It is possible to obtain information about the sales volume that would be achieved. The promotion campaign must be *arranged* before this information is available (although no costs would be incurred on the campaign), but if the sales prediction is low the campaign can be cancelled at a cost of £3,000.

What is the maximum amount that Wall Knott plc should pay for this information?

A  £1,800
B  £2,100
C  £3,000
D  £3,700

Circle your answer

A    B    C    D

### Data for questions 15 - 17

Dot Chelm, managing director of Mounter Nash Limited is currently deciding which of four mutually exclusive projects to undertake. Each of the projects could lead to different profits depending on whether demand is concentrated in the North, South, East or West of the country. The accountant has constructed the following pay-off table:

| Project | Net profit in £000 if demand is concentrated in: | | | |
|---|---|---|---|---|
|  | North | South | East | West |
| E | 75 | 98 | 120 | 100 |
| F | 135 | 90 | 112 | 108 |
| G | 105 | 120 | 85 | 105 |
| H | 120 | 92 | 100 | 95 |

**15** Using the maximin decision rule, to maximise the minimum achievable profit, which project would be selected?

A  Project E
B  Project F
C  Project G
D  Project H

Circle your answer

A    B    C    D

106

**16** Using the maximax decision rule, to maximise the highest achievable profit, which project would be selected?

A  Project E
B  Project F
C  Project G
D  Project H

*Circle your answer*

A   B   C   D

**17** Using the minimax regret decision rule, to minimise the opportunity loss, which project would be selected?

A  Project E
B  Project F
C  Project G
D  Project H

*Circle your answer*

A   B   C   D

### Data for questions 18 and 19

A company is currently appraising a possible investment in a project for which forecasts have been prepared as follows:

| | |
|---|---:|
| Initial investment (fixed assets) | £612,500 |
| Expected life | 10 years |
| Annual sales volume | 35,000 units |
| Contribution per unit | £8 |
| Annual fixed costs, excluding depreciation | £45,000 |

**18** Management are concerned about the risk associated with the project and have requested a sensitivity analysis. You are asked to test the sensitivity of the project to a 10% adverse change in a number of variables in isolation. The company's cost of capital is 15%.

To which of the following changes is the net present value of the project most sensitive?

A  10% adverse change in initial investment
B  10% adverse change in project life
C  10% adverse change in annual sales volume
D  10% adverse change in annual fixed costs

*Circle your answer*

A   B   C   D

**19** Depreciation would be based on the straight line method over 10 years to a residual value of £12,500. If the sales price per unit is £20, by how much could this price be reduced for all units sold, given sales of 35,000 units per annum, before the project ceased at least to break even annually, in marginal costing terms?

## 7: UNCERTAINTY AND DECISION MAKING

A £2
B £3
C £4
D £5

*Circle your answer*

A  B  C  D

### Data for questions 20 and 21

Al de Berry Limited are considering launching two complementary products, P and Q. The sales of the products will be interdependent, and the possible annual sales of P are as follows:

Sales of Product P
| £'000 | Probability |
|---|---|
| 40 | 0.3 |
| 50 | 0.5 |
| 60 | 0.2 |

The interdependence of the sales volumes is forecast to be as follows:

| If annual sales of Product P are: | There is a probability of: | that annual sales of Product Q will be: |
|---|---|---|
| £40,000 | 0.20 | £70,000 |
|  | 0.60 | £50,000 |
|  | 0.20 | £40,000 |
| £50,000 | 0.40 | £60,000 |
|  | 0.60 | £30,000 |
| £60,000 | 0.50 | £60,000 |
|  | 0.50 | £70,000 |

**20** What is the expected value of total annual sales from products P and Q?

A £98,600
B £102,000
C £138,600
D £179,300

*Circle your answer*

A  B  C  D

**21** What is the probability of achieving total sales of at least £100,000 per annum?

A 0.12
B 0.46
C 0.54
D 0.84

*Circle your answer*

A  B  C  D

## 7: UNCERTAINTY AND DECISION MAKING

**22** Douglas Fir-Banks Ltd sells product WX which it has been selling at a price of £20 per unit, and making a profit of £250,000 per year after covering fixed costs of £150,000. Its management is considering the effect of a price increase to £22 and has made the following estimates.

| Sales demand at a price of £22 | Probability |
|---|---|
| 39,000 units | 0.15 |
| 37,000 units | 0.50 |
| 35,000 units | 0.35 |

| Unit variable cost | Probability |
|---|---|
| £10.0 | 0.20 |
| £9.5 | 0.25 |
| £9.0 | 0.55 |

The volume of sales demand and the unit variable cost are unrelated to each other.

The management have decided that the price rise would not be justified unless there is a probability of at least 75% that contribution would increase to £450,000 or more.

What is the probability that the contribution would be £450,000 or more at a selling price of £22 per unit?

A   0.7425
B   0.8425
C   0.9300
D   1.0000

*Circle your answer*

A   B   C   D

**23** The standard costing records of Hugh Calliptos Ltd showed an adverse material usage variance of £1,200 for the latest period. Based on past experience, the management accountant believes that:

- the cost incurred if the variance is allowed to continue unchecked will be £1,050, if it is due to a controllable cause
- the cost of investigating the variance will be £300
- the probability of the variance being uncontrollable is 0.45
- the cost of corrective action, if the variance is controllable, will be £350

Ignore the time value of money.

What is the expected value of the net benefit of investigating the variance?

A   £15
B   £85
C   £235
D   £1,285

*Circle your answer*

A   B   C   D

# 7: UNCERTAINTY AND DECISION MAKING

## Data for questions 24 - 26

Lee Finnook Limited is currently appraising a project which involves the investment of a fixed amount at the beginning of the project, to generate a constant annual contribution for 5 years. The company's cost of capital is 16%.

The PV of £1 per annum for 5 years at 16% is 3.27.

Management has forecast a range of possible levels of required initial investment and annual contribution:

| Initial investment | | Annual contribution | |
|---|---|---|---|
| £m | Probability | £000 | Probability |
| 1.80 | 0.15 | 650 | 0.10 |
| 1.95 | 0.25 | 680 | 0.30 |
| 2.00 | 0.40 | 700 | 0.55 |
| 2.15 | 0.20 | 720 | 0.05 |

The different levels of investment and contribution are independent of each other.

The management accountant is carrying out a risk analysis using a computer simulation based on random numbers. Random numbers are allocated from the lowest levels of initial investment or annual contribution at 00, increasing to the highest levels at 99.

For a particular simulation run, the random numbers drawn were:

    15   for initial investment
    60   for annual contribution

**24** What is the net present value (NPV) of the project for this simulation, with the random numbers drawn?

    A  £268,800
    B  £339,000
    C  £489,000
    D  £1,550,000

*Circle your answer*

    A    B    C    D

**25** What is the expected value of the NPV of the project?

    A  £268,800
    B  £339,000
    C  £547,050
    D  £1,297,500

*Circle your answer*

    A    B    C    D

**26** The biggest worry for the management of Lee Finnook Limited is that *either* the initial investment will be £2.15m, *or* that annual contribution will be £650,000.

## 7: UNCERTAINTY AND DECISION MAKING

What is the probability that *either or both* of these events will occur?

A  0.02
B  0.28
C  0.30
D  0.32

*Circle your answer*

| A | B | C | D |

## Data for questions 27 and 28

Coker Nutt Limited intends to provide a new type of business service, and has to decide on the location of its premises. Demand for the service will arise in either the north or south of the country. The cost of setting up premises will be £200,000 in the south of the country and £180,000 in the north. The company expects no residual value from this investment. The cost of relocating the premises after 4 years is:

   from south to north            £15,000
   from north to south            £20,000

In the first 4 years, there is a 70% chance that the majority of customers will be in the south. In years 5 to 8 there is a 65% chance that the majority of customers will be in the north. Annual net cash inflow will be £80,000, *reduced by 25%* if the company is not located in the same area as the majority of customers.

The cost of capital is 15%. Ignore taxation and inflation.

The discount factor of £1 p.a. at 15%
   for years 1 - 4 is 2.86
   for years 5 - 8 is 1.63
   for years 1 - 8 is 4.49

The discount factor at 15% for £1 in year 4 is 0.57.

**27** Which location decision will produce the largest expected net present value in years 1 to 8?

A  Locate south initially; move north after 4 years

B  Locate south and remain in south for 8 years

C  Locate north initially; move south after 4 years

D  Locate north and remain in north for 8 years

*Circle your answer*

| A | B | C | D |

**28** What is the maximum expected value of NPV to the nearest £000, that can be earned in years 1 to 8?

111

## 7: UNCERTAINTY AND DECISION MAKING

A  £122,000
B  £128,000
C  £290,000
D  £293,000

*Circle your answer*

A   B   C   D

**29** The management accountant of Homaganay Limited is concerned about cash flow. He has warned the directors that there is a 60% probability that the bank overdraft limit will be exceeded if extended supplier credit cannot be negotiated. The purchasing manager has estimated that the probability of success in negotiating extended supplier credit is only 25%.

What is the probability that the overdraft limit will be exceeded?

A  0.10
B  0.15
C  0.45
D  0.85

*Circle your answer*

A   B   C   D

### Data for questions 30 and 31

A project has the following possible outcomes:

| Net income £000 | Probability |
|---|---|
| 150 | 0.2 |
| 200 | 0.5 |
| 260 | 0.3 |

The management accountant decides to use statistical analysis to measure the risk associated with the project.

**30** What is the standard deviation of the expected value of the project, to the nearest £10?

A  £10,320
B  £38,940
C  £45,210
D  £77,890

*Circle your answer*

A   B   C   D

**31** What is the coefficient of variation of the project?

A  0.05
B  0.14
C  0.19
D  0.22

*Circle your answer*

A   B   C   D

# CHAPTER 8

# PERFORMANCE MEASUREMENT AND TRANSFER PRICING

> This chapter covers the following topics:
> - Return on capital employed
> - Residual income
> - Transfer pricing

## 1. Return on capital employed

1.1 Return on capital employed (ROCE) is one of the most frequently used performance appraisal indicators. It shows how much profit has been earned in relation to the amount of capital invested. ROCE is sometimes referred to as ROI, return on investment, particularly when assessing the performance of individual divisions within an organisation.

1.2 ROCE (ROI) can be measured in a variety of different ways in management accounts, including:

- profit after depreciation as a percentage of net assets employed at the year end

- profit after depreciation as a percentage of net assets employed at the beginning of the year

- profit after depreciation as a percentage of gross assets employed, either at the beginning or end of the year

- profit after depreciation as a percentage of average assets employed.

Profit could be measured by the historical cost accounting convention, or by some form of current value accounting method. Assets could be at book value, replacement cost or some other form of current value.

The list is almost endless, so the message is: *read the question carefully to make sure that you use the correct basis of calculation for ROCE.*

1.3 An investment centre is a part of an organisation for which both the profit and the level of investment can be measured. The performance of the investment centre can then be assessed, often using ROCE (ROI). If performance is assessed using ROCE, we should expect that investment centre managers will probably undertake new capital projects *only if* these new projects are likely to increase the ROI of their centre. This can often lead to investment centre managers taking decisions which are not in the best interests of the organisation as a whole - "sub-optimal" decisions.

# 8: PERFORMANCE MEASUREMENT AND TRANSFER PRICING

> - Example of sub-optimality and a lack of goal congruence
>
> It might be group policy that investments earning 15% or more should be undertaken. If a subsidiary is currently earning an ROI of, say, 30%, its manager might want to reject a project whose return would be, say, 20%, because it would reduce the centre's overall ROI below 30%. The investment might be desirable from the group's point of view, but the manager would want to reject it. The manager's individual goals would not be congruent with the goals of the group as a whole.

## 2. Residual income

2.1 Residual income, sometimes called residual profit, is a measure of an investment centre's performance after deducting a notional or imputed interest cost based on the value of the investment in the division.

> Residual income = Divisional profit - (Notional interest rate x Divisional investment)

2.2 Residual income will increase if a new investment earns a profit after depreciation which is greater than the imputed interest charge on the value of the extra capital invested. Residual income will go up even if the extra profit only marginally exceeds the imputed interest charge. This means that 'marginally profitable' investments are likely to be acceptable to the investment centre manager. In contrast, when a manager is judged by ROI, a marginally profitable investment is likely to be rejected because it would reduce the average ROI earned by the centre as a whole.

2.3 Even so, decisions based on changes in residual income (RI) are not always congruent with decisions based on DCF appraisal techniques.

## 3. Transfer pricing

3.1 A transfer price is the price at which goods and services are transferred from one part of the organisation to another part of the same organisation. The transfer price can be established to suit the objectives of the transfer pricing system, and many different bases of calculation can be used, including full or marginal cost, standard or actual cost, market price etc.

3.2 There are several different methods of setting transfer prices and each is useful in different situations. But one overriding point must be remembered, and that is that the objective of transfer pricing is twofold:

- to motivate managers to take actions which are in the interests of the organisation as a whole

- to provide a fair basis of charging for internal transfers, so that relative performance can be judged more effectively.

# 8: PERFORMANCE MEASUREMENT AND TRANSFER PRICING

3.3 In multinational companies, a further aim of transfer prices between subsidiary companies might be to improve cash flows and tax-efficiency within the group.

3.4 There are some questions in this chapter which will test your ability to manipulate transfer prices in different situations. Meanwhile, it may be helpful to list some guidelines for identifying the optimal transfer price.

> (a) The ideal transfer price should reflect the opportunity cost of sale to the supply division and the opportunity cost to the buying division (ie purchase price available externally and/or the contribution obtainable from the extra output that could be made and sold with the transferred items).
>
> (b) The opportunity cost of transfer, when unit variable costs and unit selling prices are constant, will be:
>
> (i) external market price; or
> (ii) external market price less savings in selling costs
>
> where an external market price exists.
>
> (c) In the absence of an external market price for the transferred item, but when unit variable costs are constant, the the sales price per unit of the end-product is constant, the ideal transfer price should reflect the opportunity cost of the resources consumed by the supply division to make and supply the item.
>
> (i) In some cases, this may simply be the standard variable cost of production.
> (ii) When there is a scarce production resources, the transfer price might be the variable cost of production plus the contribution forgone by using the scarce resource, instead of putting it to its most profitable alternative use.
>
> THE TRANSFER PRICE SHOULD BE STANDARD VARIABLE COST
> + OPPORTUNITY COST OF MAKING THE TRANSFER
>
> (d) When unit variable costs and/or unit selling prices are not constant, either in the intermediate market or the end-market, a more difficult problem arises, and the ideal transfer price will only be found by sensible negotiation and careful analysis.
>
> The starting point should be to establish the output and sales quantities that will optimise the profits of the company or group as a whole.
>
> Having done this, the next step is to establish the transfer price at which both profit centres, the supply division and the buying division, would maximise their profits at this company-optimising output level.
>
> (e) There may be a range of prices within which both profit centres can agree on the output level that would maximise their individual profits and the profits of the company as a whole. Any price within the range would then be 'ideal'. However, in some circumstances, there may be just one ideal transfer price.

# 8: PERFORMANCE MEASUREMENT AND TRANSFER PRICING

# QUESTIONS

## Data for questions 1 - 3

The manager of the Containers Division has prepared the following forecasts for his division for next year:

|  | £ |
|---|---|
| Operating profit | 85,000 |
| Depreciation | 20,000 |
| Net current assets at beginning of year | 30,000 |
| Net book value of fixed assets at beginning of year | 180,000 |

The company's cost of capital is 25%.

**1** What is the forecast return on investment and residual income for the division, based on beginning of year balance sheet values?

|   | Return on investment % | Residual income £ |
|---|---|---|
| A | 31.0 | 12,500 |
| B | 31.0 | 20,000 |
| C | 36.1 | 20,000 |
| D | 40.5 | 32,500 |

*Circle your answer*

A   B   C   D

**2** The manager is now considering the sale of a machine which is included in his original forecasts. The machine earns an annual profit of £2,500 after depreciation of £500, has a net book value of £6,000 and could be sold for this amount. He would use the proceeds plus further cash from Head Office to purchase a new machine for £15,000. The new machine would earn an annual profit of £5,200, after depreciation of £2,000.

What will be the division's total return on investment, based on beginning of year balance sheet values, if the new investment is undertaken?

A  30.9%
B  31.6%
C  35.8%
D  40.0%

*Circle your answer*

A   B   C   D

116

## 8: PERFORMANCE MEASUREMENT AND TRANSFER PRICING

**3** What will be the division's total residual income, based on beginning of year balance sheet values, if the new investment detailed in the previous question is undertaken?

   A  £11,450
   B  £12,950
   C  £16,925
   D  £34,450

   *Circle your answer*

   A   B   C   D

**4** Division X of Tina Pease Ltd produced the following results in the last financial year:

|  |  | £000 |
|---|---|---|
| Net profit |  | 360 |
| Capital employed: | fixed assets | 1,500 |
|  | net current assets | 100 |

For evaluation purposes all divisional assets are valued at original cost. The division is considering a project which will increase annual net profit by £25,000 but will require average stock levels to increase by £30,000 and fixed assets to increase by £100,000. Tina Pease Ltd imposes an 18% capital charge on its divisions.

Given these circumstances, will the evaluation criteria of Return on Investment (ROI) and Residual Income (RI) motivate division X management to accept the project?

|   | ROI | RI |
|---|-----|-----|
| A | Yes | Yes |
| B | Yes | No |
| C | No  | Yes |
| D | No  | No |

   *Circle your answer*

   A   B   C   D

**5** Division Y of Glasser Milk Ltd is considering a project which will increase annual net profit after tax by £45,000, but will require average stock levels to increase by £180,000. The current target accounting return on investment is 28% and the imputed interest cost of capital is 20%.

In these circumstances would the performance evaluation systems of Return on Investment (ROI) and Residual Income (RI) motivate the managers of division Y to act in the interest of the company as a whole?

|   | ROI | RI |
|---|-----|-----|
| A | No  | No |
| B | No  | Yes |
| C | Yes | No |
| D | Yes | Yes |

   *Circle your answer*

   A   B   C   D

117

# 8: PERFORMANCE MEASUREMENT AND TRANSFER PRICING

**6** A manager of a trading division of the Bagger Marbles Group has complete discretion over the purchase and use of fixed assets and stock. Head Office keeps a central bank account, collecting all cash from debtors and paying all creditors. The division is charged a management fee for these services. The performance of the manager of the division is assessed on the basis of his controllable residual income. The Bagger Marbles Group requires a rate of return of I% from all its divisions.

|  |  |
|---|---|
| Divisional fixed assets | F |
| Divisional working capital |  |
|   Debtors | D |
|   Stock | S |
|   Creditors | (L) |
| Divisional net assets | W / Z |
|  |  |
| Divisional profit | P |
| Head office management charges | (M) |
| Divisional net profit | N |

What should be the correct formula for calculating the controllable residual income of the division?

A   N - F.I  
B   P - Z.I  
C   N - (F+S)I  
D   P - (F+S)I  

*Circle your answer*

A   B   C   D

**7** Presented below are the net income and investment base data of three divisions:

| Division | Net income | Investment base | Return on investment |
|---|---|---|---|
|  | £ | £ |  |
| X | 155,000 | 1,000,000 | 15.5% |
| Y | 200,000 | 1,250,000 | 16.0% |
| Z | 250,000 | 1,500,000 | 16.7% |

What is the maximum imputed interest charge on the investment base that will produce the same ranking of divisional performance using residual income as is produced using return on investment base?

A   15.5%  
B   16.7%  
C   18.0%  
D   20.0%  

*Circle your answer*

A   B   C   D

# 8: PERFORMANCE MEASUREMENT AND TRANSFER PRICING

**8** The following data relate to Jim Jarr plc, a manufacturing company with several divisions. Division X produces a single product which it sells to Division Y and also to outsiders.

|  | Division X Sales to Division Y £ | Division X External sales £ |
|---|---|---|
| Sales revenue: at £35 per unit |  | 350,000 |
| at £30 per unit | 150,000 |  |
| Variable costs at £18 per unit | (90,000) | (180,000) |
| Contribution | 60,000 | 170,000 |
| Fixed costs | (50,000) | (120,000) |
| Profit | 10,000 | 50,000 |

A supplier offers to supply 4,000 units at £25 each to Division Y.

Divisional managers are given freedom of choice for selling and buying decisions, and their performance is judged solely according to divisional profitability.

If Division X does not match the lower price offered by the external supplier and cannot increase its external sales, so that Division Y chooses to purchase from the external supplier:

|   | Division X profit will be | Jim Jarr's Ltd's profit will be |
|---|---|---|
| A | Nil | £28,000 lower |
| B | Nil | £20,000 higher |
| C | £12,000 | £28,000 lower |
| D | £12,000 | £20,000 higher |

Circle your answer

| A | B | C | D |

---

## Data for questions 9 - 11

A group of companies is divided into three autonomous operating divisions. The group cost of capital is 15%. In ROCE calculations, the capital employed is taken as the figure at the beginning of the year. All fixed assets are depreciated on a straight line basis.

If no new capital expenditure transactions take place, the forecast results for next year are:

| Division | Capital employed at beginning of year £000 | Net profit for year (after depreciation) £000 |
|---|---|---|
| P | 410 | 130 |
| Q | 620 | 175 |
| R | 570 | 132 |

The managers are proposing the following transactions, all of which take place at the beginning of the year.

Division P:   Invest £50,000 to increase net profit by £11,500 per annum

Continued...

## 8: PERFORMANCE MEASUREMENT AND TRANSFER PRICING

> **Division Q:** Sale at net book value of a machine which is budgeted to earn a net profit after depreciation of £7,000 next year. The original equipment cost £225,000 four years ago with an expected life of five years and no residual value. The sale proceeds would be remitted to Head Office.
>
> **Division R:** Sale, at net book value of £5,000, of a machine which is forecast to earn an annual profit after depreciation of £2,000. Head Office would invest a further £14,000 to enable the purchase for £19,000 of a machine which will earn an annual profit after depreciation of £3,500.

**9** If the proposed transactions went ahead, which divisional managers would receive a higher bonus, if such bonuses are directly related to the level of ROCE in the division?

A Managers of divisions P and Q only
B Managers of divisions Q and R only
C Manager of division P only
D Manager of division Q only

*Circle your answer*

A  B  C  D

**10** If the proposed transactions went ahead, which divisional managers would receive a higher bonus, if such bonuses are directly related to the level of Residual Income in the division?

A Divisions P and Q only
B Divisions Q and R only
C Division P only
D Division Q only

*Circle your answer*

A  B  C  D

**11** What is the incremental Residual Income on the transaction proposed by Division P?

A £4,000
B £7,500
C £9,775
D £11,500

*Circle your answer*

A  B  C  D

### Data for questions 12 - 18

Two subsidiary companies of Bowler Soups plc, E Limited and F Limited, achieved the following results last year:

|  | E Limited £000 | F Limited £000 |
|---|---|---|
| Operating profit | 1,000 | 1,600 |
| Depreciation charge included in operating profit | 200 | 250 |
| Fixed assets at cost | 7,000 | 9,400 |
| Accumulated depreciation | 5,000 | 3,100 |
| Net current assets | 180 | 230 |

*Continued...*

The straight line method is used to calculate depreciation. The group cost of capital is 15%.

For a more effective comparison of performance, certain adjustments are to be made to the above results.

- Fixed assets are to be revalued to replacement cost. Assuming cost price equals 100, the following price indices are to be used to revalue fixed assets.

    E Limited        170
    F Limited        130

- Adjustments are to be made to F Limited results to bring the accounting treatment into line with that used by E Limited:
    o  E Limited purchased a computer at the beginning of last year for £100,000, with a five-year life and no residual value. F Limited leased an identical computer at the same time for £27,000 per annum.
    o  both companies incurred £15,000 of development costs last year. E Limited wrote off the whole cost; F Limited decided to spread the cost over 3 years.

**12** What is the ROCE of E Limited, after the revaluation of fixed assets?

A   24.0%
B   26.7%
C   27.9%
D   29.4%

*Circle your answer*

A    B    C    D

**13** What is the Residual Income of E Limited, after the revaluation of fixed assets?

A   £304,000
B   £323,000
C   £350,000
D   £463,000

*Circle your answer*

A    B    C    D

**14** What is the adjusted operating profit for F Limited, after the revaluation of fixed assets and adjustments for the other factors given in the data?

A   £1,517,000
B   £1,522,000
C   £1,525,000
D   £1,597,000

*Circle your answer*

A    B    C    D

121

## 8: PERFORMANCE MEASUREMENT AND TRANSFER PRICING

**15** What is the adjusted capital employed for F Limited, after the revaluation of fixed assets and adjustment for the other factors given in the data?

A £8,257,000
B £8,407,000
C £8,420,000
D £8,487,000

*Circle your answer*

A    B    C    D

**16** What is the adjusted ROCE for F Limited, after the revaluation of fixed assets and adjustment for the other factors given in the data?

A 17.6%
B 17.9%
C 18.0%
D 18.1%

*Circle your answer*

A    B    C    D

**17** Each company is to be offered a new investment of £350,000 which will generate an annual operating profit of £70,000. Would the directors accept or reject the project, if their company performance was to be assessed on fully-adjusted ROCE figures and each company's directors will only accept the project if it improves the subsidiary's ROCE?

|   | *E Limited* | *F Limited* |
|---|---|---|
| A | Accept | Accept |
| B | Accept | Reject |
| C | Reject | Reject |
| D | Reject | Accept |

*Circle your answer*

A    B    C    D

**18** Consider again the new investment in the previous question. Would the directors accept or reject the project, if the company performance was to be assessed using Residual Income and each company's directors will only accept the project if it improves the subsidiary's ROCE?

|   | *E Limited* | *F Limited* |
|---|---|---|
| A | Accept | Accept |
| B | Accept | Reject |
| C | Reject | Reject |
| D | Reject | Accept |

*Circle your answer*

A    B    C    D

# 8: PERFORMANCE MEASUREMENT AND TRANSFER PRICING

## Data for questions 19 - 22

The following information has been provided to the Head Office of Cuppak Hokoe plc by a newly-acquired subsidiary, Mugg Limited. Mugg Limited commenced operations in 19X6 and the figures submitted need to be adjusted for group performance comparison purposes.

| Year | Purchases of fixed assets at cost Freehold premises £000 | Plant & machinery £000 | End of year price level index for plant and machinery |
|---|---|---|---|
| 19X5 | - | - | 96 |
| 19X6 | 200 | 192 | 100 |
| 19X7 | - | 80 | 116 |
| 19X8 | - | 116 | 120 |
| 19X9 | - | 120 | 125 |

All fixed asset purchases were made at the beginning of the year. Depreciation of plant and machinery is calculated on a straight line basis over 4 years. Plant and machinery is disposed of for nil value at the end of 4 years. Freehold premises are not depreciated. Mugg Limited's operating profit after depreciation for 19X9 was £240,000. Working capital at the end of 19X9 amounted to £150,000. The market value of the freehold premises has increased by 10% per annum. Mugg Limited also pays £30,000 per annum for rented premises. Group policy is to capitalise rented accommodation, for comparison purposes, on the basis of a 15% return. The Group uses year-end written down net replacement values for fixed assets in all calculations of capital employed.

**19** What is the operating profit for Mugg Limited for 19X9, after the revaluation of fixed assets and adjustments for Group accounting policy?

A £217,000
B £221,500
C £247,000
D £255,240

*Circle your answer*

A    B    C    D

**20** What is the capital employed for Mugg Limited at the end of 19X9, after the revaluation of fixed assets and adjustments for Group accounting policy?

A £624,070
B £731,250
C £814,788
D £824,070

*Circle your answer*

A    B    C    D

# 8: PERFORMANCE MEASUREMENT AND TRANSFER PRICING

**21** What is the fully adjusted Return on Capital Employed for Mugg Limited in 19X9?

A  26.3%
B  30.0%
C  34.8%
D  39.6%

*Circle your answer*

A   B   C   D

**22** What is the fully adjusted Residual Income for Mugg Limited in 19X9 using a cost of capital of 20%?

A  £52,186
B  £82,186
C  £92,186
D  £122,186

*Circle your answer*

A   B   C   D

## Data for questions 23 - 26

Smallparcel Limited, a subsidiary of the Raptin Brown Paper Group plc, has the following budgeted results for next year:

| Extract from budgeted results | £000 |
|---|---|
| Capital employed | 1,600 |
| Operating profit | 400 |

The Group uses Return on Capital Employed (ROCE) to assess the performance of subsidiary companies, valuing fixed assets at net book value at the year end, and net current assets at average value for the year. Depreciation is calculated on a straight line basis. The Group expects all investments to earn a minimum 18% DCF return over four years.

In addition to the budgeted results, Smallparcel Limited is considering the following three independent investments:

I   Invest £300,000 in plant that will reduce annual revenue costs by £100,000. The plant would be purchased at the beginning of next year, with a useful life of four years and no residual value

II  Invest £8,000 at the beginning of the year in a computerised stock control system. The investment would be regarded as a revenue expense and one extra member of staff would be employed at a cost of £9,000 per annum. The system would reduce stock levels by an average of £45,000 over the year. The extra cash generated would be remitted to Group head office.

*Continued...*

III  Increase the period of credit allowed to customers. Debtors would increase by an average of £35,000 over the year, the extra cash required being provided by Group head office. The resulting increased sales are expected to generate an annual contribution of £25,000.

Ignore taxation and inflation.

Discount factors at 14%:  PV of £1 in year 1           = £0.85
                          PV of £1 p.a. in years 1 - 4 = £2.69

**23** What would be Smallparcel Limited's ROCE for next year, if only investment I is undertaken?

  A  22.4%
  B  23.3%
  C  26.3%
  D  27.4%

  Circle your answer

  A   B   C   D

**24** What would be Smallparcel Limited's ROCE for next year, if only investment II is undertaken?

  A  24.3%
  B  24.6%
  C  24.9%
  D  25.0%

  Circle your answer

  A   B   C   D

**25** What would be Smallparcel Limited's ROCE for next year, if only investment III is undertaken?

  A  26.0%
  B  26.3%
  C  26.6%
  D  27.2%

  Circle your answer

  A   B   C   D

**26** Which of the three investments, considered separately, are likely to encourage goal congruence between Raptin Brown Paper Group plc and Smallparcel Limited for next year?

  A  Investment I only
  B  Investment II only
  C  Investments I and II only
  D  Investments I and III only

  Circle your answer

  A   B   C   D

## 8: PERFORMANCE MEASUREMENT AND TRANSFER PRICING

### Data for questions 27 - 30

Penn Fuller Fink Limited has two divisions, Division 1 and Division 2, each of which manufactures a single product. Two units of the Division 1 product are required to manufacture one unit of the Division 2 product. The output of Division 1 can be sold externally, or transferred to Division 2. All of the output of Division 2 is sold externally. Information concerning costs, prices and volumes is as follows:

|  | Division 1 £/unit | Division 2 £/unit |
|---|---|---|
| External sales price | 45 | 154 |
| Variable production costs (excluding transfer price) | 16 | 32 |
| Variable selling costs | 2 | 1 |
|  | 18 | 33 |
| Annual fixed costs | £120,000 | £160,000 |
| Annual external sales | 8,000 units | 7,000 units |
| Investment in the division | £1,950,000 | £500,000 |

The company cost of capital is 16%. The transfer price for the product between Division 1 and Division 2 is obtained by deducting the variable selling expenses from the external sales price, since these costs are not incurred on internal sales.

**27** What is the annual Return on Capital Employed for Division 1?

A  14.6%
B  22.9%
C  24.3%
D  30.1%

*Circle your answer*

A   B   C   D

**28** What is the annual Residual Income for Division 1?

A  (£27,000)
B  £134,000
C  £162,000
D  £274,000

*Circle your answer*

A   B   C   D

**29** What is the annual Return on Capital Employed for Division 2?

A  11.4%
B  17.0%
C  77.2%
D  92.6%

*Circle your answer*

A   B   C   D

## 8: PERFORMANCE MEASUREMENT AND TRANSFER PRICING

**30** What is the annual Residual Income for Division 2?

A (£23,000)
B £5,000
C £306,000
D £383,000

Circle your answer

A    B    C    D

**31** Butler Browne Nails (RBN) Ltd is a UK holding company with an overseas subsidiary. The directors of RBN Ltd wish to transfer profits from the UK to the overseas company. They are considering changing the level of the transfer prices charged on goods shipped from the overseas subsidiary to RBN Ltd and the size of the royalty payments paid by RBN Ltd to its overseas subsidiary.

In order to transfer profit from RBN Ltd to the overseas subsidiary, the directors of RBN Ltd should

A increase both the transfer prices and royalty payments

B increase the transfer prices but decrease the royalty payments

C decrease the transfer prices but increase the royalty payments

D decrease both the transfer prices and royalty payments

Circle your answer

A    B    C    D

## Data for questions 32 - 34

Boxer Trix plc has two divisions, P and Q. Division P manufactures product P, which can be sold externally or transferred to Division Q. Division Q uses three units of product P to manufacture one unit of product Q, which is sold externally. The directors of Boxer Trix consider that two possible market states could arise:

| State of market | Product P | | Product Q | |
|---|---|---|---|---|
| | External market price £/unit | External demand '000 units | External market price £/unit | External demand '000 units |
| I | 27 | Unlimited | 110 | 45 |
| II | 24 | 60 | 100 | 30 |

Other relevant information is as follows:

| | Division P | Division Q | |
|---|---|---|---|
| Standard variable cost per unit | £18 | £14 | (excluding 3 units of product of P) |
| Fixed costs per annum | £430,000 | £750,000 | |
| Budgeted annual capacity in units | 215,000 | 45,000 | |
| Maximum annual capacity in units | 215,000 | 70,000 | |

127

## 8: PERFORMANCE MEASUREMENT AND TRANSFER PRICING

**32** If Boxer Trix plc decides to set transfer prices on the basis of 'standard variable cost plus opportunity cost', what will be the transfer price if Market State I arises?

A £18
B £23
C £27
D £45

*Circle your answer*

A  B  C  D

**33** If Boxer Trix plc decides to set transfer prices on the basis of 'standard variable cost plus opportunity cost', what will be the transfer price if Market State II arises?

A £18
B £20
C £24
D £36

*Circle your answer*

A  B  C  D

**34** Division Q now receives a special order for 15,000 units of product Q at a price of £70 each. The order will not affect other sales. Consider the following four situations:

| Situation number | State of Market | Basis of transfer price |
|---|---|---|
| 1 | I | Standard variable cost per unit |
| 2 | I | Standard variable cost plus opportunity cost per unit |
| 3 | II | Fully absorbed standard cost per unit |
| 4 | II | Standard variable cost per unit |

In which of these situations would the manager of Division Q and the manager of Boxer Trix plc both want the same decision to be made concerning acceptance of the order?

A Situations 1 and 2 only
B Situations 1, 3 and 4 only
C Situations 2 and 4 only
D Situations 2, 3 and 4 only

*Circle your answer*

A  B  C  D

**35** Roy Bishbin Ltd has two divisions P and Q. Division P transfers all its output to division Q, which finishes the work. Costs and revenues at various levels of capacity are as follows.

| Output | Division P costs | Division Q costs | Total revenue (sales by Division Q) |
|---|---|---|---|
| units per day | £ | £ | £ |
| 1 | 510 | 100 | 1,400 |
| 2 | 730 | 150 | 2,100 |
| 3 | 960 | 220 | 2,550 |
| 4 | 1,200 | 320 | 2,900 |
| 5 | 1,480 | 470 | 3,200 |
| 6 | 1,800 | 630 | 3,450 |

## 8: PERFORMANCE MEASUREMENT AND TRANSFER PRICING

Each division is a profit centre, and each divisional manager wishes to maximise his/her divisional profits.

Within what ranges should the transer prices per unit be so that the managers of each division agree on what the daily volume of output should be, and so that this volume of output is one which will maximise the company's overall profits?

- A £150 - £250 per unit
- B £240 - £250 per unit
- C £240 - £280 per unit
- D £280 - £300 per unit

Circle your answer

A   B   C   D

### Data for questions 36 and 37

Division X is a profit centre which produces three products, Long, Tall and Short. Each product has an external market, but Tall can also be transferred to Division Y. The maximum quantity that might be required for transfer is 30 units of Tall. Information on the products is as follows:

|  | Long | Tall | Short |
|---|---|---|---|
| External market price per unit | £84 | £81 | £70 |
| Variable production cost in Division X, per unit | £57 | £41 | £49 |
| Labour hours required per unit in Division X | 3 | 4 | 2 |
| Maximum external sales, in units | 1,400 | 875 | 525 |

**36** If labour hours in Division X are limited to 1,170, what is the appropriate transfer price for a unit of Tall?

- A £41
- B £77
- C £81
- D £83

Circle your answer

A   B   C   D

**37** If labour hours in Division X are limited to 4,670, what is the appropriate transfer price for a unit of Tall?

- A £41
- B £68
- C £77
- D £81

Circle your answer

A   B   C   D

## 8: PERFORMANCE MEASUREMENT AND TRANSFER PRICING

**38** Division K sells all of its output to Division L. Division L processes the output further and sells the finished product externally. Changes in output can only be made in steps of 100 units, and the resulting costs and revenues for the relevant range of output are as follows:

| Units | Division K costs | Division L costs (excluding transfer price) | Division L external revenue |
|---|---|---|---|
|  | £000 | £000 | £000 |
| 100 | 15 | 25 | 80 |
| 200 | 32 | 65 | 155 |
| 300 | 54 | 107 | 230 |
| 400 | 77 | 139 | 290 |
| 500 | 110 | 186 | 360 |

Management require a transfer price which is a whole number of £ per unit. The manager of K will not transfer extra units unless it is profitable for his division to do so. The manager of L will not purchase extra units from K unless it is profitable for his division to do so.

What is the most appropriate narrow range of transfer price per unit between the two divisions, in order to maximise total company profit and to obtain *agreement* between the divisional managers about what the activity level should be?

A £221 to £229
B £231 to £279
C £231 to £329
D £281 to £329

*Circle your answer*

A  B  C  D

---

**39** PG Division of Chopin Bagge Ltd achieved the following results for the year to 31 December 19X1.

|  | £000 | £000 |
|---|---|---|
| Sales |  | 570 |
| Direct materials | 120 |  |
| Direct labour | 60 |  |
|  |  | 180 |
| Contribution |  | 390 |
| Bought-in services | 50 |  |
| Indirect materials | 15 |  |
| Nominal rental | 40 |  |
| Depreciation | 30 |  |
| Salaries | 150 |  |
|  |  | 285 |
| Profit before interest |  | 105 |
| Notional interest |  | 15 |
| Profit net of interest (residual interest) |  | 90 |

Nominal rental is a notional charge for the use of space in the company's office buildings.

The division's performance is to be measured by valued added. (Depreciation will be accounted for as an item retained within the business).

What value added (added value) did the division achieve in the year?

A £330,000
B £385,000
C £400,000
D £450,000

*Circle your answer*

A  B  C  D

# CHAPTER 9

# JOINT PRODUCT COSTING AND PROCESS COSTING

> **This chapter covers the following topics:**
>
> - Joint product and by-product costing
> - Process costing: introduction
> - Process costing: work in progress and equivalent units
> - Process costing: losses in process
> - Standard process costing

## 1. Joint product and by-product costing

1.1 Joint products are two or more products which are output from the same processing operation and which are indistinguishable from each other up to the point of separation. Each joint product has a significant sales value when compared with the sales value of the other product(s).

1.2 The point at which the joint products become separately identifiable is known as the separation point or split-off point. Costs incurred up to this point can be referred to as joint costs, common costs or pre-separation point costs.

1.3 There are basically three main methods which can be used to apportion joint costs between the joint products:

- Physical measurement.    The costs are apportioned according to the proportion of total weight or volume represented by the output of each joint product.

- Relative sales value.    The costs are apportioned according to the proportion of total sales value represented by the output of each joint product.

- Notional sales value.    Sometimes called proxy sales value, this method is appropriate when the products are not saleable at the separation point. The joint costs are apportioned on the basis of the final sales value of output less further processing costs incurred after the separation point and up to the point of sale.

1.4 Whichever method is used to apportion joint costs, you should be aware that the resulting arbitrary apportionment, like all overhead apportionment, should usually be ignored when preparing data for decision making purposes.

However, a distinction between fixed and variable joint costs can be made, and could be significant for decision-making purposes.

1.5 When a joint product is output from a process, it may be in a condition ready for immediate sale, but by processing it further it may be sold instead for a higher price. In such a situation, management may have to decide whether or not to process the product further. This is the 'joint product further processing decision'. The decision rule is:

> Joint products should only be subject to further processing if the incremental costs incurred are less than the resulting increase in sales value.

1.6 A by-product is a product which arises *incidentally* in the production of the main product or products. It has a relatively low sales value in comparison with the main product(s). The usual method of accounting for a by-product is to deduct the net realisable value of the by-product from the cost of the process, thus reducing the cost of the main product or products.

## 2. Process costing: introduction

2.1 Process costing is the costing method which is used when the production process consists of a continuous stream of identical units. A major feature of the process costing system is the task of cost accounting, which is to establish a cost per unit of production for the purposes of stock valuation, profit measurement and (possibly) cost control and pricing.

## 3. Process costing: work in progress and equivalent units

3.1 The concept of equivalent units is used to apportion process costs when there is work in progress (WIP), either at the beginning or end of a period. Units in WIP are not complete, therefore it is not 'fair' that they should be allocated the same cost as complete units. The concept of equivalent units helps us to deal with this situation.

> *Example of the concept of equivalent units, using FIFO method*
>
> If opening WIP is 200 units which are 40% complete, completed production is 5,000 units, and closing WIP is 300 units which are 20% complete, the equivalent units produced in the period are:
>
> | | *1st method of calculation* | | | *2nd method of calculation* | |
> |---|---|---|---|---|---|
> | | Completed units | 5,000 | | Completion of opening WIP | |
> | | Closing WIP (300 x 20%) | 60 | | (200 x 60%) | 120 |
> | | | 5,060 | | plus Units started and | |
> | *less* | Opening WIP (200 x 40%) | 80 | | completed in the period | 4,800 |
> | *=* | Equivalent units | | | plus Closing WIP | 60 |
> | | produced | 4,980 | = | Equivalent units produced | 4,980 |

# 9: JOINT PRODUCT COSTING AND PROCESS COSTING

3.2 Once the equivalent units of production have been established, the net process costs are apportioned over this number of units. A distinction is often made between equivalent units of materials and equivalent units of conversion costs (direct labour and production overhead). This is because the degree of completion of WIP may be different for each of these cost elements.

3.3 Closing WIP is valued at

Equivalent units of direct material x cost per equivalent unit of material
*plus* Equivalent units of conversion cost x cost per equivalent unit of conversion cost

3.4 The method of stock valuation in process costing may be FIFO, weighted average pricing or standard costing (see 5).

| *FIFO* | *Weighted average pricing* |
| --- | --- |
| • Process costs for the period exclude value of opening WIP b/fwd | • Process costs for the period include value of opening WIP b/fwd |
| • Units of opening WIP are valued at the number of equivalent units of work needed to complete them in the period | • Units of opening WIP are valued at a full equivalent unit of work done |

The cost per equivalent unit will differ according to the method of stock valuation used.

## 4. Process costing: losses in process

4.1 Losses occur in processing, from evaporation, wastage and so on. *Normal loss* is the process loss that is expected to occur in the normal course of events. Although it is a well accepted principle that the cost of normal loss should be shared out between other units of production, practice can vary and you must read all examination questions carefully to check what is the required costing treatment.

4.2 *Abnormal losses* arise when the actual process loss is higher than the normal loss and *abnormal gains* arise when the actual loss is lower than the normal loss.

- Abnormal losses and gains are usually valued at the full cost of production on the assumption that losses occur at the end of processing

- The scrap value of abnormal loss or an abnormal gain is not included in the process account - the scrap value of normal loss only is credited to the process account.

However, losses and their scrap values can be treated in a variety of ways, and not always by the 'standard' methods described above. Our advice is that you should read the question carefully to make sure that you do not simply assume that the usual costing treatment applies.

4.3 A particular difficulty that you may encounter in some management accounting examinations is when losses occur evenly throughout the processing. This makes the calculation of equivalent units a bit more tricky. The problem is that if loss occurs gradually, opening and closing WIP will have suffered some but not all of its loss already, and the differing degrees of completion make it difficult to value all opening and closing WIP on a common basis. This can be overcome by calculating the number of equivalent units which *will eventually result*, once the WIP has been fully processed.

> *Example: gradual losses and equivalent units in WIP*
>
> Normal loss in a process is 10% of completed output, occurring evenly throughout the process. All material is input at the beginning of the process. The closing work in progress of 4,280 kg is 30% complete. How many equivalent units of production are in this closing WIP?
>
> *Solution*
> For every 110 kg input, 100 kg of output is produced. If the closing stock is 30% complete, each 110 kg input will have lost 3 kg already, and still have a further 7 kg to lose.
>
> The stock therefore represents $\frac{107}{100}$ of the expected output.
>
> Equivalent units of material in closing stock = $\frac{100}{107} \times 4,280 = 4,000$
>
> and equivalent units of conversion cost in closing stock = $4,000 \times 30\% = 1,200$

## 5. Standard process costing

5.1 The basic rules of standard process costing are as follows.

- All finished output, and the equivalent units in WIP, are valued at standard cost

- There are no normal losses and abnormal losses and gains in standard process costing. Instead, there are *variances*.

- The usage and efficiency variances are calculated by taking the *equivalent units of production* as the actual output for the period. The equivalent units of production are calculated in the same way as for the FIFO method.

- The labour efficiency and material usage variances will be recorded in the process account: credit the process account with an adverse variance and debit the relevant variance account. The opposite entries obviously apply for a favourable variance.

- The labour rate variance and material price variance can either be eliminated before the labour and material cost is debited to the process account, or they can be included in the process account. Once more, you will have to *read the question* to see which of the differing accounting treatments to use. There are a couple of questions in this chapter to help you make sure that you know how to do this.

# QUESTIONS

## Data for questions 1 - 3

Wynne Donsomble Limited has a manufacturing process which produces two joint products, X and Y, and a by-product, Z. A standard input mix of 40% material M and 60% material N produces the following output:

|  | % of input |
|---|---|
| Product X | 30 |
| Product Y | 45 |
| By-product Z | 15 |
| Loss by evaporation | 10 |
|  | 100 |

*Costs of production are:*

| Material M | £5 per kg |
|---|---|
| Material N | £3 per kg |
| Labour | £4 per kg of input material |
| Fixed overhead | £45,000 per month |

Any amount of output can be sold each month at the following prices:

|  | £/kg |
|---|---|
| X | 14 |
| Y | 10 |
| Z | 4 |

---

**1** What must be the monthly output and sales of product X, in order to break even?

A 9,000 kg
B 12,000 kg
C 13,500 kg
D 15,000 kg

*Circle your answer*

A   B   C   D

**2** What monthly profit will result from 75,000 kg of material input?

A £45,500
B £67,500
C £84,500
D £112,500

*Circle your answer*

A   B   C   D

## 9: JOINT PRODUCT COSTING AND PROCESS COSTING

**3** A potential overseas customer has recently made enquiries about the purchase of 1,500 kg of product X. Wynne Donsomble Limited would have to hire extra factory space for £500, and additional export and shipping costs would amount to £250 in total. What would be the absolute minimum price that the company could charge, to break even on this export order? Extra output of product Y and by-product Z would be sold at their normal price.

A  £3.50 per kg
B  £9.00 per kg
C  £9.50 per kg
D  £26.50 per kg

Circle your answer

A   B   C   D

### Data for questions 4 - 7

Tenner Sachs Limited produces two types of chemical sealant - product P and product Q - in three consecutive processes. Output of product P next year is budgeted to be 95,000 litres. A description of the processes is as follows:

Process 1: Raw materials E and F are mixed in equal proportions and filtered. There is an evaporation loss of 25% of input.

Process 2: The mixture from process 1 is boiled to reduce the volume by 30%. The resulting liquid is then distilled into 40% product P and 60% product Q.

Process 3: Both products are poured into 1 litre containers, resulting in a further loss amounting to 5% of the eventual total liquid output. There is no loss of containers in this process.

Costs are as follows:

Raw material E: £0.20 per litre
Raw material F: £0.45 per litre
1 litre containers: £0.30 per container

|  | Conversion cost per litre of input processed |
|---|---|
| Process 1: | £0.41 |
| Process 2: | £0.56 |
| Process 3: | £0.20 |

Joint process costs are apportioned on the basis of output.

**4** What is the budgeted input of material E for next year?

A  190,000 litres
B  237,500 litres
C  238,095 litres
D  475,000 litres

Circle your answer

A   B   C   D

136

## 5

What is the cost per litre of output from Process 1?

A  £0.74
B  £0.84
C  £0.91
D  £0.98

*Circle your answer*

A   B   C   D

## 6

What is the cost per litre of output from Process 2?

A  £0.80
B  £1.30
C  £1.54
D  £2.20

*Circle your answer*

A   B   C   D

## 7

What is the cost per litre of finished product P?

A  £1.31
B  £2.52
C  £2.82
D  £2.84

*Circle your answer*

A   B   C   D

### Data for questions 8 and 9

Pickle Low Limited produces two products - Jay and Kay. The products are manufactured together in process 1, then Jay is processed further in process 2, and Kay is processed further in process 3. Neither product is saleable at the end of process 1. The total cost of the output from process 1 during April was £117,000. There were no losses in any process. Data for process 2 and 3 for April are as follows:

|  | | Process 2 litres | | Process 3 litres |
|---|---|---|---|---|
| Opening work in progress | | 24,000 | | 6,500 |
| Input from process 1 | | 192,000 | | 78,000 |
| Completed output | (Jay) | 206,400 | (Kay) | 80,600 |
| Closing work in progress | | 9,600 | | 3,900 |
| Processing costs incurred | | £69,720 | | £39,650 |
| Sales price per litre of completed output: | (Jay) | £1.00 | (Kay) | £0.75 |

All opening and closing work in progress was complete as to material input and was 50% processed. No further materials are added in processes 2 and 3.

## 9: JOINT PRODUCT COSTING AND PROCESS COSTING

**8** Using the notional (proxy) sales value at the separation point to apportion joint costs, what was the cost of output of Jay and Kay from process 1 in April, to the nearest £1?

|   | Jay | Kay |
|---|---|---|
| A | £54,321 | £62,679 |
| B | £66,857 | £50,143 |
| C | £100,859 | £16,141 |
| D | £101,189 | £15,811 |

*Circle your answer*

A   B   C   D

**9** Pickle Low Limited is considering the use of an alternative form of notional sales value as the basis for apportioning joint process costs. This notional sales value would be calculated after allowing for a notional profit on post-separation point costs. The notional profit percentage is to be taken as the average rate of profit mark up earned on all products, calculated to 2 decimal places.

What is the total cost of output of Jay and Kay from process 1, to the nearest £, if this basis is used for joint cost apportionment?

|   | Jay | Kay |
|---|---|---|
| A | £89,213 | £27,787 |
| B | £103,248 | £13,752 |
| C | £103,858 | £13,142 |
| D | £104,312 | £12,688 |

*Circle your answer*

A   B   C   D

**10** Forte and Antey Limited manufactures three joint products - Exe, Wye and Zed. Each of the products is processed further after the separation point, although they are all saleable without further processing. Data for the latest period are as follows:

|   | Exe | Wye | Zed |
|---|---|---|---|
| Sales price per kg - after further processing | £15 | £22 | £18 |
|                     - at separation point | £10 | £17 | £12 |
| Total product costs per kg, including apportionment of joint costs | £11 | £10 | £16 |
| Output in kilograms | 6,000 | 3,000 | 2,000 |

Joint costs of £77,000 have been apportioned according to the weight of the joint products. There was no work in progress in any process.

Which of the products should be sold at the separation point, and not processed further, in order to maximise profits?

A   Products Exe and Wye only
B   Products Exe and Zed only
C   Product Wye only
D   Product Zed only

*Circle your answer*

A   B   C   D

# 9: JOINT PRODUCT COSTING AND PROCESS COSTING

**11** A chemical manufacturer produces three joint products in process 1 - Alpha, Bravo and Charlie. Although each product can be sold at the end of process 1, they are normally processed further - in processes 2, 3 and 4 respectively. Accounts for these processes last month are as follows:

*Process 2*

|  | kg | £ |  | kg | £ |
|---|---|---|---|---|---|
| Opening work in progress | 8,000 | 5,780 | Output of refined Alpha | 243,000 | 360,080 |
| Transfer from Process 1 | 240,000 | 288,000 | Closing work in process |  |  |
| Processing costs |  | 72,675 |  | 5,000 | 6,375 |
|  | 248,000 | 366,455 |  | 248,000 | 366,455 |

*Process 3*

|  | kg | £ |  | kg | £ |
|---|---|---|---|---|---|
| Opening work in process | 4,000 | 8,200 | Output of refined Bravo | 112,000 | 226,600 |
| Transfer from Process 1 | 120,000 | 144,000 | Closing work in process |  |  |
| Processing costs |  | 91,200 |  | 12,000 | 16,800 |
|  | 124,000 | 243,400 |  | 124,000 | 243,400 |

*Process 4*

|  | kg | £ |  | kg | £ |
|---|---|---|---|---|---|
| Opening work in progress | 2,000 | 1,800 | Output of refined Charlie | 91,000 | 226,250 |
| Transfer from Process 1 | 90,000 | 108,000 | Closing work in process |  |  |
| Processing costs |  | 117,975 |  | 1,000 | 1,525 |
|  | 92,000 | 227,775 |  | 92,000 | 227,775 |

All opening and closing work in process is complete as to material content and is one quarter processed. All processing costs in processes 2, 3 and 4 would have been avoidable if the processing had not taken place.

Sales prices of the products are as follows:

|  | Alpha £ per kg | Bravo £ per kg | Charlie £ per kg |
|---|---|---|---|
| At the end of process 1 | 4.20 | 7.10 | 6.80 |
| Refined product after processing further | 4.80 | 7.60 | 8.30 |

If the manufacturer had attempted to maximise profits, which of the products should have been subject to further processing?

A Products Alpha and Bravo only
B Products Alpha and Charlie only
C Product Bravo only
D Product Charlie only

*Circle your answer*

A    B    C    D

# 9: JOINT PRODUCT COSTING AND PROCESS COSTING

## Data for questions 12 and 13

Fran Shorn Limited manufacture four products in one process. Basic raw material is processed in 100 kg batches, and the standard output per batch is as follows:

| Product | Output per 100 kg input | Sales value per kg at separation point |
|---------|-------------------------|----------------------------------------|
| S | 30 kg | £12 |
| T | 20 kg | £2 |
| U | 10 kg | £6 |
| V | 40 kg | £3 |

Only 50,000 kg of basic raw material is available per period. The cost of processing this quantity of material is £270,000. All of the products can be processed further before sale, and the relevant costs of further processing are as follows:

| Product | Labour hours used per kg processed | Other direct costs per kg processed | Sales value per kg after further processing |
|---------|-----------------------------------|-------------------------------------|---------------------------------------------|
| S | 1.0 hours | £8 | £28 |
| T | 1.5 hours | £3 | £14 |
| U | 0.5 hours | £7 | £18 |
| V | 2.0 hours | £12 | £24 |

Labour is paid £5 per hour for all further processing, and labour costs are not included in the 'other direct costs' in the table above. There are no fixed costs of further processing.

---

**12** What is the maximum profit which Fran Shorn Limited can earn per period?

- A £72,500
- B £92,500
- C £362,500
- D £512,500

*Circle your answer*

A   B   C   D

---

**13** A temporary labour shortage now restricts the total labour hours available for further processing to 10,000 hours only per period. What is the maximum profit which Fran Shorn Limited can now earn per period?

- A £50,000
- B £55,000
- C £175,000
- D £325,000

*Circle your answer*

A   B   C   D

# 9: JOINT PRODUCT COSTING AND PROCESS COSTING

## Data for questions 14 - 16

Morgan Recital Limited produces a cleaning powder in a single process. Information for this process last month is as follows:

Opening work in progress — 6,000 kg, valued at £15,000 for direct material and £7,600 for conversion costs

Material input during month
- 16,000 kg of material X at £0.75 per kg
- 20,000 kg of material Y at £3 per kg

Conversion costs during month — £157,500

Output during month
- 25,000 kg of finished product
- 5,000 kg of scrap

All opening and closing work in progress is complete as to material content and one quarter processed. The FIFO convention is used to value all production and stocks. Scrap arises at the *end of the process* and has a value of 30 pence per kg. Normal scrap for the month was 3,000 kg. Normal losses are not given a cost, but the scrap value of *all* losses is set off against the cost of materials in the process account. No allowance for eventual scrapping of units is included in closing stock values.

**14** What was the average cost per kg of finished output during the month?

A £7.05
B £7.68
C £7.84
D £7.86

*Circle your answer*

A  B  C  D

**15** What was the value of closing work in progress at the end of the month?

A £39,000
B £42,432
C £44,040
D £94,080

*Circle your answer*

A  B  C  D

## 9: JOINT PRODUCT COSTING AND PROCESS COSTING

**16** What was the cost of abnormal loss in the month?

A £13,917
B £14,000
C £15,605
D £15,680

*Circle your answer*

A    B    C    D

---

### Data for questions 17 and 18

Acoustigi Tar Limited uses standard costing to control process costs. Standards are currently being set for next year and data relating to one particular process is as follows.

Two joint products, Dot and Dash, are produced in a single process.
Materials M and N are mixed in a standard proportion 70:30. The standard output from a total input of 100 kg is:

20 kg of Dot
60 kg of Dash
20 kg of scrap, which has a value of £0.60 per kg

Standard prices for raw materials are M = £4 per kg, N = £3 per kg. Standard processing time for 100 kg of input is 2 hours, at a cost of £27 per hour.

The standard value of scrap is credited to the process account.

---

**17** If joint process costs are to be apportioned on the basis of weight at the separation point, what is the standard cost per 100 kg of good output?

A £412.00
B £501.50
C £515.00
D £530.00

*Circle your answer*

A    B    C    D

---

**18** The sales prices per kg of Dot and Dash are £20 and £10 respectively. If joint process costs are to be apportioned on the basis of sales value at the separation point, what is the standard cost per 100 kg of each product?

|   | Dot | Dash |
|---|---|---|
| A | £164.80 | £247.20 |
| B | £274.67 | £137.33 |
| C | £824.00 | £412.00 |
| D | £1,030.00 | £515.00 |

*Circle your answer*

A    B    C    D

## 9: JOINT PRODUCT COSTING AND PROCESS COSTING

### Data for questions 19 - 24

Tom Bone Limited manufactures a chemical in a single process, and uses standard process costing to control costs. The standard cost per unit of output is as follows:

|  |  | £ per unit |
|---|---|---|
| Direct material | 8 litres @ £2 per litre | 16 |
| Direct labour | 2 hours @ £5 per hour | 10 |
| Production overhead | 2 hours @ £4 per hour | 8 |
|  |  | 34 |

**Actual data for March:**

Opening work in progress    170 units; 100% complete in materials, 40% complete in labour and overhead

Output of finished product    9,500 units

Closing work in progress    670 units; 100% complete in materials, 70% complete in labour and overhead

Actual costs incurred:                                £
  Direct materials      78,000 litres        163,800
  Direct labour         21,000 hours         109,200
  Production overhead                         60,000
  Total actual costs                         333,000

Direct material price variances are calculated when the material is purchased, and direct labour rate variances are calculated as the labour cost is incurred. Raw material stocks are, therefore, issued to production at standard price and labour hours are charged to production at standard rate.

**19** What value of closing work in progress would be shown in the process account for March?

  A  £6,834
  B  £14,338
  C  £19,162
  D  £22,780

*Circle your answer*

A    B    C    D

**20** What would be the debit entry for direct material cost in the process account for March?

  A  £152,000
  B  £156,000
  C  £160,000
  D  £163,800

*Circle your answer*

A    B    C    D

143

## 9: JOINT PRODUCT COSTING AND PROCESS COSTING

**21** What would be the debit entry for direct labour cost in the process account for March?

A £95,000
B £99,010
C £105,000
D £109,200

*Circle your answer*

A   B   C   D

**22** What bookkeeping entries would be made to record the direct material usage variance for March?

A   Debit   Process account   £4,000
      Credit   Material usage variance account   £4,000

B   Debit   Material usage variance account   £4,000
      Credit   Process account   £4,000

C   Debit   Process account   £4,200
      Credit   Material usage variance account   £4,200

D   Debit   Material usage variance account   £4,200
      Credit   Process account   £4,200

*Circle your answer*

A   B   C   D

**23** What bookkeeping entries would be made to record the direct labour efficiency variance for March?

A   Debit   Process account   £10,000
      Credit   Labour efficiency variance account   £10,000

B   Debit   Labour efficiency variance account   £10,000
      Credit   Process account   £10,000

C   Debit   Process account   £5,990
      Credit   Labour efficiency variance account   £5,990

D   Debit   Labour efficiency variance account   £5,990
      Credit   Process account   £5,990

*Circle your answer*

A   B   C   D

## 9: JOINT PRODUCT COSTING AND PROCESS COSTING

**24** What is the production overhead efficiency variance for March?

A £4,792 adverse
B £8,000 adverse
C £16,000 favourable
D £19,208 favourable

*Circle your answer*

A    B    C    D

**25** Eyebrow Tastes Ltd manufactures Gunge in a continuous process. There is a normal loss in process, equal to 10% of the eventual good output, which occurs evenly throughout the processing. All material is added at the start of processing. On 1 May there were 6,300 kg of unfinished work in process, which was 50% complete. During May, 45,000 kg of output were finished and transferred to finished goods store. At the end of May, there was 5,350 kg of unfinished work in progress, which was 30% complete. There was no abnormal loss during the month.

What were the equivalent kilograms of production in May, to the nearest kg, measured in equivalent kilograms of eventual good output?

| | Materials | Processing cost |
|---|---|---|
| A | 43,991 kg | 43,500 kg |
| B | 44,000 kg | 43,500 kg |
| C | 44,050 kg | 43,455 kg |
| D | 44,110 kg | 43,410 kg |

*Circle your answer*

A    B    C    D

### Data for questions 26 - 29

Vylin Bow Limited manufactures a product in a single process, and uses standard process costing to control costs. The standard cost per 100 kg of output is as follows:

|  | £ per 100 kg output |
|---|---|
| Direct material: 120 kg at £3 per kg | 360 |
| Direct labour: 40 hours at £4 per hour | 160 |
| Production overhead: 40 hours at £2 per hour | 80 |
| | 600 |

All material is added at the start of the process and losses occur evenly throughout the processing.

*Actual data for October*

Costs incurred:
| | | £ |
|---|---|---|
| Direct material, 62,000 kg | | 179,800 |
| Direct labour, 19,000 hours | | 79,800 |
| Production overhead | | 57,000 |
| | | 316,600 |

Production and work in progress (WIP):

| | Kilos | Degree of completion |
|---|---|---|
| Opening WIP | 5,500 | 50% |
| Completed production | 50,000 | 100% |
| Closing WIP | 4,240 | 70% |

No abnormal losses occurred during the month.

145

## 9: JOINT PRODUCT COSTING AND PROCESS COSTING

**26** What were the equivalent kilograms of production in October, to the nearest kg, measured in kilograms of eventual good output?

|   | Materials | Labour and production overhead |
|---|---|---|
| A | 48,444 kg | 50,121 kg |
| B | 48,740 kg | 50,218 kg |
| C | 48,878 kg | 50,262 kg |
| D | 49,000 kg | 50,300 kg |

*Circle your answer*

A    B    C    D

**27** What was the direct material usage variance for October?

- A  £6,000 adverse
- B  £9,280 adverse
- C  £9,600 adverse
- D  £10,536 adverse

*Circle your answer*

A    B    C    D

**28** What was the direct labour efficiency variance for October?

- A  £2,400 favourable
- B  £4,000 favourable
- C  £4,480 favourable
- D  £4,704 favourable

*Circle your answer*

A    B    C    D

**29** What was the production overhead efficiency variance for October?

- A  £1,200 favourable
- B  £2,000 favourable
- C  £2,240 favourable
- D  £2,352 favourable

*Circle your answer*

A    B    C    D

# SECTION 2

## MARKING SCHEDULES AND COMMENTS

# 1: MARKING SCHEDULE

| Question | Correct answer | Marks for correct answer | Question | Correct answer | Marks for correct answer | Question | Correct answer | Marks for correct answer |
|---|---|---|---|---|---|---|---|---|
| 1 | D | 1 | 12 | B | 1 | 23 | C | 1 |
| 2 | A | 3 | 13 | C | 2 | 24 | D | 1 |
| 3 | C | 1 | 14 | C | 1 | 25 | D | 1 |
| 4 | C | 2 | 15 | D | 1 | 26 | B | 1 |
| 5 | C | 2 | 16 | B | 1 | 27 | C | 2 |
| 6 | B | 1 | 17 | B | 1 | 28 | A | 1 |
| 7 | A | 1 | 18 | D | 1 | 29 | B | 2 |
| 8 | A | 1 | 19 | B | 1 | 30 | A | 2 |
| 9 | C | 1 | 20 | D | 1 | 31 | A | 2 |
| 10 | C | 1 | 21 | B | 1 | | | |
| 11 | D | 1 | 22 | B | 1 | | | |

## YOUR MARKS

Total marks available  **40**   Your total mark

---

**GUIDELINES - If your mark was:**

**0 - 11**  You are obviously having a lot of difficulty with this topic. Go back to your study text and work through it again carefully.

**12 - 20**  Still quite a few weaknesses. You need to do a little better.

**21 - 30**  Good. You have a sound grasp of the basic principles, but there might be one or two gaps in your knowledge still - could it be problems with the learning curve, or activity based costing?

**31 - 40**  Very good. You have a clear understanding of the essential principles of this topic.

# COMMENTS

## Question

### 1

*Factor D:* An increase in the rate of pay for direct labour will increase the direct labour cost. Ignoring overtime, it will not affect the production overhead nor the number of direct labour hours. This factor is therefore unlikely to have contributed to the increase in the overhead absorption rate.

*Factors A and B:* A reduction in the level of activity and improved productivity could both lead to a reduction in the number of direct labour hours, and therefore to an increase in the overhead absorption rate.

*Factor C:* Higher depreciation charges resulting from increased mechanisation could cause a rise in overhead costs. Mechanisation is also likely to reduce the labour hours. Both of these factors will lead to an increase in an overhead absorption rate that is based on direct labour hours.

### 2

A problem here is that the costs of department P are to be apportioned on the basis of personnel, but 10% of the personnel are in department P itself. A cost centre cannot give itself a charge, therefore the apportionment must be based on the location of the remaining 90% of the personnel. For instance, 18% of the personnel are in department Q, therefore 18/90 of P's costs should be apportioned to Q.

Let P be the total overhead apportioned from department P

Let Q be the total overhead apportioned from department Q

$$P = 20,000 + \frac{2,000}{60,000} Q \qquad \text{(i)}$$

$$Q = 48,000 + \frac{18}{90} P = 48,000 + 0.2P \qquad \text{(ii)}$$

Simplify (i)  $\quad P = 20,000 + \frac{1}{30} Q \qquad \text{(iii)}$

Multiply (iii) by 30  $\quad 30P = 600,000 + Q \qquad \text{(iv)}$

From (ii)  $\quad 0.2P = -48,000 + Q \qquad \text{(v)}$

(iv) - (v)  $\quad 29.8P = 648,000$
$\quad P = 21,745$

Substituting in (ii)

$$Q = 48,000 + (0.2 \times 21,745)$$
$$= 52,349$$

# 1: OVERHEADS AND COST BEHAVIOUR

## Question

The final apportionment can now be calculated:

|  | Department 1 £ |
|---|---|
| Initial allocation | 72,800 |
| Apportion P (23/90 x 21,745) | 5,557 |
| Apportion Q (8,000/60,000 x 52,349) | 6,980 |
| Total cost centre overhead | 85,337 |
| | |
| Direct labour hours | 20,000 |
| Overhead absorption rate | £4.27  per direct labour hour |

**3** If marginal costing is used to value stock instead of absorption costing, then the difference in profits will be equal to the change in stock volume multiplied by the fixed production overhead absorption rate:

80 units x £34 = £2,720

Since closing stocks are higher than opening stocks, the marginal costing profit will be lower than the absorption costing profit. This is because the marginal costing profit does not 'benefit' from an increase in the amount of fixed production overheads taken to stock (rather than to the P & L account).

**4** To establish the amount of fixed overhead that is included in the stock valuation, we should first calculate how much overhead was absorbed in Year 2:

|  | £ |
|---|---|
| Overhead incurred | 30,000 |
| Under-absorbed | 10,000 |
| ∴ Overhead absorbed | 20,000 |

∴ Fixed overheads are $\frac{£20,000}{£100,000}$ = 20% of the full cost of production

∴ Variable costs = (100% - 20%) = 80% of full cost

The profit and loss account can now be restated, using marginal costing:

|  | £ | £ |
|---|---|---|
| Sales |  | 128,000 |
| Opening stock (80% x 20,000) | 16,000 |  |
| Variable cost of production | 80,000 |  |
|  | 96,000 |  |
| Closing stock (80% x 36,500) | 29,200 | 66,800 |
| Contribution |  | 61,200 |
| Fixed production overhead |  | 30,000 |
| General overhead |  | 14,300 |
| Profit |  | 16,900 |

## Question

### 5

Next, we need to establish the amount of fixed overhead absorbed in Year 3:

|  | £ |
|---|---|
| Overhead incurred | 30,000 |
| Underabsorbed | 6,000 |
| ∴ Overhead absorbed | 24,000 |

∴ Fixed overheads are $\frac{£24,000}{£88,000}$ of the full cost of production

= 27.2727% of the full cost of production

∴ Variable costs = 72.7273% of full cost

The profit and loss account can now be restated, using marginal costing:

|  | £ | £ |
|---|---|---|
| Sales |  | 128,000 |
| Opening stock (as per question 4) | 29,200 |  |
| Variable cost of production (72.7273% x 88,000) | 64,000 |  |
|  | 93,200 |  |
| Closing stock (72.7273% x 36,300) | 26,400 | 66,800 |
| Contribution |  | 61,200 |
| Fixed production overhead |  | 30,000 |
| General overhead |  | 14,300 |
| Profit |  | 16,900 |

### 6

If a variable cost is linear, then the total cost increases at a constant rate. The graph will therefore be a straight line through the origin - Graph 2.

### 7

The total fixed cost remains constant at any level of activity within the relevant range. The graph is therefore a straight line parallel to the horizontal axis - Graph 1.

### 8

The variable cost per unit remains constant within the relevant range. The graph is therefore a straight line parallel to the horizontal axis - Graph 1.

# Question

**9** The fixed cost per unit falls as output increases, but not in a linear fashion. Some data may help to illustrate this:

| Units produced | Fixed cost | Fixed cost per unit |
|---|---|---|
| | £ | £ |
| 1 | 300 | 300 |
| 2 | 300 | 150 |
| 3 | 300 | 100 |
| 4 | 300 | 75 |
| 5 | 300 | 60 |

Graph 4 is therefore correct, not graph 3.

**10** Total cost will start from a fixed cost base at zero activity. As activity increases the total cost will increase, but at progressively lower unit rates. Graph 5 is therefore correct.

**11** At zero activity there will be no wages cost. As activity increases the total cost increases at progressively higher rates. Since the increases are in small steps, the cost line can be shown as a curve rather than as a large number of small straight line segments. This is a description of a concave curvilinear variable cost - Graph 6.

**12** *Condition 1:* If costs are fluctuating as a result of any factor other than the level of activity, then adjustments must be made before the analysis is carried out. This means that fluctuations caused by factors such as technology changes and inflation must be eliminated.

*Condition 2:* Linear regression analysis will produce a straight line equation for any set of data. The analyst must check first that there is in fact an underlying linear relationship.

*Condition 3:* It is important to use a spread of activity levels which is as *wide* as possible. Otherwise serious error margins can occur when the cost line is extrapolated back to the vertical axis.

*Condition 4:* If costs in the future are unlikely to be similar to costs in the past, then it is wrong to use past data as a basis for forecasts.

## COMMENTS

## Question

**13** As a first step, you need to remove the cost differences caused by inflation. The quickest method is to express the appropriate costs in terms of year 6 prices, using a price index of 180. The high-low method can then be applied to the inflation-adjusted figures.

Using the figures for the highest and lowest volume:

| Volume | Cost | | Cost at year 6 prices |
|---|---|---|---|
| | £ | | £ |
| 90,000 (High) | 209,100 | x 180/123 | 306,000 |
| 60,000 (Low) | 201,600 | x 180/144 | 252,000 |
| 30,000 | | | 54,000 |

Therefore, variable cost per unit = £54,000 / 30,000

= £1.80

and fixed cost = £252,000 - £(1.80 x 60,000) = £144,000

|  |  | £ |
|---|---|---|
| Total distribution cost for year 6 | = fixed cost | 144,000 |
| | + variable cost (1.80 x 85,000) | 153,000 |
| | | 297,000 |

**14** This group of costs would also include the costs of quality inspection.

**15** Such equipment would help operators to improve product quality and/or avoid failure. The costs of training operators to improve quality would also belong to this group of costs.

**16** Warranty costs are the costs of carrying out repairs etc that customers claim free of charge under warranties. Other costs of failure after production include product liability claims, handling costs of product returns, refunds and the (difficult to measure) costs of lost reputation.

Group 1 costs include costs of scrap, costs of re-worked items, and so on.

**17** Budgeted overhead for actual production = Budgeted fixed overhead per period + (Standard machine hours produced x Standard variable overhead per hour)

Continued...

# 1: OVERHEADS AND COST BEHAVIOUR

## Question

The high-low method can be used to analyse the budgeted overhead:

| Period | Activity hours | Budgeted overhead £ |
|---|---|---|
| 2 | 4,930 | 10,122 |
| 4 | 4,180 | 9,072 |
|   | 750 | 1,050 |

∴ Standard variable overhead per hour = $\frac{£1,050}{750}$ = £1.40

**18** Using the data for period 2,

|  | £ |
|---|---|
| Standard variable overhead = 4,930 hours x £1.40 | = 6,902 |
| Total budgeted overhead | = 10,122 |
| ∴ Budgeted fixed overhead per period | = 3,220 |

**19**

Total overhead absorbed = Standard machine hours produced × Standard overhead absorption rate per hour

∴ Standard overhead per hour = $\frac{£58,002}{27,620}$ = £2.10 per hour, for both fixed and variable overhead

∴ Standard fixed overhead per hour = £2.10 total - £1.40 variable

= £0.70

Fixed overhead per hour = $\frac{\text{Budgeted fixed overhead}}{\text{Activity level used for absorption}}$

∴ Activity level used for absorbing fixed overhead = $\frac{£3,220}{£0.70}$

= 4,600 standard machine hours

**20** A cost driver is a resource-consuming activity that incurs overhead costs. To make a product, a variety of such activities will be incurred (such as the costs of product design, engineering, manufacturing, distribution, selling, and so on) and the principle of *activity-based costing* (ABC) is that overhead costs ought to be allocated to products on the basis of multiple cost drivers, not just on the basis of one or two over-simplistic apportionment bases such as £x per direct labour hour, £y per machine hour or z% of sales price.

## Question

**21** The principles of activity-based costing have been set out by Professors Robert Kaplan and Robin Cooper of Harvard Business School. Statement 1 is correct. Short term variable costs, as defined by Kaplan and Cooper, vary with the volume of activity, and should be allocated to product costs accordingly.

Statement 2 is not fully correct. Kaplan and Cooper argued that many overhead costs, traditionally regarded as fixed costs, vary *in the long run* with the volume of certain activities, although they do not vary immediately. The activities they vary with are *principally* related to the complexity ahd diversity of production, *not* to sheer volume of output - for example product design and set up costs vary in the long run with the number of different products made and the number of production runs scheduled, not the number of *units* produced.

Statement 3 is correct. Kaplan and Cooper argue that long-run variable costs vary eventually according to such items as the number of production runs, the number of goods received notes, the number of despatch orders, the number of materials requisitions and so on, which relate to activities undertaken by support department personnel.

Statement 4 is also correct. Kaplan and Cooper argue that cost drivers are activities that cause costs, and so costs should be allocated to them directly. Products should then be allocated a share of these costs according to the scale of these activities that they have required. Cost drivers should be established for non-production overhead costs as well as for production overheads.

**22** Direct labour hours

$$\begin{array}{lll} P & 3{,}000 \times \tfrac{1}{2} & = 1{,}500 \\ Q & 2{,}000 \times 1 & = 2{,}000 \\ R & 1{,}500 \times \tfrac{1}{3} & = \phantom{0}\underline{\phantom{0}500} \\ & & \phantom{00}4{,}000 \end{array}$$

Absorption rate for overhead = £165,000 ÷ 4,000
= £41.25 per direct labour hour.

Unit cost of R = £(8 + 2 + $\tfrac{1}{3}$ of 41.25) = £23.75.

**23** Machine hours (3,000 x 2) + (2,000 x 1) + (1,500 x 2) = 11,000.
Absorption rates:
   Materials handling (£35,000 ÷ £70,000) = 50% of direct materials cost

   Other overheads $\dfrac{£(165{,}000 - 35{,}000)}{11{,}000 \text{ machine hours}}$ = £11.82 per machine hour.

| Cost per unit of R | £ |
|---|---:|
| Direct materials | 8.00 |
| Direct labour | 2.00 |
| Materials handling overhead (50% of £8) | 4.00 |
| Other overhead (£11.82 x 2 machine hours) | 23.64 |
| | 37.64 |

# Question

## 24

Overhead rates

| | | | |
|---|---|---|---|
| Machining | £71,500 ÷ 11,000 machine hours | = | £6.5 per machine hour |
| Set-up costs | £10,500 ÷ 20 production runs | = | £525 per run |
| Materials handling | £35,000 ÷ 40 materials deliveries | = | £875 per delivery |
| Packing costs | £22,500 ÷ 15 deliveries to customers | = | £1,500 per delivery |
| Engineering | £25,500 ÷ 50 production orders | = | £510 per order |

Product R overhead costs

| | | £ |
|---|---|---|
| Machinery | (3,000 machine hours x £6.5) | 19,500 |
| Set up costs | 10 production runs x £525 | 5,250 |
| Materials handling | 20 deliveries x £875 | 17,500 |
| Packing costs | 10 customer deliveries £1,500 | 15,000 |
| Engineering | 15 production orders x £510 | 7,650 |
| | | 64,900 |

Cost per unit of R

| | £ |
|---|---|
| Direct materials | 8.00 |
| Direct labour | 2.00 |
| Overhead (£64,900 ÷ 1,500 units of R) | 43.27 |
| | 53.27 |

## 25

If labour operations involve a set of complex repetitive activities (factor 1), then a learning curve might apply. However, if labour is not a significant proportion of total cost (factor 2) the effort involved in attempting to calculate the learning effect may not be worthwhile.

Also, a high rate of labour turnover (factor 3) may mean that employees do not stay in Department Y long enough for the learning to be remembered. If there is a long time delay (factor 4) then the learning curve should not be applied, because the learning will be forgotten.

## 26

A 90% learning effect means that every time output doubles, the average time per unit (for all units produced so far) is reduced to 90% of the *previous* average.

| Cumulative production (units) | Average time per unit (hours) | Average labour cost £ per unit | Materials cost £ per unit | Average overhead cost £ per unit | Total cost £ |
|---|---|---|---|---|---|
| 1 | 100 | | | | |
| 2 | x 90% = 90 | | | | |
| 4 | x 90% = 81 | (x £6) 486 | 500 | (8,000/4) 2,000 | 2,986 |

# COMMENTS

## Question

**27** The data provided relates to initial measurements for 200 units. If the customer is now considering increasing the order to 300 units, the learning effect will mean that a lower price can be quoted.

It is first necessary to isolate the items which will be affected by learning:

|  | Unit £ |
|---|---|
| Direct labour - department 2 | 180 |
| Variable overhead - 10% | 18 |
| Fixed overhead - department 2 | 90 |
|  | 288 |
| Profit and general overhead - 10% | 28.8 |
|  | 316.8 |

300 units = 1.5 x original measurement of 200 units, and so from the learning curve, the affected items will reduce to 87.6% of £316.8 per unit.

Therefore, the unit price can be reduced by  (100 - 87.6)% x £316.8
 = 12.4% x £316.8
 = £39.28
Unit price for an order of 300 units  = £572 - £39.28
 = £532.72

**28** Since the customer is not guaranteeing to take 300 units, the whole of the discount cannot be passed on immediately. However, in the solution to the previous question we calculated the amount which the company wished to receive for a total order of 300 units. If we deduct the amount which the customer has already paid for 200 units, then the price per unit for the last 100 units can be determined:

|  | £ |
|---|---|
| Sales revenue required from order totalling 300 units = 300 x £532.72 | 159,816 |
| *Less:* Revenue already received for 200 units = 200 x £572 | 114,400 |
| Revenue required from second order for 100 units | 45,416 |
| Price per unit | £454.16 |

**29** The first thing to determine is whether any overtime work will be necessary:

|  | Hours per unit |
|---|---|
| Direct labour hours for 75 units = | 10 |
| for 150 units = 10 x 70% = | 7 |
| for 300 units = 7 x 70% = | 4.9 |

| | |
|---|---|
| Total time for 300 units = 300 x 4.9 = | 1,470 hours |
| Current workload | 1,800 hours |
| Total workload, including contract | 3,270 hours |
| Capacity available, normal time | 3,000 hours |
| Overtime required | 270 hours |

Continued...

# 1: OVERHEADS AND COST BEHAVIOUR

## Question

|  |  |  |
|---|---|---|
| Overtime premium (x £2 per hour) |  | £540 |
| Overtime premium per unit |  | £1.80 |

Lastly, the price per unit can be calculated:

|  |  | Unit £ |
|---|---|---|
| Direct material |  | 30.00 |
| Direct labour | 4.9 hours x £4 | 19.60 |
| Production overhead | 4.9 hours x £7 | 34.30 |
| Overtime premium |  | 1.80 |
|  |  | 85.70 |
| Add 20% |  | 17.14 |
| Selling price |  | 102.84 |

**30** In the learning curve equation, the learning index b is given by:

$$b = \frac{\log(1 - \text{proportionate decrease})}{\log 2}$$

For a 90% curve, $b = \frac{\log 0.9}{\log 2}$ = (from tables) $\frac{\bar{1}.9542}{0.3010} = \frac{-1 + 0.9542}{0.3010}$

$$b = \frac{-0.0458}{0.3010} = -0.152$$

Placing the available data in the formula, we have:

Average labour hours per unit at the start of the period = $220 \times 190^{-0.152}$
= 99.0951
Average labour hours per unit at the end of the period = $220 \times (190 + 25)^{-0.152}$
= 97.2505

The production can therefore be recorded as:

|  | Cumulative units | Average time per unit | Total time |
|---|---|---|---|
| At beginning of period | 190 | x 99.0951 | = 18,828.069 hours |
| At end of period | 215 | x 97.2505 | = 20,908.857 hours |
|  | 25 |  | 2,080.788 hours |

Average time allowance per unit = $\frac{2,080.788}{25}$ = 83.2 hours

## COMMENTS

## Question

**31** You could answer this by hit and miss, trying all the learning rates in the question. Here, our solution uses the learning curve formula in reverse.

Average time per unit to date = (104 ÷ 15) = 6.933 hours.

Since $y = ax^b$
$6.933 = 28(15^b)$
$15^b = 6.933 \div 28 = 0.2476$
Since log 15 = 1.1761
and log 0.2476 = $\bar{1}.3938$ = -1 + 3938 = -0.6062:

$$b = \frac{\log 0.2476}{\log 15} = \frac{-0.6062}{1.1761} = -0.515$$

$$b = \frac{\log \text{ of learning rate}}{\log 2}$$

$$-0.515 = \frac{\log \text{ of learning rate}}{0.3010}$$

Log of learning rate = -0.515 × 0.3010
= -0.155
= $\bar{1}.845$

Using antilogarithms $\bar{1}.845$ converts back to 0.70. This learning rate is 70%.

## 2: MARKING SCHEDULE

| Question | Correct answer | Marks for correct answer | Question | Correct answer | Marks for correct answer | Question | Correct answer | Marks for correct answer |
|---|---|---|---|---|---|---|---|---|
| 1 | C | 1 | 11 | A | 1 | 21 | B | 1 |
| 2 | B | 2 | 12 | C | 2 | 22 | B | 1 |
| 3 | D | 1 | 13 | D | 2 | 23 | C | 2 |
| 4 | D | 1 | 14 | D | 1 | 24 | C | 1 |
| 5 | A | 2 | 15 | C | 1 | 25 | A | 1 |
| 6 | C | 2 | 16 | C | 1 | 26 | C | 1 |
| 7 | C | 2 | 17 | C | 1 | 27 | A | 1 |
| 8 | C | 2 | 18 | B | 1 | 28 | D | 1 |
| 9 | A | 2 | 19 | D | 1 | 29 | B | 1 |
| 10 | B | 1 | 20 | B | 1 | | | |

### YOUR MARKS

Total marks available: 38     Your total mark: ____

---

**GUIDELINES - If your mark was:**

**0 - 11**: This topic is causing you great difficulty. Go back to the study text and concentrate particularly on the inter-relationships of the various functional budgets.

**12 - 20**: You are still weak in this important area of management accounting. Think carefully about the reasons for your errors.

**21 - 31**: Good. Although you still have to perfect your knowledge, you are well on the way to a thorough understanding of this subject area.

**32 - 38**: Very good. You have a thorough understanding of the essential principles of budgeting.

# COMMENTS

## Question

**1** Rolling budgets, sometimes called continuous budgets, are continuously updated short term budgets. In the case of Castle Ltd the budget could be revised and updated each quarter, so that it represents a realistic target for planning and control purposes. At the end of each quarter, budget managers could be required to add another quarter to the end of the annual budget and to update the unexpired portion. In this way they would always have a 12-month, rolling, up-to-date budget available.

Flexible budgets are designed to adapt to changes in activity indicators, such as the level of output or the number of employees. They are not particularly useful for adapting to changes in economic variables.

Zero base budgets are designed to ensure the efficient allocation of resources. While they could be useful to Castle Limited generally, they would not provide the solution to their planning and control difficulties in this volatile situation.

**2** Raw material requirements depend on the level of production, which in turn depends on sales and finished goods stock requirements:

|  | February kg | March kg | April kg | May kg |
|---|---|---|---|---|
| Required finished stock: |  |  |  |  |
| Base stock | 6,000 | 6,000 | 6,000 | 6,000 |
| + 25% of next month's sales | 2,250 | 2,250 | 2,000 | 1,750 |
| = Required stock | 8,250 | 8,250 | 8,000 | 7,750 |
| + Sales |  | 9,000 | 9,000 | 8,000 |
|  |  | 17,250 | 17,000 | 15,750 |
| *Less* opening stock |  | 8,250 | 8,250 | 8,000 |
| = Finished production required |  | 9,000 | 8,750 | 7,750 |
| + 10% for losses = Raw material required for production |  | 9,900 | 9,625 | 8,525 |

Now that the requirements for production are known, raw material stock requirements must be taken into account to determine the level of purchases:

|  | February kg | March kg | April kg |
|---|---|---|---|
| Required material stock: |  |  |  |
| Base stock | 5,000 | 5,000 | 5,000 |
| + 25% of material required for next month's production | 2,475 | 2,406.25 | 2,131.25 |
| = Required closing material stock | 7,475 | 7,406.25 | 7,131.25 |
| + Production requirements |  | 9,900 | 9,625 |
|  |  | 17,306.25 | 16,756.25 |
| *Less* opening material stock |  | 7,475 | 7,406.25 |
| = Required purchases |  | 9,831.25 | 9,350 |

# Question

## 3

Using the purchases figures calculated in the previous solution.

|  | March | April |
|---|---|---|
| Purchases | 9,831.25 kg | 9,350 kg |
| x £3 per kg | £29,493.75 | £28,050 |

Therefore, budgeted payments to suppliers in April are:

|  | £ |
|---|---|
| 80% x March purchases £29,493.75 = | 23,595 |
| 20% x April purchases £28,050 = | 5,610 |
|  | 29,205 |

## 4

None of the factors would be included in the profit and loss account, and factor 2 is the only one which does not affect cash flow. The revaluation of a fixed asset would be shown as an increase in reserves, but there will be no cash movement until the asset is sold.

## 5

The first step is to determine the variable production cost. Since the fixed production overhead is treated as a period cost, there must be a charge of £15,000 included in each period's cost of production:

|  | January £ | February £ | March £ |
|---|---|---|---|
| Cost of production | 56,920 | 62,180 | 49,120 |
| Fixed production overhead | 15,000 | 15,000 | 15,000 |
| Variable production cost | 41,920 | 47,180 | 34,120 |
| Material cost (x 30%) | 12,576 | 14,154 | 10,236 |
| ∴ Material purchases | 14,154 | 10,236 |  |
|  |  |  |  |
| 50% paid in the month | 7,077 | 5,118 |  |
| 50% paid in following month |  | 7,077 |  |
| ∴ Payment to suppliers in February |  | 12,195 |  |

## 6

The selling and distribution cost is clearly not wholly fixed. The high-low technique can be used to separate the fixed and variable costs:

|  | Selling costs £ | Sales value £ |
|---|---|---|
| High | 6,000 | 80,000 |
| Low | 5,625 | 65,000 |
|  | 375 | 15,000 |

$$\therefore \text{Variable selling and distribution costs} = \frac{£375}{£15,000} \times 100\% = 2.5\% \text{ of sales value}$$

∴ Fixed selling and distribution costs = £6,000 - (2.5% x £80,000) = £4,000

We are told that 20% of this fixed element is depreciation, which is not a cash payment.
∴ Cash payment in March = £5,625 - (20% x £4,000) = £4,825

# COMMENTS

## Question

**7** The opening cash balance of £4,820 must be adjusted for the cash flows budgeted for February:

|  | £ | £ |
|---|---:|---:|
| Opening cash balance |  | 4,820 |
| Receipts from customers: |  |  |
|    20% x £80,000 x 97% |  | 15,520 |
|    80% x £75,000 from January |  | <u>60,000</u> |
|  |  | 80,340 |
| Payments to material suppliers | 12,195 |  |
| Remaining variable production cost for February |  |  |
|    70% x £47,180 | 33,026 |  |
| Fixed production overhead - £15,000 - £3,000 depreciation | 12,000 |  |
| Selling & distribution overhead - £6,000 - £800 depreciation | 5,200 |  |
| Administration overhead - £5,100 - £500 depreciation | <u>4,600</u> |  |
|  |  | <u>67,021</u> |
| ∴ Closing cash balance |  | <u>13,319</u> |

**8** Ben Clone Ltd will start September with an opening cash balance of £2,400 and add £12,420 budgeted cash inflow. This means that there will be sufficient cash to take advantage of available discounts:

|  | Cash balance £ | Payments to material suppliers £ |
|---|---:|---:|
| Opening balance | 2,400 |  |
| Cash inflow | <u>12,420</u> |  |
|  | 14,820 |  |
| *Less* payments to material suppliers |  |  |
|   for August purchases | (5,800) | 5,800 |
|   for September purchases |  |  |
|     £5,900 x 25% x 96% | <u>(1,416)</u> | <u>1,416</u> |
|  | <u>7,604</u> | <u>7,216</u> |

Taking advantage of the full discount still leaves a cash balance well above £2,500.

**9** Ability to take discounts will again depend on the amount of cash available.

|  | Cash balance £ | Payment to material suppliers £ |
|---|---:|---:|
| Opening balance (from previous solution) | 7,604 |  |
| Net cash flow, excluding materials | 281 |  |
| Payment for remainder of September purchases |  |  |
|   75% x 5,900 | <u>(4,425)</u> | 4,425 |
| Leaves a cash balance of | 3,460 |  |
| Required minimum cash balance | <u>2,500</u> | <u>960</u> |
| Immediate payments to suppliers, taking discount | <u>960</u> | <u>5,385</u> |

## Question

**10** Cash flows for November are clearly going to result in an overdraft. Scott will not therefore settle any supplier accounts on immediate payment terms. However, the company must pay for the remainder of October purchases. £960 was paid in October, net of 4% discount. This represents a gross payment of £1,000 cleared from the balance owing to suppliers.

|  | Cash balance £ |
|---|---:|
| Opening balance (from previous solution) | 2,500 |
| Net cash outflow excluding materials payments | (2,490) |
| Payment for remainder of October purchases = £6,200 - £1,000 | (5,200) |
|  | (5,190) |

**11** The balance sheet trade debtors of £612,500 represents two months sales - November and December. Cash from November sales will be received in January:

$$\text{November sales} = \frac{0.75}{1.75} \times £612,500 = £262,500$$

**12** Let November purchases = x
∴ December purchases = 0.5x
The balance sheet trade creditors of £160,000 represent $1\frac{1}{2}$ months' purchases - half of November and all of December.

| ∴ Trade creditors at 31 Dec | = $\frac{1}{2}$ November purchases | 0.5x |
|---|---|---|
|  | + December purchases | 0.5x |
|  |  | 1.0x |

∴ Trade creditors at 31 Dec = x = £160,000

∴ November purchases = x = £160,000 and December purchases = £80,000.

Payments made in January will be for the purchases in the 2nd half of November and the 1st half of December:

|  | £ |
|---|---:|
| November - $\frac{1}{2}$ x £160,000 = | 80,000 |
| December - $\frac{1}{2}$ x £80,000 = | 40,000 |
|  | 120,000 |

## Question

### 13

This first step is to determine the maximum number of paid hours required in a period, allowing for inefficiencies and absences.

| Period | Standard hours of production | × $\frac{100}{70}$ = | Attendance time for output | × | Allowance for paid absence | = | Paid hours required |
|---|---|---|---|---|---|---|---|
| 1 | 10,090.5 | | 14,415 | × | $\frac{100}{93}$ | | 15,500 |
| 2 | 9,765.0 | | 13,950 | | as above | | 15,000 |
| 3 | 9,569.7 | | 13,671 | | as above | | 14,700 |
| 4 | 9,937.2 | | 14,196 | × | $\frac{100}{91}$ | | 15,600 |
| 5 | 9,809.8 | | 14,014 | | as above | | 15,400 |
| 6 | 9,576.9 | | 13,680 | × | $\frac{100}{90}$ | | 15,200 |

The highest number of paid hours is required in period 4 - 15,600 hours. The labour force must be large enough to provide this level of hours, taking into account the maximum allowed overtime.

Maximum hours per employee in a 4 week period
    =     160 basic hours + (160 × 15%) overtime hours
    =     184 hours
∴ Number of employees required
    =     $\frac{15,600}{184}$ = 85 employees

### 14

The total labour cost budget will depend on the amount of overtime to be paid for.

85 employees work a basic 160 hours each per period = 13,600 hours. Paid hours required for output are calculated in the previous solution.

| Period | Paid hours required for output hours | Paid hours available normal time hours | Paid hours overtime required hours |
|---|---|---|---|
| 1 | 15,500 | 13,600 | 1,900 |
| 2 | 15,000 | 13,600 | 1,400 |
| 3 | 14,700 | 13,600 | 1,100 |
| 4 | 15,600 | 13,600 | 2,000 |
| 5 | 15,400 | 13,600 | 1,800 |
| 6 | 15,200 | 13,600 | 1,600 |
| | | | 9,800 |

The labour cost budget can now be calculated:

| | £ |
|---|---|
| Basic pay - 13,600 hours × £4 × 6 periods | 326,400 |
| Overtime pay - 9,800 hours × £6 | 58,800 |
| Other wages costs - £16 × 4 weeks × 6 periods × 85 employees | 32,640 |
| | 417,840 |

## Question

**16** Direct materials are the only wholly variable cost, and administration is the only wholly fixed cost. The high-low technique can be used to analyse the other costs:

Production labour and overheads:

| | Production units | Total cost £'000 |
|---|---|---|
| | 7,500 | 115 |
| | 6,000 | 100 |
| | 1,500 | 15 |

∴ Variable cost per unit = £15,000 ÷ 1,500 = £10 per unit

∴ Fixed cost = £115,000 - (7,500 x £10) = £40,000.

Selling and distribution costs:

| | Sales units | £'000 |
|---|---|---|
| | 7,000 | 37.5 |
| | 5,000 | 28.5 |
| | 2,000 | 9.0 |

∴ Variable cost per unit = $\frac{£9,000}{2,000}$ = £4.50 per unit

∴ Fixed cost = £37,500 - (7,000 x £4.50) = £6,000

The budget cost allowance can now be calculated:

| | | £'000 |
|---|---|---|
| Direct materials - 6,200 x £10 | | 62 |
| Production labour and overheads: | fixed | 40 |
| | variable 6,200 x £10 | 62 |
| Administration costs | | 20 |
| Selling and distribution costs: | fixed | 6 |
| | variable 6,200 x £4.50 | 27.9 |
| Budget cost allowance | | 217.9 |

**17** Before any analysis can be performed, the cost figures must be adjusted to remove the effects of inflation:

| Period | £ | | Inflation adjusted £ | Cost | Index 1 | Index 2 | Index 3 | Index 4 |
|---|---|---|---|---|---|---|---|---|
| 1 | 11,400 | | 11,400 | | | | | |
| 2 | 11,676 x | $\frac{100}{101}$ | 11,560 | + | + | - | + | + |
| 3 | 11,975 x | $\frac{100}{102}$ | 11,740 | + | + | + | + | + |
| 4 | 11,474 x | $\frac{100}{103}$ | 11,140 | - | - | - | - | - |
| 5 | 12,072 x | $\frac{100}{104}$ | 11,608 | + | - | - | + | + |
| 6 | 11,722 x | $\frac{100}{105}$ | 11,164 | - | - | + | - | + |

*Direction of movement (up = +, down = -)*

Continued...

# COMMENTS

## Question

The last five columns of this table are used to show which index moves in harmony with the costs incurred. Index No 3 is the only one which moves in the same direction as the cost.

### 18

Using Index No 3 and the inflation-adjusted costs, the high-low technique can be used to separate fixed and variable costs:

|  | Index 3 | Cost (at Period 1 prices) £ |
|---|---|---|
| High | 145 | 11,740 |
| Low | 95 | 11,140 |
|  | 50 | 600 |

∴ Variable cost per student registration processed = $\frac{£600}{50}$ = £12

and fixed cost = £11,740 - (145 × £12) = £10,000.

The budget cost allowance can now be calculated:

|  | £ |
|---|---|
| Variable cost = Index No 3, 100 × £12 = | 1,200 |
| Fixed cost | 10,000 |
|  | 11,200 |
| Adjust for inflation | × 108/100 |
| = Budget cost allowance for period 9 | 12,096 |

### 19

The data for Year 3 can be used to work out the total costs and revenues, which can then be adjusted for the budgeted changes in Year 4:

|  | Year 3 | | | Year 4 | |
|---|---|---|---|---|---|
|  | £'000 | £'000 | | £'000 | £'000 |
| Sales |  | 8,400 | (× 1.05 × 1.10) |  | 9,702 |
| Materials (40%) | 3,360 | | (+ 10%) | 3,696 | |
| Other var.costs (20%) | 1,680 | | (+ 10% | 1,848 | |
|  | | 5,040 | | | 5,544 |
| Contribution |  | 3,360 |  |  | 4,158 |
| Fixed costs (150 × 12) |  | 1,800 | (+ 8%) |  | 1,944 |
| Profit |  | 1,560 |  |  | 2,214 |

### 20

Budgeted working capital can be calculated using the cost and revenue data derived in the previous solution.

|  |  | £'000 |
|---|---|---|
| Raw material stock | = 1/12 × £3,696 | 308 |
| Finished goods stock | = 2/12 × £5,544 (see note) | 924 |
| Debtors | = 2/12 × £9,702 | 1,617 |
|  |  | 2,849 |
| Creditors | = 2/12 × £3,696 | 616 |
| Balance sheet value of working capital |  | 2,233 |

*Note.* The data on cost structure states that stocks are valued at variable cost.

## Question

**21** The priority scores must be calculated first, so that the different levels of expenditure can be ranked.

| Level of activity | Office cleaning | | | Staff canteen | | | Storekeeping | | |
|---|---|---|---|---|---|---|---|---|---|
| | Incremental cost £'000 | Weighting | Priority score | Incremental cost £'000 | Weighting | Priority score | Incremental cost £'000 | Weighting | Priority score |
| 1 | 24 x | 1.0 = | 24.0 | 37 x | 0.9 = | 33.3 | 28 x | 0.9 = | 25.2 |
| 2 | 22 x | 0.7 = | 15.4 | 11 x | 0.8 = | 8.8 | 16 x | 0.8 = | 12.8 |
| 3 | 7 x | 0.6 = | 4.2 | 13 x | 0.3 = | 3.9 | 15 x | 0.7 = | 10.5 |
| 4 | 8 x | 0.4 = | 3.2 | 8 x | 0.2 = | 1.6 | 12 x | 0.3 = | 3.6 |

Available funds can now be allocated according to the ranking of the priority scores:

| Operation | Level | Score | Expenditure £'000 | Cumulative expenditure £'000 |
|---|---|---|---|---|
| Staff canteen | 1 | 33.3 | 37 | 37 |
| Storekeeping | 1 | 25.2 | 28 | 65 |
| Office cleaning | 1 | 24.0 | 24 | 89 |
| Office cleaning | 2 | 15.4 | 22 | 111 |
| Storekeeping | 2 | 12.8 | 16 | 127 |
| Storekeeping | 2 | 10.5 | 15 | 142 |
| Staff canteen | 2 | 8.8 | 11 | 153 |
| Office cleaning | 3 | 4.2 | 7 | 160 |

It is not possible to include the third increment of staff canteen expenditure, which is next in the ranking. Only £5,000 is available, but the incremental cost is £13,000.

Staff canteen activity should therefore be budgeted at level 2. The allocated expenditure is £37,000 for level 1 + £11,000 for level 2 = £48,000.

**22** In the matrix, Row P column P shows how much total output is required from P to produce one unit of external sale for P.

Similarly, Row P column Q gives the input required by department Q from department P to obtain 1 unit of output from department Q. Production of P can be calculated as follows:

|  |  |  | P units |
|---|---|---|---|
| In department P: | for external sales of P | = 2,850 x 1.0526 | 3,000 |
|  | for transfer to Q | = 5,700 x 0.26316 | 1,500 |
|  |  |  | 4,500 |

# Question

**23** In the same way, row Q gives elements of the required output from department Q. Row Q column Q shows the output required from Q to achieve one unit of external sale of Q. Row Q column P gives the input required by department P from department Q to obtain 1 unit of output from department P.

|  |  | Q units |
|---|---|---|
| In department Q: for external sales of Q | = 5,700 x 1.05263 | 6,000 |
| for transfer to P | = 2,850 x 0.2105 | 600 |
|  |  | 6,600 |

**24** A stochastic model is one which allows for uncertainty by attaching probabilities to some or all of the variables. Models 2 and 3 are therefore stochastic models.

Models 1 and 4 use single estimates for the variables and are therefore deterministic models - model 1 is an optimising deterministic model; model 4 is a satisficing deterministic model.

**25** Exponential smoothing forecasts use the formula:

new forecast = old forecast + $\alpha$ (most recent observation - old forecast)

The forecast for period 5 will be:
forecast = 4,800 + 0.2 (4,950 - 4,800)
= 4,830 units

**26** The forecast material cost can be obtained by using the indices to adjust Year 8, remembering also to allow for the increase in production volume:

| Year 8 material cost |  | £175,000 |
|---|---|---|
| Adjust for | - material usage | x 0.98 |
|  | - material price | x 1.10 |
|  | - production volume | x 1.08 |
| Forecast Year 9 material cost |  | £203,742 |

**27** The fixed and variable labour costs must be dealt with separately. Note that the fixed element is not affected by changes in efficiency or in production volume.

|  |  | Variable | Fixed | Total |
|---|---|---|---|---|
| Year 8 cost |  | £50,000 | £28,000 | £78,000 |
| Adjust for | - labour efficiency | x 1.01 | - |  |
|  | - labour rate | x 1.05 | x 1.05 |  |
|  | - production volume | x 1.08 | - |  |
| Forecast Year 9 labour cost |  | £57,267 | £29,400 | = £86,667 |

## Question

**28** This definition of value analysis comes from the CIMA Official Terminology.

Quality costing is concerned with achieving a certain product quality standard at an acceptable level of cost, but deals specifically with 'quality costs' such as inspection costs, costs of scrap, warranty costs, cost of customer refunds and so on. In contrast, value analysis is wider in scope.

**29** In *contrast* to the 'traditional' responses to lower costs - longer production runs, economic batch quantities, few products in the product range and standarisation etc - JIT systems are based on:

(a) recognising the need for a wider product range and so greater flexibility in production, shorter production runs and so *more* resources spent on setting up new runs;

(b) recognising the importance of product quality and production quality;

(c) recognising the need for flexible materials/components supply in such a flexible system, and so short lead times from suppliers who can also supply high quality items.

Since *more* time is spent on set ups in JIT, setting targets for reducing set-up times is *not* a cost improver.

## 3: MARKING SCHEDULE

| Question | Correct answer | Marks for correct answer | Question | Correct answer | Marks for correct answer | Question | Correct answer | Marks for correct answer |
|---|---|---|---|---|---|---|---|---|
| 1 | C | 1 | 11 | A | 1 | 21 | D | 1 |
| 2 | B | 1 | 12 | C | 1 | 22 | A | 1 |
| 3 | D | 1 | 13 | C | 1 | 23 | D | 1 |
| 4 | C | 1 | 14 | A | 1 | 24 | D | 1 |
| 5 | C | 1 | 15 | B | 1 | 25 | D | 1 |
| 6 | C | 1 | 16 | C | 1 | 26 | B | 1 |
| 7 | B | 1 | 17 | D | 1 | 27 | C | 1 |
| 8 | A | 1 | 18 | D | 1 | 28 | B | 1 |
| 9 | C | 1 | 19 | A | 1 | 29 | A | 1 |
| 10 | A | 1 | 20 | C | 1 | 30 | D | 1 |

YOUR MARKS

Total marks available   30         Your total mark

---

**GUIDELINES - If your mark was:**

**0 - 10**   You are obviously having problems with the topic.

**11 - 16**  Still a number of weaknesses. Try writing out the variance formulae and memorising them, just to get you started. Do this before you try the next chapter.

**17 - 25**  Quite good. You are still making a few mistakes, but you can calculate most of the basic variances.

**26 - 30**  Very good. You have got to grips with basic variances and should be ready to try the next chapter.

# 3: BUDGETARY CONTROL AND STANDARD COSTING I

Question

Question

# COMMENTS

**1** Standard costing systems can be established in an automated manufacturing system. Variances might identify controllable causes (eg inefficient maintenance) and automation does *not* mean that ideal and attainable standards are the same. However, direct labour costs will become a much smaller proportion of total costs, and so the significance of any direct labour cost variances will be much less than in non-automated systems or systems with a bigger labour element.

**2** A feedforward control system involves forecasting future outcomes, and comparing these with desired outcomes. Control action is then taken to minimise or remove any differences. Models 1 and 3 are therefore feedforward control models. Model 2 is a feedback control model, because it provides information on what has already happened, for comparison with a standard or plan (which in this case is the maximum or minimum stock level).

**3** The CIMA defines an attainable standard as one which relates to reasonable attainable future performance and objectives. Option D is therefore correct. The other options are different types of standard:

Option A describes a current standard;
Option B describes a basic standard;
Option C describes an ideal standard.

**4** A 0.05 or 95% significance level rule states that variances should be investigated if they exceed 1.96 standard deviations from the standard.

The upper control limit is therefore
£18,000 + (1.96 × 1,700) = £21,332

**5** Std purchase cost per 100 kg = £(500 + 20 + 20 - 30)
= £510 = £5.10 per kg

Std usage per unit of product P = (5.5 + 0.3 + 0.2) kg
= 6 kg

Std material cost per unit = £5.1 × 6 = £30.6

## COMMENTS

## Question

**6**

The standard data can be used to determine the standard price per litre for each material:

$$W = \frac{£1,400}{700} = £2 \text{ per litre}$$

$$P = \frac{£600}{400} = £1.50 \text{ per litre}$$

The next problem is: should the calculation of the price variance be based on materials used or materials purchased? Since stocks are valued at standard price, all of the price variance is eliminated immediately the stocks are received, therefore the variance should be based on purchases.

|  |  | Should cost £ |  | Did cost £ | Price variance £ |
|---|---|---|---|---|---|
| 670 litres of W | (x 2) | 1,340 |  | 1,474 | 134 (A) |
| 320 litres of P | (x 1.5) | 480 | (x 1.6) | 512 | 32 (A) |
|  |  | 1,820 |  | 1,986 | 166 (A) |

**7**

The actual usage of each material must be determined from the stock and purchases data:

|  | W litres | P litres | Total litres |
|---|---|---|---|
| Opening stock | 650 | 380 |  |
| Purchases | 670 | 320 |  |
|  | 1,320 | 700 |  |
| Less closing stock | 680 | 295 |  |
| = Usage | 640 | 405 | 1,045 |

|  |  | W |  | P |
|---|---|---|---|---|
| 900 litres of output should use | (x 0.7) | 630 litres | (x 0.4) | 360 litres |
| did use |  | 640 litres |  | 405 litres |
| Usage variance |  | 10 litres (A) |  | 45 litres (A) |
|  |  | x £2 std cost |  | x £1.5 std cost |
|  |  | £20 (A) | + | £67.5 (A) |
|  |  | = £87.5 (A) |  |  |

**8**

The total material used was 1,045 litres (see previous solution). The standard mix of this input must be compared with the actual mix:

| Material |  | Standard mix of actual input litres | Actual mix litres | Difference litres | At std price £ | Variance £ |
|---|---|---|---|---|---|---|
| W | (x 700/1,100) | 665 | 640 | 25 (F) | 2.00 | 50.00 (F) |
| P | (x 400/1,100) | 380 | 405 | 25 (A) | 1.50 | (37.50) (A) |
|  |  | 1,045 | 1,045 |  |  | £12.50 (F) |

# Question

## 9

From the standard data, 1,100 litres input should yield 1,000 litres output, at a cost of £2,000 or £2 per litre of output.

Therefore, 1,045 litres of material input should yield ( x $\frac{1,000}{1,100}$ )  950 litres output

|   |   |
|---|---|
| but did yield | 900 litres |
| a shortfall of | 50 litres (A) |
| x standard cost per litre produced | £2 |
| = yield variance | £100 Adverse |

## 10

|   |   |
|---|---|
| Adverse materials usage  in £ | £3,150 |
| in kg (÷ £10.5) | 300 (A) |
| Actual output = 80% of budget | = 3,200 kg |
| Adverse usage variance | 300 kg (A) |
| Actual materials usage | = 3,500 kg |

Actual cost per kg: £32,480 ÷ 3,500 kg = £9.28

## 11

In this question, the exchange rate variance part of the price variance is calculated separately, and so the remaining price variance is a variance caused by price factors other than exchange rate changes.

|   |   |
|---|---|
| 80,000 litres did cost, in $, (£420,000 x 1.5) | $630,000 |
|  | £ |
| At standard exchange rate of $1.60 = £1, this should have cost (630,000 ÷ 1.6) | 393,750 |
| did cost | 420,000 |
| Adverse exchange rate variance | 26,250 (A) |

|   |   | £ at standard exchange rate |
|---|---|---|
| 80,000 litres | did cost $630,000 | 393,750 |
|  | should cost, in £ (x 4.8) | 384,000 |
| Price variance |  | 9,750 (A) |

## 12

|   | Actual mix gm | Standard mix gm | Mix variance gm | £ |
|---|---|---|---|---|
| X | 4,000 | (1) 5,000 | 1,000 (F) x 2p | 20 (F) |
| Y | 14,000 | (3) 15,000 | 1,000 (F) x 1p | 10 (F) |
| Z | 12,000 | (2) 10,000 | 2,000 (A) x 4p | 80 (A) |
|   | 30,000 | 30,000 |  | 50 (A) |

Continued...

## COMMENTS

## Question

|  |  |  |
|---|---|---|
| 30,000 gm of input should yield (x 100/150) | | 20,000 gm of output |
| did yield | | 19,000 gm |
| Yield variance | | 1,000 gm (A) |
| x Std cost per gm of output | | (325p ÷ 100) |
| Yield variance in £ | | £32.5 (A) |

## 13

|  |  | Should cost £ | Did cost £ | Rate variance £ |
|---|---|---|---|---|
| 8,700 hrs of Grade 1 labour | (x 3) | 26,100 | 26,970 | 870 (A) |
| 3,270 hrs of Grade 2 labour | (x 5) | 16,350 | 15,696 | 654 (F) |
|  |  | 42,450 | 42,666 | 216 (A) |

## 14

7,200 standard hours of production, allowing for an 80% efficiency level, should take

| 7,200 ÷ 0.8 | = | 9,000 hours |
|---|---|---|
| 60% should be Grade 1 | = | 5,400 hours |
| 40% should be Grade 2 | = | 3,600 hours |

|  | | Grade 1 | Grade 2 |
|---|---|---|---|
| 7,200 hours | should take | 5,400 hrs | 3,600 hrs |
|  | did take | 8,700 hrs | 3,270 hrs |
| Efficiency variance | | 3,300 hrs (A) | 330 hrs (F) |
| Standard labour rate per hour | | £3 | £5 |
|  | | £9,900 (A) + | £1,650 (F) |
|  | = £8,250 (A) | | |

## 15

The direct labour mix variance is calculated in the same way as the direct materials mix variance:

| Grade | | Standard mix of actual hours | Actual mix | Difference hours | Std rate x per hour | £ |
|---|---|---|---|---|---|---|
| 1 | 60% | 7,182 | 8,700 | 1,518 (A) | £3 | 4,554 (A) |
| 2 | 40% | 4,788 | 3,270 | 1,518 (F) | £5 | 7,590 (F) |
|  |  | 11,970 | 11,970 | | Mix variance | 3,036 (F) |

## 16

The direct labour productivity variance values the shortfall in expected output at the standard wage rate.

| Average standard wage rate per hour: | Grade 1 = £3 x 0.6 = | £1.80 |
|---|---|---|
|  | Grade 2 = £5 x 0.4 = | £2.00 |
| Average rate per hour worked | | £3.80 |
| Allow for standard output efficiency ÷ | | 0.80 |

Continued...

# Question

|  | = Average labour rate per standard hour produced | £4.75 |

The variance can now be calculated:

| 11,970 labour hours should produce (x 0.8) | 9,576 std hours |
| but did produce | 7,200 std hours |
| shortfall | 2,376 std hours |
| at average rate | £4.75 |
| | = £11,286 (A) |

## 17

Standard direct labour cost per unit £192,000 ÷ 8,000 = £24

|  | £ |
|---|---|
| 9,000 units should cost (x £24) | 216,000 |
| did cost | 227,000 |
| Total direct labour variance | 11,000 (A) |
| Efficiency variance | 4,000 (F) |
| Rate variance | 15,000 (A) |

|  | £ |
|---|---|
| Actual labour cost | 227,000 |
| Rate variance | 15,000 (A) |
| Standard labour cost | 212,000 |

$$\frac{\text{Actual cost}}{\text{Standard cost}} = \frac{£227,000}{£212,000} = 107.08\%.$$

## 18

The direct labour efficiency variance = Total variance - Rate variance
= £920F - £3,220A = £4,140 Favourable

Considering each of the statements in turn:

*Statement 1:* levels of efficiency higher than standard result in a favourable efficiency variance - consistent. Higher bonuses than budgeted result in an adverse rate variance - also consistent.

*Statement 2:* an unrealistically low standard is likely to cause an adverse rate variance - consistent.

*Statement 3:* use of more higher skilled labour may result in a favourable efficiency variance - consistent. A higher hourly rate of pay would cause an adverse rate variance - also consistent.

## COMMENTS

## Question

**19** The idle time variance is simply the number of idle hours multiplied by the standard labour rate per hour:

$$200 \text{ hours} \times £7 = £1,400 \text{ Adverse}$$

**20** Once the idle time has been eliminated, all other variance calculations must be based on active hours only, which in this case is (1,600 - 200) = 1,400 hours.

| | | |
|---|---|---|
| 1,800 units should take (× 1 hour) | | 1,800 hours |
| did take | | 1,400 hours |
| | | 400 hours (F) |
| × Standard variable overhead rate per hr | | £3 |
| | | =£1,200 (F) |

**21**

| | | £ |
|---|---|---|
| 1,400 hours of work should cost (× £3) | | 4,200 in variable overhead |
| did cost | | 6,000 |
| Variable overhead expenditure variance | | 1,800 (A) |

**22**

| | £ |
|---|---|
| Budgeted fixed overhead (2,000 × £4) | 8,000 |
| Actual fixed overhead expenditure | 8,200 |
| Fixed overhead expenditure variance | 200 (A) |

**23** The fixed overhead capacity (volume) variance shows the potential under- or over-absorbed fixed overhead which is caused by utilising less or more of the available capacity than expected. Remember to use active hours only.

| | |
|---|---|
| Budgeted hours | 2,000 hours |
| Actual hours | 1,400 hours |
| Capacity/volume variance | 600 hours (A) |
| Fixed overhead rate per hour | £4 (A) |
| Variance in £ | £2,400 (A) |

**24** The fixed overhead efficiency variance is calculated in a similar way to the variable overhead efficiency variance and is the same in hours.

| | |
|---|---|
| Efficiency variance | 400 hours (F) |
| Fixed overhead rate per hour | £4 |
| Fixed overhead efficiency variance | = £1,600 (F) |

# Question

## 25
*Analysing each statement in turn:*

*Statement 1:* Over-absorbed fixed overhead is represented by a favourable total overhead variance. This statement is therefore correct.

*Statement 2:* If production output is higher than budget, the sum of the efficiency and capacity variances should be favourable. In this case the sum is:
£8,000 (A) + £7,000 (F) = £1,000 (A)

*Statement 3:* If labour hours utilised are higher than expected in the original budget then the fixed overhead capacity (volume) variance would be favourable. The statement is therefore correct.

*Statement 4:* If labour is taking longer than the standard time allowance for the actual production, then the potentially under-absorbed overhead will result in an adverse efficiency variance. The statement is therefore correct.

## 26
Expenditure variance = Budgeted fixed overhead - Actual fixed overhead
= P - Q. Here, this is a favourable variance

Total volume variance = Budgeted standard hours produced - Actual standard hours produced, valued at the standard fixed overhead recovery rate. This is the difference between the large and the small dotted rectangles in the diagram, which is reflected in distance PR (adverse) on the graph.

## 27
If the variance is investigated:

| Process | Costs (C) £ | Benefits (B) £ | (B-C) £ | Probability | EV £ |
|---|---|---|---|---|---|
| In control | (2,000) | - | (2,000) | 0.8 | (1,600) |
| Out of control | (2,000) | *11,900 | 9,900 | 0.2 | 1,980 |
| | | | | EV = | 380 |

(*£3,400 x $3\frac{1}{2}$)

Since the EV is positive, the decision rule would be to investigate the variance.

## 28
Let the probability that the process is *out* of control be p, and so the probability that the process in *in* control is (1 - p). "Breakeven" is where

$$\begin{aligned}
p(B - C) &= (1 - p)C \\
p(10{,}000 - 3{,}600) &= (1 - p)3{,}600 \\
6{,}400p &= 3{,}600 - 3{,}600p \\
10{,}000p &= 3{,}600 \\
p &= 0.36
\end{aligned}$$

Continued...

# COMMENTS

## Question

**29**

The probability that the system is out of control must be at least 0.36 if it is to be worth investigating.

B = benefit from control action if variance is found to be due to a controllable cause.
B = £(5,250 - 1,500) = £3,750 with the prediction error
B = £(5,250 - 2,800) = £2,450 if correctly predicted.

On the basis of current estimates, the decision would be to investigate the variance, and the EV of the NPV of this decision would be:

in £ 
p (B-C) + (1-p)C
0.3(3,750 - 800) + 0.7(-800)
= £885 - £560 = £325.

If the costs of correcting the variance were £2,800, and B = £2,450, the decision would be *not* to investigate the variance, and the EV of the NPV of this decision would be

in £ 0.3(2,450 - 800) + 0.7(-800)
= £495 - £560 = -£65.

The expected PV of the prediction error is therefore

|  | EV £ |
|---|---|
| If decision is taken to investigate, realistic EV of net cost | (65) |
| Expected PV of benefit on current estimates | 325 |
| EV of prediction error | 390 |

*Note.* You could argue that the only *actual* cost to the company, measured in EV terms, is the EV of cost of £65 if the decision is taken to investigate the variance. However, although this argument is valid, it is not offered as a possible solution here.

**30**

Let p = probability that the variance can be eliminated
B = net benefit of correcting the variance if it is found after investigation that it can be eliminated
C = cost of investigating the causes of the variance

B = £(1,000 x 4) - £700 = £3,300
C = £1,100 (variable cost only)

The minimum value of p is where

p(B-C) = (1-p)C
p(3,300-1,100) = (1-p)1,100
2,200p = 1,100 - 1,100p
3,300p = 1,100
p = 0.333

180

# 4: MARKING SCHEDULE

| Question | Correct answer | Marks for correct answer | Question | Correct answer | Marks for correct answer | Question | Correct answer | Marks for correct answer |
|---|---|---|---|---|---|---|---|---|
| 1 | A | 1 | 10 | B | 1 | 19 | C | 1 |
| 2 | A | 1 | 11 | A | 1 | 20 | B | 1 |
| 3 | B | 1 | 12 | D | 1 | 21 | B | 1 |
| 4 | B | 1 | 13 | A | 1 | 22 | B | 1 |
| 5 | C | 1 | 14 | B | 2 | 23 | B | 1 |
| 6 | C | 1 | 15 | D | 1 | 24 | B | 1 |
| 7 | C | 1 | 16 | A | 1 | 25 | C | 1 |
| 8 | A | 1 | 17 | A | 1 | | | |
| 9 | D | 1 | 18 | A | 1 | | | |

YOUR MARKS

Total marks available  **26**  Your total mark

---

**GUIDELINES - If your mark was:**

**0 - 8**  These more advanced applications of variance analysis are causing you difficulty. Go back and make sure you understand the basics of variance analysis before you try this chapter again.

**9 - 14**  You made several mistakes in this chapter. Read the comments carefully and make sure that you understand the reasons for your errors.

**15 - 21**  Good. However a bit more practice should improve your ability in this subject area.

**22 - 26**  Very good. Even the more tricky questions did not catch you out. Well done.

# COMMENTS

## Question

**1.** The sales price variance can be calculated for each product, and then added to arrive at the total variance:

| Product | | Actual selling price £ | Standard selling price £ | Difference £ | Units sold | Variance £ | |
|---|---|---|---|---|---|---|---|
| Red | (64,220/2,600) | 24.70 | 25 | 0.3 (A) | 2,600 | 780 | (A) |
| White | (191,840/4,400) | 43.60 | 42 | 1.6 (F) | 4,400 | 7,040 | (F) |
| Blue | (167,000/5,000) | 33.40 | 36 | 2.6 (A) | 5,000 | 13,000 | (A) |
| | | | | | | 6,740 | (A) |

**2.** Similarly the sales volume variance can be calculated for each product:

| Product | Actual sales units | Budgeted sales units | Difference (units) | Standard profit margin £ | Variance £ | |
|---|---|---|---|---|---|---|
| Red | 2,600 | 2,000 | 600 (F) | 7 | 4,200 | (F) |
| White | 4,400 | 5,000 | 600 (A) | 15 | 9,000 | (A) |
| Blue | 5,000 | 3,000 | 2,000 (F) | 9 | 18,000 | (F) |
| | | | | | 13,200 | (F) |

**3.**

| Product | Actual sales mix (units) | Standard mix of actual sales (units) | | Difference (units) | Standard profit margin £ | Variance £ | |
|---|---|---|---|---|---|---|---|
| Red | 2,600 | (20%) | 2,400 | 200 (F) | 7 | 1,400 | (F) |
| White | 4,400 | (50%) | 6,000 | 1,600 (A) | 15 | (24,000) | (A) |
| Blue | 5,000 | (30%) | 3,600 | 1,400 (F) | 9 | 12,600 | (F) |
| | 12,000 | → | 12,000 | 0 | | 10,000 | (A) |

**4.** First calculate the standard weighted average profit margin:

| | | | £ |
|---|---|---|---|
| | Red | £7 x 20% | 1.40 |
| | White | £15 x 50% | 7.50 |
| | Blue | £9 x 30% | 2.70 |
| Standard weighted average profit margin | | | 11.60 |

Sales quantity variance = [Actual sales units in total − Budgeted sales units in total] x Standard weighted average profit margin

= (12,000 − 10,000) x £11.60
= £23,200 Favourable

# Question

## 5

| Budgeted sales | | £ | Profit/sales ratio | |
|---|---|---|---|---|
| | Red | 50,000 | (7 ÷ 25) | 28% |
| | White | 210,000 | (15 ÷ 42) | 35.71428% |
| | Blue | 108,000 | (9 ÷ 36) | 25% |
| | | 368,000 | | |

| | Actual sales at standard revenue | | Standard mix of sales | | Sales mix variance In £ std revenue | | In profit £ | |
|---|---|---|---|---|---|---|---|---|
| | | £ | | £ | | | | |
| Red | (2,600x25) | 65,000 | (x50/368) | 58,397 | 6,603 (F) | x 28% | 1,849 | (F) |
| White | (4,400x42) | 184,800 | (x210/368) | 245,266 | 60,446 (A) | x 35.71428% | 21,595 | (A) |
| Blue | (5,000 x 36) | 180,000 | (x108/368) | 126,137 | 53,863 (F) | x 25% | 13,466 | (F) |
| | | 429,800 | → | 429,800 | Mix variance = | | 6,280 | (A) |

*Note.* The sales quantity variance calculated by the revenue method would be

£(429,800 - 368,000) x Weighted average budgeted profit/sales ratio
= £61,800 (F) x 116/368
= £19,480 (F)

This gives a total sales volume variance of £13,200 (F).

## 6

The first thing to calculate is the original (ex ante) standard cost per unit and then compare this with the revised (ex post) standard cost.

Ex ante standard cost = $\frac{£4,050}{270}$ = £15 per unit

Ex post standard cost          £18 per unit

Planning variance per unit     £3 per unit (A)

Multiplied by units produced   300

= Planning variance in £:      £900 Adverse

## 7

The operational variances must all be based on the ex post standard:

| | | £ |
|---|---|---|
| 1,140 hours | should cost (x £4.50) | 5,130 |
| | did cost | 5,586 |
| | Rate variance | 456 (A) |

# Question

## 8

| 300 units | should take (x 4) | 1,200 hrs |
|---|---|---|
| | did take | 1,140 hrs |
| | Efficiency variance | 60 hrs (F) |
| | x £4.5 per hour | £270 (F) |

## 9

It can be seen in retrospect that Lowke Hilary plc set an unrealistically low standard price. Even if they had selected the right material, the lowest price that could have been achieved was £11 per kilogram. The planning error was therefore £(11 - 8) = £3 per kilogram.

Planning variance caused by unrealistic standard = £3 x 6kg per unit
= £18 per unit
(x 730 units produced)
= £13,140 Adverse

## 10

If the company had been using Laird instead of Greece throughout the period, they would have saved £1 per kg.

Planning variance caused by choice of more
expensive material = £1 x 6kg per unit
= £6 per unit
(x 730 units produced)
= £4,380 Adverse

## 11

Using the revised and realistic (ex post) standard allowance of £12 per kg for *Greece* (the actual material used) the operational price variance is as follows.

| | £ |
|---|---|
| 4,350 kg should cost (x £12) | 52,200 |
| did cost | 52,000 |
| Price variance | 200 Favourable |

## 12

| 730 units | should use (x 6) | 4,380 kg |
|---|---|---|
| | did use | 4,350 kg |
| | Usage variance | 30 kg (F) |
| | x Standard price per kg of Greece £12 = | £360 Favourable |

184

## Question

### 13

Statement 1 is consistent with the variances because a fairly large favourable price variance arose at the same time as an adverse usage variance, which could have been caused by the higher wastage.

Statement 2 is consistent with the variances because the trend is for higher percentage variances. Even is these variances are still within any control limits set by Welsh Limited, the persistent trend is probably worthy of investigation.

Statement 3 is not consistent, because more effective use of material should produce a favourable usage variance.

### 14

The actual material cost and the two material variances can be used to derived the standard material cost of production.

|  |  | £ |
|---|---|---|
| Total actual direct material cost |  | 2,400 |
| Add back variances: | Material price variance | (800) |
|  | Material usage variance | 400 |
| Standard direct material cost of production |  | 2,000 |
| Divided by the standard material cost per unit |  | £10 |
| = Number of units produced |  | 200 |

### 15

Since there was no change in stocks in the month, the usage variance can be used to calculate the material purchases, which can then be divided into the actual material cost.

Material usage variance = £400 favourable

Therefore, the saving in material used compared with standard = $\frac{£400}{£2}$ = 200 kg

| | |
|---|---|
| Standard material usage (200 units x 5kg) | 1,000 kg |
| Usage variance | 200 kg(F) |
| Actual usage of material | 800 kg |

### 16

| | | £ |
|---|---|---|
| 200 units | should sell for (x £70) | 14,000 |
| | did sell for | 15,200 |
| | Sales price variance | 1,200 (F) |

# COMMENTS

## Question

### 17

Budgeted sales volume per month = $\dfrac{\text{Budgeted material cost of sales}}{\text{Standard material cost per unit}}$

$= \dfrac{£2,300}{£10} = 230$ units

Budgeted profit margin per unit = $\dfrac{\text{Budgeted monthly profit margin}}{\text{Budgeted monthly sales in units}}$

$= \dfrac{£6,900}{230} = £30$

| | |
|---|---|
| Budgeted sales | 230 units |
| Actual sales | 200 units |
| Sales volume variance in units | 30 units Adverse |
| Standard profit per unit | x £30 |
| Sales volume variance in £ | £900 Adverse |

### 18

The opportunity cost variance is the variance caused by wrongly estimating costs and so budgeting for a sub-optimal level of output that failed to maximise profits.

(1) *Ex ante budget*

| | | |
|---|---|---|
| | Revenue | = 60Q |
| | Costs | = (10 + 0.25Q)Q = 10Q + 0.25Q² |
| Marginal revenue | (MR) | = 60 |
| Marginal cost | (MC) | = 10 + 0.5Q |
| Profits maximised where | MR | = MC |
| | 60 | = 10 + 0.5Q |
| | Q | = 100 |

(2) *Ex post budget*

| | | |
|---|---|---|
| | Costs | = (16 + 0.2Q)Q |
| | | = 16Q + 0.2Q² |
| Marginal cost | MC | = 16 + 0.4Q |
| Profits maximised where | MR | = MC |
| | 60 | = 16 + 0.4Q |
| | Q | = 110 |

The opportunity cost variance is the loss of profit from producing only 100 units of output instead of 110 units.

| | 100 units | 110 units |
|---|---|---|
| | £ | £ |
| Revenue (60Q) | 6,000 | 6,600 |
| Costs (16Q + 0.2Q²) | 3,600 | 4,180 |
| Profit | 2,400 | 2,420 |
| | | |
| Profit difference | | £20 |

## Question

### 19

|  | £ |
|---|---|
| Budgeted fixed overhead expenditure (3,200 units x £29) | 92,800 |
| Fixed overhead expenditure variance | 2,200 (A) |
| Actual fixed overhead expenditure | 95,000 |

### 20

The first thing we need to know is the actual sales volume. Since there was no change in stocks, production = sales for the month. The overhead total volume variance (capacity volume variance + efficiency variance) can be used to determine the production quantity.

|  | units |  |
|---|---|---|
| Budgeted production | 3,200 |  |
| Total volume variance (£8,700 ÷ £29) | 300 | (F) |
| Actual production | 3,500 | units |

The marginal costing sales volume variance can now be calculated, remembering to use the standard contribution instead of the standard profit margin:

|  |  |  |
|---|---|---|
| Sales volume variance in units | 300 | (F) |
| Standard volume variance per unit (£82 - 47) | £35 |  |
| Sales volume variance | £10,500 | (F) |

### 21

There is no volume variance with marginal costing, because under- or over-absorption due to volume changes cannot arise. The only fixed overhead variance in a marginal costing statement is the fixed overhead expenditure variance - the difference between budgeted and actual overhead expenditure.

### 22

We are not told how many units were sold, but we can calculate the percentage difference in sales volume in the year:

|  | £ |
|---|---|
| Actual sales at actual prices | 204,120 |
| Actual sales at standard prices (x 100/108) | 189,000 |
| Standard sales | 180,000 |
| Increase in sales at standard prices | 9,000 |

Percentage increase in sales = $\dfrac{£9,000}{£180,000}$ = 5% increase

─── COMMENTS ───

## Question

**23** Part of the calculations above can be used to determine the sales price variance:

|  | £ |
|---|---|
| Actual sales at standard prices = | 189,000 |
| Actual sales revenue | 204,120 |
| Sales price variance | 15,120 Favourable |

**24** If you think carefully about the sales volume variance you will see that it measures the increase in standard contribution resulting from the higher level of sales.

Since there was a 5% increase in sales, sales volume variance = 5% x £60,000
= £3,000    Favourable

**25**

| Expected variable cost, with a 5% increase in sales | = 1.05 x £120,000 |
|---|---|
|  | = £126,000 |
| Actual variable cost | = £136,700 |
| Variable cost variance | = £10,700    Adverse |

## 5: MARKING SCHEDULE

| Question | Correct answer | Marks for correct answer | Question | Correct answer | Marks for correct answer | Question | Correct answer | Marks for correct answer |
|---|---|---|---|---|---|---|---|---|
| 1 | B | 1 | 15 | C | 2 | 29 | A | 2 |
| 2 | A | 1 | 16 | D | 2 | 30 | D | 1 |
| 3 | C | 1 | 17 | B | 1 | 31 | A | 1 |
| 4 | A | 1 | 18 | C | 1 | 32 | D | 1 |
| 5 | A | 1 | 19 | A | 1 | 33 | D | 1 |
| 6 | B | 1 | 20 | C | 1 | 34 | B | 1 |
| 7 | D | 1 | 21 | A | 1 | 35 | C | 1 |
| 8 | B | 2 | 22 | B | 1 | 36 | D | 1 |
| 9 | A | 1 | 23 | B | 2 | 37 | D | 1 |
| 10 | B | 1 | 24 | D | 1 | 38 | A | 1 |
| 11 | B | 1 | 25 | D | 1 | 39 | C | 1 |
| 12 | D | 1 | 26 | A | 1 | 40 | C | 1 |
| 13 | A | 1 | 27 | B | 1 | | | |
| 14 | D | 1 | 28 | C | 1 | | | |

### YOUR MARKS

Total marks available   45   Your total mark   ☐

---

**GUIDELINES - If your mark was:**

**0 - 14** The important techniques in this chapter are causing you difficulty. Go back to your study text and look again through each chapter.

**15 - 25** Fairly good. But several of the questions have caught you out. If there is one particular technique which has caused you problems, go back to the study text and read through the relevant chapters carefully.

**26 - 37** Good. There may still be one particular section of this chapter which has caused you difficulty. Check whether this is so, and refer to the study text if there is a clear gap in your knowledge.

**38 - 45** Very good. You have a good understanding of these management accounting principles.

# COMMENTS

## Question

**1**

Breakeven point = $\dfrac{\text{fixed costs}}{\text{contribution per unit}}$

Present method = $\dfrac{£24,400}{£(14 - 6)}$ = 3,050 units

New method = $\dfrac{£31,720}{£(15 - 5)}$ = 3,172 units

Breakeven will increase by 122 units

**2**

If we use v to indicate the relevant sales volume, the cost and revenue structures of the two different production methods can be represented algebraically:

contribution - fixed costs = profit

| present method | | new method |
|---|---|---|
| £(14 - 6)v - 24,400 | = | £(15 - 5)v - 31,720 |
| 8v - 24,400 | = | 10v - 31,720 |
| v | = | 3,660 |

**3**

The budgeted profit statement can be adjusted for the differences:

|  | £ | £ |
|---|---:|---:|
| Sales (480,000 x 115% volume increase x 97% for bulk price reduction) | | 535,440 |
| Direct materials (140,000 x 115% x 98% for bulk discount) | 157,780 | |
| Direct labour (110,000 + [110,000 x 15% x 1.5 for shift premium]) | 134,750 | |
| Variable overhead (50,000 x 115%) | 57,500 | 350,030 |
| Contribution | | 185,410 |
| Fixed cost (130,000 + 2,000) | | 132,000 |
| Revised profit | | 53,410 |

**4**

Current weekly contribution = 12% x £280,000 = £33,600

|  | £ |
|---|---:|
| Loss on Z per week 3,000 x £(1.90 - 2.20 - 0.15) | (1,350) |
| Extra contribution from 5% increase in sales: 5% of £33,600 | 1,680 |
| Net increase in contribution/profit per week | 330 |

# Question

## 5

| | £ |
|---|---|
| Sales | 145,000 |
| Variable cost £(32,000 + 50,000 + 5,000) | 87,000 |
| Contribution | 58,000 |

| | |
|---|---|
| Contribution per unit (÷ 20,000) | £2.90 |

| | £ |
|---|---|
| Loss of contribution from sales irretrievably lost (9,000 x £2.90) | 26,100 |
| Extra variable costs incurred to meet sales for 11,000 units (x 50% of £2.50 per unit) | 13,750 |
| Adverse effect on company's profit | 39,850 |

*Note* Answer B is incorrect. If you assumed that variable overhead costs per hour would be 50% higher than normal, as for direct labour, this would be incorrect. We are told that variable overhead varies with hours worked, not with direct labour cost.

## 6

You have probably recognised that machine capacity is a limiting factor. The decision rule is therefore to maximise the contribution per week of machine capacity, subject to the other constraints, about minimum output for each product and machine suitability for making products W and Y.

| | W | X | Y | Z |
|---|---|---|---|---|
| Contribution per unit | £115 | £80 | £160 | £125 |
| x Units per machine week | 22 | 8 | 14 | 16 |
| = Contribution per week | £2,530 | £640 | £2,240 | £2,000 |
| Ranking | 1 | 4 | 2 | 3 |

Since W and Y are the most profitable products and 12 of the machines are unsuitable for their manufacture, the 9 machines which are suitable for all products should be used exclusively for W and Y. Since W is preferable to Y, the minimum amount of 500 units of Y should be manufactured, leaving the remainder of this capacity for W.

| | *Machine suitable for W and Y machine weeks* | |
|---|---|---|
| Weeks available (46 x 9) | 414 | |
| Minimum allocation to Y (500/14 per week) | 36 | (whole weeks only) |
| Remainder allocated to W | 378 | |

Using the remaining 12 machines for X and Z, the minimum requirement of the least profitable product, X, should be manufactured, leaving the remainder of the capacity for product Z:

| | *Machines suitable for all products* | |
|---|---|---|
| Weeks available (46 x 12) | 552 | |
| Minimum allocated to X (500/8) | 63 | (whole weeks only) |
| Remainder allocated to Z | 489 | |

Continued...

## COMMENTS

## Question

Calculation of profit achievable from this product mix:

|  |  | £ |
|---|---|---|
| W | 378 machine weeks x £2,530 | 956,340 |
| X | 63 machine weeks x £640 | 40,320 |
| Y | 36 machine weeks x £2,240 | 80,640 |
| Z | 489 machine weeks x £2,000 | 978,000 |
|  | Total contribution | 2,055,300 |
|  | Fixed costs | 1,200,000 |
|  | Maximum profit | 855,300 |

### 7

The shadow price of a scarce resource is the amount by which profit could be increased if one more unit of resource is obtained.

Since there is unlimited demand, product W would be produced if another week's capacity was obtained, because it earns the highest weekly contribution. The shadow price is therefore the weekly contribution from W - £2,530.

### 8

This is a make-or-buy decision involving a limiting factor. If all of the components are manufactured in-house, 78,000 machine hours will be required. Some sub-contracting will therefore be necessary, since only 50,000 machine hours are available.

Costs can be kept at their lowest by minimising the extra variable costs of sub-contracting per machine hour saved.

|  | P | Q | R |
|---|---|---|---|
|  | £ | £ | £ |
| Variable cost of manufacture | 45 | 70 | 56 |
| Sub-contractor price | 65 | 78 | 80 |
| Extra cost of buying | 20 | 8 | 24 |
| Machine hours saved by buying | 9 | 5 | 12 |
| Extra cost of buying per hour saved | £2.22 | £1.60 | £2.00 |

The priority for internal manufacture will be in the order: P, R, Q. This will minimise the extra cost of buying per hour saved. The production and purchasing plan for components should therefore be:

|  |  |  | Hours used |  | Cost |
|---|---|---|---|---|---|
|  |  |  |  |  | £ |
| Manufacture | 3,000 x P | (x 9 hrs) | 27,000 | (x £45) | 135,000 |
|  | 1,916 x R | (x 12 hrs) | 22,992 | (x £56) | 107,296 |
|  |  |  | 49,992 |  |  |
| Purchase | 1,084 x R (balance of requirement) |  |  | (x £80) | 86,720 |
|  | 3,000 x Q |  |  | (£78) | 234,000 |
| Minimum cost of satisfying component requirements |  |  |  |  | 563,016 |

# Question

## 9

If a product is discontinued, the only costs to be saved would be the variable costs and the attributable fixed costs.

The first step, then, is to calculate these costs for Oblong. We will at the same time calculate the variable costs and contribution for the other products, because this data is needed for the next two questions.

Variable costs and attributable fixed costs:

|  | Square £000 | Round £000 | Oblong £000 |
|---|---|---|---|
| *Variable costs* |  |  |  |
| Material | 16 | 14 | 24 |
| Labour (note 1) | 40 | 50 | 90 |
| Variable production overhead | 20 | 42 | 40 |
| Selling costs - 5% commission | 11 | 13 | 19 |
|  | 87 | 119 | 173 |
| Sales revenue | 220 | 260 | 380 |
| Contribution | 133 | 141 | 207 |
| *Attributable fixed costs of Oblong* |  |  |  |
| Fixed production overhead (note 2) |  |  | 82 |
| Delivery costs (note 3) |  |  | 28 |
| Attributable profit |  |  | 97 |

*Notes:*

1  Since the total labour cost includes a 20% surcharge added to the variable cost, the variable labour cost is calculated by dividing the total cost by 1.2.

2  The apportioned general fixed production overhead must be excluded from the analysis, because it would not be saved if the product was discontinued.

   Attributable fixed production overhead = £102,000 - (50% x £40,000) = £82,000.

3  Similarly, the apportioned general delivery costs must be excluded:

   Attributable fixed delivery cost = £40,000 - (50% x £24,000) = £28,000

We are now in a position to calculate the effect of discontinuing Oblong:

|  | £000 |
|---|---|
| Original budgeted profit | 28 |
| Less attributable profit from Oblong | 97 |
| Forecast loss | (69) |

## 10

|  | £000 |
|---|---|
| Original budgeted contribution from Round | 141 |
| Add back original budgeted commission | 13 |
|  | 154 |

Continued...

## Question

**10**

| | |
|---|---:|
| This will increase by 8% with the extra sales volume = | 166,320 |
| Less revised commission (£260,000 original sales x 1.08 x 7% commission) = | 19,656 |
| Revised contribution from Round | 146,664 |
| Original budgeted contribution from Round | 141,000 |
| Overall gain | 5,664 |
| Original budgeted profit | 28,000 |
| Revised profit | 33,664 |

**11**

| | £000 |
|---|---:|
| Gain in contribution from increased sales of Round (141 x 25%) | 35,250 |
| Loss of contribution from reduced sales of Square (133 x 15%) | 19,950 |
| Net gain in contribution | 15,300 |
| Cost of advertising campaign | 10,000 |
| Overall gain | 5,300 |
| Original budgeted profit | 28,000 |
| Revised profit | 33,300 |

**12**

Since fixed costs are the same for every option, we can include them in the calculation because they will not affect the differential costs.

| To produce 40,000 units Option | | Total cost £000 | |
|---|---|---|---|
| Nil on X, | 40,000 on Y | (33 + 138) | 171 |
| 10,000 on X, | 30,000 on Y | (55 + 100) | 155 |
| 20,000 on X, | 20,000 on Y | (79 + 62) | 141 |
| 30,000 on X, | 10,000 on Y | (104 + 36) | 140 * least cost option |
| 40,000 on X, | Nil on Y | (140 + 19) | 159 |

**13**

| Production and sales units | Least cost option | Total cost £000 | Total revenue £000 | Loss £000 |
|---|---|---:|---:|---:|
| 10,000 | (Nil on X, 10,000 on Y) | 69 | 30 | (39) |
| 20,000 | (10,000 on X, 10,000 on Y) | 91 | 60 | (31) |
| 30,000 | (20,000 on X, 10,000 on Y) | 115 | 90 | (25) |
| 40,000 | (30,000 on X, 10,000 on Y) | 140 | 120 | (20) |
| 50,000 | (30,000 on X, 20,000 on Y) | 166 | 150 | *(16) |
| 60,000 | (40,000 on X, 20,000 on Y) | 202 | 180 | (22) |
| 70,000 | (40,000 on X, 30,000 on Y) | 240 | 210 | (30) |
| 80,000 | (40,000 on X, 40,000 on Y) | 278 | 240 | (38) |

Loss-minimising*

The product is making a loss, although this is after bearing some apportioned fixed overhead and depreciation charges. Management will presumably wish to consider methods of improving profitability or disposing of the machines.

# 5: DECISION ACCOUNTING

## Question

**14** Consider each material in turn, and remember one golden rule: the historical or book value of material is never relevant for decision accounting. It is a past cost which cannot now be recovered.

|  |  | £ |
|---|---|---|
| *Material P:* will have to be purchased at £40 per unit | 400 × £40 | 16,000 |

*Material Q:* there are existing stocks but if these are used on the special job a further 100 units would have to be purchased to replace them. The relevant price is therefore the replacement price    230 × £64    14,720

*Material R:* 200 of the units required are already in stock. They have no other use and if not used for this job they could be sold. The opportunity cost of using these 200 units is therefore the sales revenue forgone    200 × £23    4,600

The remaining 150 units would have to be purchased    150 × £59    8,850

*Material S:* 140 of the units required are already in stock. There are two alternative uses for these units. They can be sold, to realise 140 × £12 = £1,680, or they can be used as a substitute for material V. The saving on material V would be 225 units × £10 = £2,250, therefore this is the best alternative use for the stock of material S. The opportunity cost of using them is the saving forgone    2,250

The remaining units will have to be purchased    30 × £49    1,470

*Material T:* The full requirement is already in stock. If they are used on this contract, Lovell Crossing will be saved the cost of having them disposed of. This saving is the relevant opportunity 'cost'    (160)

Total relevant cost    **47,730**

**15** If the 2,500 machine hours released (50% of the budgeted capacity) they would be used making L, M or N so as to maximise total contribution.

|  | L | M | N |
|---|---|---|---|
| Contribution per machine hour | £2 | £3 | £4 |
| Ranking | 3rd | 2nd | 1st |
| Maximum demand | 250 units | 125 units | 1,250 units |

The opportunity cost of *making* L, M or N is the need to purchase motors externally, saving (5,000 hrs ÷ 8,000 units) 0.625 machine hours per motor purchased at an extra cost of £2 per motor. This represents an opportunity cost of £2 ÷ 0.625 machine hours = £3.20 per machine hour saved.

Only product N offers a contribution in excess of £3.20 per machine hour, and so it would be more profitable to make N and buy motors, but it would not be profitable to make L or M.

# COMMENTS

## Question

**16**  PHC 1   costs per year are 20n + 12,500
PHC 2   costs per year are 18n + 16,000
PHC 3   costs per year are 15n + 20,500

(a)   PHC 1 is cheaper than PHC 2 up to where
20n + 12,500 = 18n + 16,000
n = 1,750

(b)   PHC 1 is cheaper than PHC 3 up to where
20n + 12,500 = 15n + 20,500
n = 1,600

(c)   PHC 2 is cheaper than PHC 3 up to where
18n + 16,000 = 15n + 20,500
n = 1,500

*Conclusion*  PHC 1 is the cheaper up to n = 1,600, and then PHC 3 is cheapest.

**17**

| Number of salesmen | Sales per area units | Increment units | Area S Contribution £ | Area S Incremental contribution £ | Area N Contribution £ | Area N Incremental contribution £ |
|---|---|---|---|---|---|---|
| 1 | 50,000 |  | (x5) 250,000 |  | (x4) 200,000 |  |
| 2 | 60,000 | 10,000 | (x5) | 50,000 | (x4) | 40,000 |
| 3 | 66,000 | 6,000 | (5,000x5) + (1,000x4) | 29,000 | (5,000x4) + (1,000x3) | 23,000 |
| 4 | 70,000 | 4,000 | (x4) | 16,000 |  |  |

Since a salesman's incremental costs are £23,500 per annum, it would be profitable to have a second salesman in Area N but not a third, and to hire a third salesman in Area S but not a fourth.

**18**  Skilled labour:
The relevant cost of skilled labour is the variable cost plus the contribution forgone from not being able to put the labour to its alternative use:                                £
27 hours x £(7 + 8)     405

Semi-skilled labour:
Semi-skilled labour are being paid anyway, so their wages are not relevant. The incremental cost to be incurred will be the wages paid to the unskilled labour taken on to replace them:                    14 hours x £2      28

Unskilled labour:
There is no information which indicates that there is any opportunity cost associated with unskilled labour, therefore the relevant hourly wage rate is £2
20 hours x £2      40
Relevant cost of labour     473

# Question

## 19

Production overhead:
Unskilled labour hours are used as the overhead absorption base, at a rate of (£2 x 50%) per hour = £1 per hour. We are told that 60% of this overhead (60p per hour) is variable. Fixed overhead will be incurred anyway, therefore it is not relevant.

£

Variable production overhead = £0.60 per hour x 20 hours =    12

Machine costs:
Depreciation is not relevant because it is a non-cash cost. The relevant cost is the opportunity cost of the rental income forgone:    175

Drawings cost:
The £280 already spent is a sunk cost and is not relevant. The relevant cost is the forgone opportunity to sell the drawings    250

Administration cost:
Apportioned administration cost is not incremental to the contract. It would be incurred anyway and is therefore not relevant.    0

Relevant overhead cost    437
Relevant labour cost (see previous solution)    473
Total relevant costs = minimum contract price    910

## 20

The required mark-up can be obtained from the formula:

$$\text{Mark up} = \frac{\text{Investment in product}}{\text{Total annual costs}} \times \text{Required return on investment}$$

$$= \frac{£(160{,}000 + 52{,}500)}{£250{,}000} \times 20\%$$

$$= 17\%$$

## 21

The price elasticity of demand indicates the percentage change in the quantity demanded which will arise from a percentage change in price:

$$\eta = \frac{\text{percentage change in quantity demanded}}{\text{percentage change in price}}$$

If demand is elastic, the percentage change in demand will be greater than the percentage change in price, and Statement 2 is therefore correct.

If the price falls, demand will increase by a greater proportion than the reduction in price. *Total* revenue will increase and Statement 1 is correct.

An increase in price will cause a greater proportionate reduction in demand. *Total* revenue will fall. Profits could rise or fall, depending on how costs are affected (as well as revenue) by the fall in demand. Statement 3 could be correct or incorrect.

# COMMENTS

## Question

### 22

To solve this question you will need to use differential calculus, to derive a formula for marginal cost (MC) and a formula for marginal revenue (MR).

First, derive functions for marginal cost and marginal revenue:

$$TC = 48{,}000 + 75Q + 0.3Q^2$$

$$MC = \frac{dTC}{dQ} = 75 + 0.6Q$$

We do not yet have a function for total revenue, but it can be derived from the price function:

$P = 89 - 0.7Q$
Since Revenue = Price x Quantity

Revenue, $R = (89 - 0.7Q) \times Q$
$R = 89Q - 0.7Q^2$

$$MR = \frac{dR}{dQ} = 89 - 1.4Q$$

To maximise profits, $MC = MR$
$75 + 0.6Q = 89 - 1.4Q$
$\therefore 2Q = 14$
$\therefore Q = 7$

We can now substitute $Q = 7$ in the price equation:

$P = 89 - 0.7Q$
$= 89 - (0.7 \times 7)$
$= \underline{\underline{£84.10}}$

### 23

*Current situation*

$P = (280 - 0.3x)$
Total revenue, $R = x(280 - 0.3x)$
$R = 280x - 0.3x^2$

Marginal revenue  $MR = \frac{dR}{dx} = 280 - 0.6x$

Marginal cost  $MC = \frac{dTC}{dx} = 100$

Profits are maximised where $MC = MR$
$100 = 280 - 0.6x$
$x = 300$ units; Price $P = £190$

Profit $= £(190 \times 300) - £10{,}000 - £100(300)$
$= £17{,}000$

Continued...

# Question

*Proposed change* MC now 70

Profits maximised where  MC = MR
70 = 280 - 0.6x
x = 350 units

Since there will be no capacity above 340 units, output and sales will be restricted to 340 units. Price P = £178

Profit = £(178 x 340) - £18,000 - £70(340)
= £60,520 - £18,000 - £23,800
= £18,720. Profits will increase

## 24

As in the previous question, the solution to this question lies in applying differential calculus to determine the marginal revenue function.

First it is necessary to use the data supplied to determine the demand function. We know that the function is a straight line:

where  P = a + bQ
P = price
Q = quantity demanded

Substituting the two sets of data given in the question:

145 = a + 5,000b        (1)
120 = 1 + 11,250b       (2)
Subtract 25 = -6,250b
∴ b = -0.004

Substitute in (1),  145 = a - (5,000 x 0.004)
∴ a = 165

Therefore, the demand function is    P = 165 - 0.004Q
Since Revenue (R) = Price x Quantity, R = 165Q - 0.004Q²
and Marginal Revenue = $\frac{dR}{dQ}$ = 165 - 0.008Q

We are told that marginal costs = £27. Therefore, to maximise profit at the point where marginal cost = marginal revenue,

27 = 165 - 0.008Q
∴ Q = 17,250

Next, substitute for Q in the demand function
P = 165 - 0.004Q
= 165 - (0.004 x 17,250)
∴ Optimum price, P = £96

## COMMENTS

## Question

**25** This is a test of your ability to recognise the correct definition of a stock control term. The important thing to notice is that the analysis concentrates on *total* annual usage cost. An individual item can have a low unit value, but if used frequently it may represent a large proportion of annual usage cost and would therefore be included in Group A for analysis purposes.

**26** The formula for the economic order quantity is:

$$EOQ = \sqrt{\frac{2cd}{h}}$$

where  c = cost of placing an order
d = annual demand
h = cost of holding one unit in stock for one year.

In this question, h is given in terms of the cost for a month, therefore you must remember to convert this to the annual cost:

$$EOQ = \sqrt{\frac{2 \times 5 \times 42,000}{0.50 \times 12}} = 264.6$$

To the nearest 5 units, the economic order quantity is 265 units.

**27** The first step is to calculate the economic order quantity:

$$EOQ = \sqrt{\frac{2cd}{h}}$$

$$= \sqrt{\frac{2 \times £10 \times 20,000}{£0.50 \times 20\%}}$$

$$= 2,000 \text{ units}$$

Next, compare the total annual cost of the current policy, with the total annual cost of the EOQ policy:

Remember that stock control theory states that average stock is equal to half of the quantity ordered.

*Current policy*
Quantity ordered each time = 20,000 ÷ 4 = 5,000 units
Stockholding cost per annum:  £  £

Average stock = $\frac{5,000}{2}$ = 2,500 units

∴ Holding cost = 2,500 x £0.50 x 20% =  250
Ordering cost = 4 orders per annum x £10 per order =  40
Total annual cost    290

Continued...

200

## Question

|  | £ | £ |
|---|---|---|

*Economic policy*
Stockholding cost per annum:

Average stock = $\frac{20,000}{2}$ = 1,000 units

∴ Holding cost = 1,000 × £0.50 × 20% =          100

Ordering cost = $\frac{20,000}{2,000}$ = 10 orders per annum × £10          100

Total annual cost                                                                                        200
Annual cost saving                                                                                    90

**28** To determine the optimum order quantity when there are discounts available, the first step is to ignore the discount and calculate the Economic Order Quantity:

$$EOQ = \sqrt{\frac{2cd}{h}}$$

$$= \sqrt{\frac{2 \times £2 \times 300,000}{£1.20}}$$

= 1,000 units

This may not be the optimum quantity, because of the discounts available. The total cost of ordering in batches of 1,000 units will be compared with the total cost of ordering in batch sizes that are just big enough to earn each size of discount.

| Order quantity (units) | 1,000 | 1,200 | 1,600 | 2,000 |
|---|---|---|---|---|
| Annual costs | £ | £ | £ | £ |
| Ordering costs: | | | | |
| 300 orders × £2 | 600 | | | |
| 250 orders × £2 | | 500 | | |
| 187.5 orders × £2 | | | 375 | |
| 150 orders × £2 | | | | 300 |
| Stockholding costs: | | | | |
| Average stock × £1.20 | 600 | 720 | 960 | 1,200 |
| Purchase costs: | | | | |
| 300,000 × £0.05 | 15,000 | | | |
| £15,000 × 95% | | 14,250 | | |
| £15,000 × 92.5% | | | 13,875 | |
| £15,000 × 92% | | | | 13,800 |
| Total annual cost | 16,200 | 15,470 | 15,210 | 15,300 |

The optimum order quantity to minimise total cost is 1,600 units.

## Question

### 29

| Month | Op'ng stock | Pur- chases | Total stock av'ble | Op'ng unfilled orders | Orders rec'd | Total orders | Sales | Unfilled orders c/f | Clos'g stock |
|---|---|---|---|---|---|---|---|---|---|
| | 000 | 000 | 000 | 000 | 000 | 000 | 000 | 000 | 000 |
| 1 | 2 | 12 | 14 | - | 15 | 15 | 14 | 1 | - |
| 2 | - | 11 | 11 | 1 | 14 | 15 | 11 | 4 | - |
| 3 | - | 15 | 15 | 4 | 11 | 15 | 15 | - | - |
| | 2 | 38 | | | | | 40 | 5 | |

|  | £000 |
|---|---|
| Sales 40,000 units at £50 | 2,000 |
| less penalty for unfilled orders (5,000 x 10% of £50) | (25) |
| | 1,975 |

|  | £000 | |
|---|---|---|
| Opening stock (2,000 x £30) | 60 | |
| Purchases: 38,000 units at £30 | 1,140 | |
| | 1,200 | |
| less closing stock | 0 | |
| | 1,200 | |
| Add penalty for shortfalls in orders below 12,000 per month (1,000 x £7) | 7 | |
| Add extra cost of purchases above 12,000 in a month (3,000 x £12) | 36 | |
| Stockholding costs (2,000 x £2) | 4 | 1,247 |
| | | 728 |
| Fixed costs | | 500 |
| Profit | | 228 |

### 30

| Month | Op'ng stock | Pur- chases | Total stock av'ble | Op'ng unfilled orders | Orders rec'd | Total orders | Sales | Unfilled orders c/f | Clos'g stock |
|---|---|---|---|---|---|---|---|---|---|
| | 000 | 000 | 000 | 000 | 000 | 000 | 000 | 000 | 000 |
| 1 | 2 | 12 | 14 | - | 15 | 15 | 14 | 1 | - |
| 2 | - | 12 | 12 | 1 | 14 | 15 | 12 | 3 | - |
| 3 | - | 14 | 14 | 3 | 11 | 14 | 14 | - | - |
| | 2 | 38 | | | | | 40 | 4 | |

|  | £000 |
|---|---|
| Sales | 2,000 |
| less penalty for unfilled orders (4,000 x 10% of £50) | (20) |
| | 1,980 |

|  | £000 | |
|---|---|---|
| Opening stock (2,000 x £30) | 60 | |
| Purchases: 38,000 units at £30 | 1,140 | |
| | 1,200 | |
| less closing stock | 0 | |
| | 1,200 | |
| Add penalty for shortfalls in orders below 12,000 per month (2,000 x £12) | 0 | |
| Add extra cost of purchases above 12,000 in a month (2,000 x £12) | 24 | |
| Stockholding costs (2,000 x £2) | 4 | 1,228 |
| | | 752 |
| | c/f | |

Continued...

## 5: DECISION ACCOUNTING

## Question

|  | £000 | £000 |
|---|---|---|
| c/f |  | 752 |
| Fixed costs |  | 500 |
| Profit |  | 252 |
| Profit under previous situation |  | 228 |
| Increase in profit |  | 24 |

This suggests that the alternative purchasing policy considered in this question might be more profitable than the policy that is currently in operation.

### 31

The figure in the bottom right hand corner of the tableau indicates that the optimum contribution is £29,000. The solution column shows that 1,000 units of product p will be produced. Each unit of product p earns £8 contribution. The remainder of the £29,000 contribution must come from q:

∴ Contribution from q = £29,000 - (£8 × 1,000) = £21,000

Divided by the contribution per unit = £14
∴ Production of q = 1,500 units

### 32

*Statement 1:* Unused machine hours is represented by the slack variable, k, which does not feature as a variable in the solution - therefore this statement is incorrect.

*Statement 2:* Unused material is represented by the slack variable, l. There is a value of 125 for l in the solution column, indicating that there will be 125 tonnes of material unused. This statement is therefore incorrect.

*Statement 3:* Unsatisfied demand for product p is represented by the slack variable, m. There is a value of 200 for m in the solution column, indicating that there will be 200 units of satisfied demand. This statement is therefore correct.

### 33

The breakeven price is the variable cost of the scarce resources plus its shadow price. The shadow price can be read from the solution row. The shadow price is the amount by which contribution will increase if one more unit of resource is made available, assuming that each extra unit of the resource will cost its normal variable cost. The breakeven price is therefore £5 + £4 = £9 per hour.

### 34

The figures in the k column tell us that for each extra machine hour made available, 2 less units of product p would be produced. Since p = 1,000 in the optimal tableau, there is a limit to the number of times this reduction could take place:

$$\frac{1,000 \text{ units}}{2 \text{ units per hour}} = 500 \text{ machine hours}$$

# COMMENTS

## Question

**35** The figures in the j column show that for every extra skilled labour hour made available, the output of product p would increase by 1 unit, and the output of product q would fall by 1 unit and the output of product q would fall by 0.5 units. The change in contribution would be (1 x £8) - (0.5 x £14) = £1. This is the shadow price, y, of skilled labour hours.

**36** The figures in the k column show that if one extra machine hour is made available, output of product q would *increase* by 1.5 units, since the value in the q row, k column is +1.5.

**37** If you haven't seen this method of presenting a linear programming solution before, it can take a bit of sorting out. However, your ability (or otherwise) to do this sorting out is a test of your understanding of linear programming.

Since materials M1 and M3 have positive dual prices (£2 and £4), the available quantities of both must be fully used up in the optimal solution. In contrast, there is a surplus of 425 kg of M2 in the optimal solution.

**38** The allowable decrease in the contribution per unit of P, before the optimal production quantities change, is £12 (given in the "allowable decrease" column of the objective coefficient ranges). Since the current unit contribution is £20 per unit, the contribution can fall to £(20 - 12) = £8 per unit before the optimal solution changes.

**39** The contribution per unit of product R must increase by £2.6667 per unit before the optimal production and sales quantities of P, Q and R begin to change. This is given in the "allowable increase" column of the objective coefficient ranges. Since the current unit contribution is £16, the contribution per unit of R would need to rise by over £(16 + 2.6667) = £18.6667, rounded to £18.67 in the question.

**40** The dual price of £2 per kg applies to M1 only within the range indicated by the "allowable increase" and "allowable decrease" columns in the "right hand side ranges" table of figures. Since the current maximum availability of M1 is 6,000 kg, the range within which the dual price of £2 per kg applies is (maximum, allowable increase) 6,000 + 400 = 6,400 kg and (minimum, allowable decrease) 6,000 - 106.25 = 5,893.75kg.

# 6: MARKING SCHEDULE

| Question | Correct answer | Marks for the correct answer | Question | Correct answer | Marks for the correct answer |
|---|---|---|---|---|---|
| 1 | C | 1 | 15 | B | 1 |
| 2 | A | 1 | 16 | B | 2 |
| 3 | A | 1 | 17 | A | 1 |
| 4 | C | 1 | 18 | C | 3 |
| 5 | C | 1 | 19 | A | 1 |
| 6 | C | 1 | 20 | D | 2 |
| 7 | D | 1 | 21 | B | 1 |
| 8 | A | 1 | 22 | A | 1 |
| 9 | C | 2 | 23 | B | 1 |
| 10 | C | 2 | 24 | A | 1 |
| 11 | B | 1 | 25 | C | 1 |
| 12 | D | 2 | 26 | B | 1 |
| 13 | D | 2 | 27 | B | 3 |
| 14 | C | 1 | 28 | A | 3 |

YOUR MARKS

Total marks available  40     Your total mark  ☐

---

**GUIDELINES** - If your mark was:

**0 - 11**  Disappointing. You need to revise thoroughly the computations involved in investment appraisal.

**12 - 20**  You are still not quite fluent with investment appraisal computations. Read the comments carefully and make sure that you understand the reasons for your errors.

**21 - 30**  Good. Although there are probably still one or two gaps in your knowledge, you are well on the way to a thorough understanding of investment appraisal.

**31 - 40**  Very good. You have a broad and thorough understanding of the principles of investment appraisal.

# COMMENTS

## Question

### 1

Always use cash flows to calculate the payback period, so subtract depreciation from running costs.

|  | £ |
|---|---|
| Cash flow in years 1 and 2: | |
| Contribution = 6 million x £60 per 1,000 | 360,000 |
| *less* Cash running costs = 276,000 - 70,000 depreciation | 206,000 |
| | 154,000 |
| | |
| Cash flow in years 3 and 4: | |
| Contribution = 5 million x £60 per 1,000 | 300,000 |
| *less* Cash running costs | 206,000 |
| | 94,000 |

Residual value of machine = £300,000 - (4 years x £70,000 depreciation) = £20,000. This is the estimated disposal value at the end of year 4.

The net cash flows can be summarised:

| Year | | £ | Cumulative £ |
|---|---|---|---|
| 0 | | (300,000) | (300,000) |
| 1 | | 154,000 | (146,000) |
| 2 | | 154,000 | 8,000 |
| 3 | | 94,000 | |
| 4 | (94,000 + 20,000 residual value) | 114,000 | |

Payback therefore occurs during year 2. Assuming even cash flows throughout the year, interpolation can be used to find the exact payback period:

Number of years = $1 + \frac{146,000}{154,000} = 1.95$

Payback period = 1.95 years

### 2

The Accounting Rate of Return is always based on profits *after* depreciation.

| Year | | Cash flow £ | Depreciation £ | Accounting profit £ |
|---|---|---|---|---|
| 1 | | 154,000 | 70,000 | 84,000 |
| 2 | | 154,000 | 70,000 | 84,000 |
| 3 | | 94,000 | 70,000 | 24,000 |
| 4 | (excluding residual value) | 94,000 | 70,000 | 24,000 |
| | | | | 216,000 |

÷ 4, = average accounting profit = £54,000

# Question

Average Accounting Rate of Return based on the original investment =

$$\frac{£54,000}{£300,000} \times 100\% = 18.0\%$$

**3** Average net book value (NBV)

$$= \frac{£300,000 + £20,000 \text{ residual value}}{2} = £160,000$$

∴ Average Accounting Rate of Return, based on average NBV

$$= \frac{£54,000}{£160,000} \times 100\% = 33.8\%$$

**4** Using the cash flows derived in question 1:

| Year | Cash flow £ | 20% discount factor | Present value £ |
|---|---|---|---|
| 0 | (300,000) | 1.00 | (300,000) |
| 1 | 154,000 | 0.83 | 127,820 |
| 2 | 154,000 | 0.69 | 106,260 |
| 3 | 94,000 | 0.58 | 54,520 |
| 4 | 114,000 | 0.48 | 54,720 |
|   |   | Net present value | 43,320 |

**5** We already have the Net Present Value at 20% - £43,320. Try 30%.

| Year | Cash flow £ | 30% discount factor | Present value £ |
|---|---|---|---|
| 0 | (300,000) | 1.00 | (300,000) |
| 1 | 154,000 | 0.77 | 118,580 |
| 2 | 154,000 | 0.59 | 90,860 |
| 3 | 94,000 | 0.46 | 43,240 |
| 4 | 114,000 | 0.35 | 39,900 |
|   |   | Net present value | (7,420) |

The Internal Rate of Return (IRR) lies between 20% and 30%.

Using interpolation: IRR = 20% + [ $\frac{43,320}{(43,320 + 7,420)}$ x 10% ]

= 28.5% (approx)

## COMMENTS

## Question

**6**

There are no present value tables for 16.5%, therefore you will have to calculate your own discount factors.

Remember that the discounting factor is $\dfrac{1}{(1+r)^n}$

where  r = cost of capital
       n = number of years

| Year | | 16.5% factor | Cash flow £ | Present value £ |
|---|---|---|---|---|
| 1 | $\dfrac{1}{(1+0.165)} =$ | 0.86 | 149,000 | 128,140 |
| 2 | $\dfrac{1}{(1+0.165)^2} =$ | 0.74 | 128,000 | 94,720 |
| 3 | $\dfrac{1}{(1+0.165)^3} =$ | 0.63 | 84,000 | 52,920 |
| 4 | $\dfrac{1}{(1+0.165)^4} =$ | 0.54 | 70,000 | 37,800 |
| | | | Present value | 313,580 |
| | | | Initial outlay | 280,000 |
| | | | Net present value | 33,580 |

**7**

Let the annual rent be £R. At a discount rate of 17%, the Net Present Value of the investment must be equal to zero.

∴ £R x (annuity for 5 years at 17%) = £27,200
∴ £R x 3.20                          = £27,200
∴ £R                                 = £27,200/3.20
Annual rent                          = £8,500

**8**

The *Net Terminal Value (NTV)* is the cash balance which would remain at the end of a project if the initial investment was borrowed at the cost of capital, and the cash flows from the project were used to repay the principal and interest. A positive NTV indicates that the investment will be financially worthwhile.

| Year | Opening balance b/f £ | Interest at 16% £ | Cash flow in year £ | Closing balance c/f £ |
|---|---|---|---|---|
| 0 | | | | (27,200) |
| 1 | (27,200) | (4,352) | 9,000 | (22,552) |
| 2 | (22,552) | (3,608) | 9,000 | (17,160) |
| 3 | (17,160) | (2,746) | 9,000 | (10,906) |
| 4 | (10,906) | (1,745) | 9,000 | (3,651) |
| 5 | (3,651) | (584) | 9,000 | 4,765 |

# 6: INVESTMENT APPRAISAL

## Question

### 9

Let the rental in year 1 be £X.

| Item | Cash flow | Discount factor at 17% | Present value |
|---|---|---|---|
| | £ | | £ |
| Capital cost | (27,200) | 1.00 | (27,200) |
| Rent | X | 0.85 | 0.8500 X |
| Rent | X | 0.73 | 0.7300 X |
| Rent | 1.10 X | 0.62 | 0.6820 X |
| Rent | 1.10 X | 0.53 | 0.5830 X |
| Rent | 1.21 X | 0.46 | 0.5566 X |
| | | | (27,200) + 3.4016 X |

For an NPV = 0,  3.4016 X = 27,200
X = £7,996
= £8,000 to the nearest £1,000.

### 10

In this question, investment funds are a limiting factor. We should therefore follow the decision rules of maximising the return from the limiting factor.

The first step is to rank the projects in order of their NPV per £1 of investment:

| Project | NPV at 20% | Investment | NPV per £1 invested | Ranking |
|---|---|---|---|---|
| | £000 | £000 | £ | |
| P | 16.5 | 40 | 0.41 | 4 |
| Q | 17.0 | 50 | 0.34 | 5 |
| R | 18.8 | 30 | 0.63 | 1 |
| S | 14.0 | 45 | 0.31 | 6 |
| T | 7.4 | 15 | 0.49 | 3 |
| U | 10.8 | 20 | 0.54 | 2 |

Available funds can now be allocated according to this ranking:

| Project | Investment | NPV |
|---|---|---|
| | £000 | £000 |
| R | 30 | 18.8 |
| U | 20 | 10.8 |
| T | 15 | 7.4 |
| P | 40 | 16.5 |
| Q (balance) | 25 | ($\frac{1}{2}$) 8.5 |
| | 130 | |
| Maximum Net Present Value = | | 62.0 |

## COMMENTS

## Question

**11** The first step is to think about the value of a perpetuity. £1,000 invested to earn 25% in perpetuity yields an NPV, at a 20% cost of capital, of

$$\left(\frac{£1,000 \times 0.25}{0.20}\right) - £1,000 = £250$$

The NPV from the suggested combinations can now be tested:

| Projects | Required internal investment £000 | Funds remaining for external investment £000 | NPV of external investment £000 | NPV from projects £000 | Total NPV £000 |
|---|---|---|---|---|---|
| P and Q | 90 | 5 (x 250/1,000) | 1.25 | (16.5 + 17.0) 33.5 | 34.75 |
| P and R | 70 | 25 | 6.25 | (16.5 + 18.8) 35.3 | 41.55 |
| Q and R | 80 | 15 | 3.75 | (17.0 + 18.8) 35.8 | 39.55 |
| All invested | 0 | 90 | 22.50 | 0 | 22.50 |

The best investment plan is to undertake projects P and R, and to invest £25,000 of surplus funds externally.

**12** The first step is to calculate the Net Present Value of operating a vehicle for 2, 3, 4 or 5 years. Trade-in prices are shown as a negative cost.

| Year | 15% factor | 2 years Cash flow £ | 2 years NPV at 15% £ | 3 years Cash flow £ | 3 years NPV at 15% £ | 4 years Cash flow £ | 4 years NPV at 15% £ | 5 years Cash flow £ | 5 years NPV at 15% £ |
|---|---|---|---|---|---|---|---|---|---|
| 0 | 1.00 | 9,600 | 9,600 | 9,600 | 9,600 | 9,600 | 9,600 | 9,600 | 9,600 |
| 1 | 0.87 | 1,890 | 1,644 | 1,890 | 1,644 | 1,890 | 1,644 | 1,890 | 1,644 |
| 2 | 0.76 | 3,180 (2,400) | 593 | 3,180 | 2,417 | 3,180 | 2,417 | 3,180 | 2,417 |
| 3 | 0.66 | | | 3,230 (1,600) | 1,076 | 3,230 | 2,132 | 3,230 | 2,132 |
| 4 | 0.57 | | | | | 3,480 (1,220) | 1,288 | 3,480 | 1,984 |
| 5 | 0.50 | | | | | | | 4,620 (380) | 2,120 |
| PV of cost at 15% | | | 11,837 | | 14,737 | | 17,081 | | 19,897 |

These PVs of cost cannot be directly compared, because they relate to different time periods. They must be converted to annualised equivalents, using the cumulative discount factors for 2, 3, 4 and 5 years:

|  | 2 years | 3 years | 4 years | 5 years |
|---|---|---|---|---|
| NPV at 15% | £11,837 | £14,737 | £17,081 | £19,897 |
| ÷ Cumulative 15% factor | 1.63 | 2.28 | 2.86 | 3.35 |
| Annualised equivalent cost | £7,262 | £6,464 | £5,972 | £5,939 |

The minimum cost option is to replace vehicles every 5 years.

# Question

## 13

Let the maximum sales capacity be £x.

| Year | 16% discount factor | Costs £ | PV of costs £ | Sales revenue £ | PV of revenues £ |
|---|---|---|---|---|---|
| 0 | 1.00 | 12,000 | 12,000 | - | |
| 1 | 0.86 | 2,600 | 2,236 | 0.30x | 0.258x |
| 2 | 0.74 | 5,400 | 3,996 | 0.45x | 0.333x |
| 3 | 0.64 | 17,800 | 11,392 | 0.60x | 0.384x |
| 4 | 0.55 | 21,000 | 11,550 | 0.75x | 0.413x |
| 5 | 0.48 | 24,000 | 11,520 | 1.00x | 0.480x |
| 6 | 0.41 | 24,000 | 9,840 | 1.00x | 0.410x |
| | | | 62,534 | | 2.278x |

For a 16% DCF yield, the PV of the costs must be exactly equal to the PV of the revenues:

∴ £62,534 = 2.278x
∴ x = £27,451

Maximum sales capacity must be £27,451, or £27,000 to the nearest £1,000.

## 14

The incremental yield is based on the incremental cash flows of the 25kg machine compared with 20kg.

|  | £000 |
|---|---|
| Incremental investment (52 - 35) | 17 |
| Incremental savings (22 - 17) | 5 |

The DCF yield of the incremental investment is where the PV of £5,000 pa for 10 years = £17,000

∴ Sum of 10 year cumulative discount factors = 17/5 = 3.4

We are looking for a cumulative discount rate of £1 pa for 10 years to be equal to 3.4.

Looking along the 10 year line on the cumulative present value tables, we find:

| 10 year cumulative factor - | 20% = | 4.19 |
|---|---|---|
| | 30% = | 3.09 |
| Difference | | 1.10 |

Using interpolation, the incremental yield is $20\% + \left[ \dfrac{(4.19 - 3.4)}{1.10} \times 10\% \right]$

$= 27.2\%$

# Question

## 15

Let the annual advertising expenditure be £x thousands. Notice that the expenditure is to be incurred at the *beginning* of the year, which for discounting purposes can be taken as the end of the previous year.

| Year | 17% discount factor | Net cash flow £000 | PV of Net cash flow* £000 | Advertising £ | PV of advertising £ |
|---|---|---|---|---|---|
| 0 | 1.00 | (400) | (400) | x | 1.00x |
| 1 | 0.85 | 210 | 178.5 | x | 0.85x |
| 2 | 0.73 | 240 | 175.2 | x | 0.73x |
| 3 | 0.62 | 320 | 198.4 |   |   |
|   |   |   | 152.1 |   | 2.58x |

\* Before advertising costs

For a 17% yield, the PV of the net cash inflow (before deducting the PV of advertising costs) must be exactly equal to the PV of advertising costs.

$$152.1 = 2.58x$$
$$\therefore x = 58.953$$

Annual advertising must be £59,000 (to the nearest £1,000).

## 16

| | | |
|---|---|---|
| Original material cost estimate = | £28,000 | per annum |
| Revised material cost estimate = | £35,000 | per annum |
| Annual cost increase | £7,000 | per annum |
| x 17% cumulative discount factor for 3 yrs | 2.21 | |
| = PV of cost increase | £15,470 | |

This amount must be saved from unskilled labour.

Present value of unskilled labour costs -

| Year | | Present value £ |
|---|---|---|
| 1 | £52,000 x 0.85 | 44,200 |
| 2 | £61,000 x 0.73 | 44,530 |
| 3 | £68,000 x 0.62 | 42,160 |
|   |   | 130,890 |

|   | £ |   |
|---|---|---|
| A 2% saving amounts to 2% x £130,890 = | 2,618 | in present value terms |
| *less* Investment required per machine | 1,500 | |
| = Present value of net saving, per machine | 1,118 | |

Total saving required = PV of material cost increase = £15,470.

$$\therefore \text{Number of machines required} = \frac{£15,470}{£1,118} = 14 \text{ machines}$$

## 6: INVESTMENT APPRAISAL

## Question

### 17

Most cumulative present value tables do not extend as far as 25 years, therefore you should know how to derive the PV factor from the available data.

(1) PV factor at 16%, years 1 - 15 =                 5.58
(2) Year 15 value of cumulative PV factor for years 16 - 25
    (= years 1 - 10) = 4.83
(3) Year 0 value of PV factor for years 16 - 25
    = year 15 value x 16% PV factor for year 15
    = 4.83 x 0.11 =                                              0.53
Cumulative 16% factor for years 1 to 25                      6.11

There will be some rounding errors, since the factors are taken to only 2 decimal places.

Present value of contribution = £40,000 x 6.11 = £244,000, to the nearest £000.

### 18

First, calculate the tax effect of the Writing Down Allowance (WDA):

|  | £ |  | £ | Year of claim | Year of tax saving |
|---|---|---|---|---|---|
| Capital cost | 86,000 |  |  |  |  |
| 25% WDA | 21,500 | x 35% | 7,525 | 0 | 1 |
| Written Down Value WDV | 64,500 |  |  |  |  |
| 25% WDA | 16,125 | x 35% | 5,644 | 1 | 2 |
| WDV | 48,375 |  |  |  |  |
| 25% WDA | 12,094 | x 35% | 4,233 | 2 | 3 |
| WDV | 36,281 |  |  |  |  |
| 25% WDA | 9,070 | x 35% | 3,175 | 3 | 4 |
| WDV | 27,211 |  |  |  |  |
| Sold for | 15,000 |  |  |  |  |
| ∴ Balancing allowance | 12,211 | x 35% | 4,274 | 4 | 5 |

The net cash flows and NPV of the project can now be calculated.

| Year | Machinery | Cont'n | 35% tax on cont'n | Tax saved on capital allowances | Net cash flow | 8% discount factor | Present value |
|---|---|---|---|---|---|---|---|
|  | £ | £ | £ | £ | £ |  | £ |
| 0 | (86,000) |  |  |  | (86,000) | 1.00 | (86,000) |
| 1 |  | 41,000 |  | 7,525 | 48,525 | 0.93 | 45,128 |
| 2 |  | 41,000 | (14,350) | 5,644 | 32,294 | 0.86 | 27,773 |
| 3 |  | 41,000 | (14,350) | 4,233 | 30,883 | 0.79 | 24,398 |
| 4 | 15,000 | 41,000 | (14,350) | 3,175 | 44,825 | 0.74 | 33,171 |
| 5 |  |  | (14,350) | 4,274 | (10,076) | 0.68 | (6,852) |
|  |  |  |  | Net present value |  |  | 37,618 |

= £37,600
to the nearest £100

213

## COMMENTS

## Question

**19** If the company is discounting the actual money cash flows for electricity, then the rate of inflation in electricity prices has already been taken into account.

We need a money discount rate to apply to the money cash flows, and this is the company's cost of capital, 20%. You might have been tempted to use the formula
= 1.20 x 1.10 = 1.32

However, a money cost of capital of 32% would be to suppose that the *real* cost of capital is 20% - an extraordinarily high figure!

**20** Since we are given a money cost of capital, the actual money cash flows must be used in the appraisal:

| Year | Investment | Fixed costs | Contribution | Net cash flow | 14% factor | Present value |
|---|---|---|---|---|---|---|
| | £ | £ | £ | £ | | £ |
| 0 | (700,000) | | | (700,000) | 1.00 | (700,000) |
| 1 | | (200,000) | 620,000 | 420,000 | 0.88 | 369,600 |
| 2 | + 5% | (210,000) | (+7%) 663,400 | 453,400 | 0.77 | 349,118 |
| 3 | + 5% | (220,500) | (+7%) 709,838 | 489,338 | 0.67 | 327,856 |
| 4 | + 5% | (231,525) | (+7%) 759,527 | 528,002 | 0.59 | 311,521 |
| | | | | Net Present Value | | 658,095 |

= £658,000 to the nearest £1,000

**21** The present value of the payments which the company wishes to make is:

(£12,000 x 0.87) + (£14,500 x 0.76) + (£16,200 x 0.66) = £32,152

We require an annuity which has a present value of £32,152 over 3 years at 15%.

3 year annuity factor at 15% = 2.28

∴ Required payment = $\frac{£32,152}{2.28}$

= £14,100 to the nearest £100

**22** The present value of an annuity in perpetuity is A/r, where A is the amount of the annuity and r is the discount rate.

PV of annuity = $\frac{£3,600}{0.18}$ = £20,000

*less* initial investment  £18,000
Net present value of investment = £2,000

# 6: INVESTMENT APPRAISAL

## Question

### 23

Social costs and social benefits might have monetary values in the first place, such as the rise or fall in property values arising from a decision to site a new airport, road or shopping centre. They might also be measurable in quantitative terms, so that 'money values' can be attributed to them - such as measured deterioration in water pollution or air pollution, increased number of specific illnesses, number of crimes avoided, number of extra educational qualifications conferred, number of lives saved and so on.

Statements 1 and 2 help to explain how CBA might be used to carry out DCF project evaluation for 'public works' spending. Statement 3 is incorrect, because CBA analysis measures a value for social costs or benefits in a project, but does not consider how these costs or benefits are shared out amongst different groups in the population. Statement 4 is incorrect - techniques cannot replace the need for some judgement in non-routine decision-making.

### 24

| Year | Discount factor at 20% | Running costs Estimated | Running costs Present value | Savings Estimated | Savings Present value |
|---|---|---|---|---|---|
|  |  | £ | £ | £ | £ |
| 1 | 0.83 | 80,000 | 66,400 | 150,000 | 124,500 |
| 2 | 0.69 | 100,000 | 69,000 | 160,000 | 110,400 |
| 3 | 0.58 | 120,000 | 69,600 | 170,000 | 98,600 |
| 4 | 0.48 | 150,000 | 72,000 | 180,000 | 86,400 |
|  |  |  | 277,000 |  | 419,900 |

If running costs were 20% higher than estimated, their PV would be higher by 20% of £277,000 = £55,400.

|  | £ |
|---|---|
| Original NPV | 22,900 |
| Higher PV of running costs | 55,400 |
| Minimum amount by which PV of savings must be higher | 32,500 |

The PV of savings must now be higher by at least £32,500 or (÷ 419,900) 7.7% for the project to have an NPV of zero or better.

### 25

If savings were 10% lower than originally estimated, their PV would be lower by 10% of £419,900 = £41,990.

|  | £ |
|---|---|
| Original NPV | 22,900 |
| Lower PV of savings | 41,990 |
| Minimum amount by which PV of running costs must be lower | 19,090 |

The PV of running costs must be lower by at least £19,090 or (÷ £277,000) 6.9% for the project to have an NPV of zero or better.

## COMMENTS

## Question

### 26

|  | Year 0 £ | Year 1 £ | Year 2 £ | Year 3 £ | Year 4 £ |
|---|---|---|---|---|---|
| Capital outlay | (300,000) | | | | |
| Direct materials | | (80,000) | (84,000) | (88,200) | (92,610) |
| Direct labour and expenses | | (100,000) | (106,000) | (112,360) | (119,102) |
| | | (180,000) | (190,000) | (200,560) | (211,712) |
| Sales revenue | | 300,000 | 309,000 | 318,270 | 327,818 |
| Net cash flow | (300,000) | 120,000 | 119,000 | 117,710 | 116,106 |
| Discount factor at 18% | 1.00 | 0.85 | 0.72 | 0.61 | 0.52 |
| Present value | £(300,000) | £102,000 | £85,680 | £71,803 | £60,375 |

Net present value = -£300,000 + £319,858 = +£19,858

### 27

This question is more tricky than it might seem at first. There is the problem that if sales volume is different from expectation, variable costs will be different too. The differing rates of inflation on materials and labour costs add to the complication.

Let sales in Year 1 be £X

| Year | Sales £ | Direct materials £ | Direct labour £ | Total v'ble costs £ | Contribution £ |
|---|---|---|---|---|---|
| 1 | X | 0.26667X | 0.33333X | 0.60000X | 0.40000X |
| 2 | 1.03X | 0.28000X | 0.35333X | 0.63333X | 0.39667X |
| 3 | 1.0609X | 0.2940X | 0.37453X | 0.66853X | 0.39237X |
| 4 | 1.09273X | 0.3087X | 0.39700X | 0.70570X | 0.38703X |

| Year | Contribution £ | Discount factor at 18% | Present value |
|---|---|---|---|
| 1 | 0.40000X | 0.85 | 0.3400X |
| 2 | 0.39667X | 0.72 | 0.2856X |
| 3 | 0.39237X | 0.61 | 0.2393X |
| 4 | 0.38703X | 0.52 | 0.2013X |
| | | | 1.0662X |

The PV of benefits is 1.0662X, and since the investment in year 0 is £300,000, X must be at least £300,000 ÷ 1.0662 = £281,373 in year 1 for the project to be viable. This is £18,627 or 6.2% below the current estimate.

*Note.* A quicker method of reaching the 1.0662X figure is as follows.

$$\frac{\text{PV of benefits on initial estimate (see previous solution)}}{\text{Year 1 sales}} = \frac{£319,858}{£300,000} = 1.0662$$

# Question

## 28

Again, this question might have been difficult for you to sort out.

The PV of labour costs can rise by no more than £19,858 (the NPV of the project) before the project ceases to be viable.

| Year | Original labour cost estimate £ | Discount factor 18% | PV of labour costs £ |
|---|---|---|---|
| 1 | 100,000 | 0.85 | 85,000 |
| 2 | 106,000 | 0.72 | 76,320 |
| 3 | 112,360 | 0.61 | 68,540 |
| 4 | 119,102 | 0.52 | 61,933 |
| | | | 291,793 |
| | Add NPV of project | | 19,858 |
| | Maximum labour costs permissible | | 311,651 |

Interpolation can be used to test the maximum growth rate in the PV of labour costs, given costs of £100,000 in year 1, that could be permitted. It works out at 11%.

| Year | Labour costs (growth 11% pa) £ | Discount factor 18% | PV of labour costs £ |
|---|---|---|---|
| 1 | 100,000 | 0.85 | 85,000 |
| 2 | 111,000 | 0.72 | 79,920 |
| 3 | 123,210 | 0.61 | 75,158 |
| 4 | 136,763 | 0.52 | 71,117 |
| | | | * 311,195 |

* Almost equal to £311,651, and so the most appropriate answer here, to the nearest whole percentage number.

# 7: MARKING SCHEDULE

| Question | Correct answer | Marks for correct answer | Question | Correct answer | Marks for correct answer | Question | Correct answer | Marks for correct answer |
|---|---|---|---|---|---|---|---|---|
| 1 | B | 1 | 12 | A | 2 | 23 | B | 1 |
| 2 | C | 1 | 13 | C | 1 | 24 | B | 2 |
| 3 | A | 1 | 14 | B | 1 | 25 | A | 1 |
| 4 | C | 1 | 15 | D | 1 | 26 | B | 1 |
| 5 | D | 1 | 16 | B | 1 | 27 | D | 2 |
| 6 | C | 1 | 17 | D | 2 | 28 | B | 1 |
| 7 | B | 1 | 18 | C | 1 | 29 | C | 1 |
| 8 | C | 1 | 19 | D | 1 | 30 | B | 1 |
| 9 | C | 1 | 20 | A | 1 | 31 | C | 1 |
| 10 | C | 2 | 21 | B | 1 | | | |
| 11 | B | 1 | 22 | A | 1 | | | |

## YOUR MARKS

Total marks available  36    Your total mark  ☐

---

**GUIDELINES - If your mark was:**

**0 - 10** This topic is obviously causing you a lot of difficulty. Go back to your study text and try to get to grips with it.

**20 - 29** Good. Your knowledge still isn't perfect, but you are well on the way to a thorough understanding.

**11 - 19** Still quite a few weaknesses. You need to revise your study material again and then attempt the questions once more.

**30 - 36** Very good. You understand clearly the essential principles of uncertainty in decision making.

# 7: UNCERTAINTY AND DECISION MAKING

# COMMENTS

## Questions

**1**

We first need to know the probabilities of the highest two sales values. Since these are predicted to be the only possible outcomes, the sum of the probabilities must be equal to 1. The probability of each of the two highest sales levels is therefore
(1 - 0.10 - 0.15 - 0.35) ÷ 2 = 0.2.

The expected value of annual sales is therefore:

(£2m x 0.10) + (£2.2m x 0.15) + (£2.4m x 0.35) + (£2.6m x 0.20) + (£2.8m x 0.20) = £2.45m

|  | £ |
|---|---|
| Expected value of contribution = £2.45m x 25% = | 612,500 |
| *less* Fixed costs (£48,000 x 12) | 576,000 |
| = Expected value of annual profit | 36,500 |

**2**

To break even, the contribution must be equal to the annual fixed costs
∴ contribution required = £576,000
Divide by the contribution/sales ratio, ÷ 25%
∴ Sales required = £2,304,000

The probability of achieving sales in excess of £2,304,000 is 0.35 + 0.20 + 0.20 = 0.75

**3**

To earn a profit of £100,000, contribution required =     fixed costs + profit
= £576,000 + £100,000
= £676,000

Divided by the contribution/sales ratio, 25%
∴ Required sales                                                                        = £2,704,000

The probability of achieving sales in excess of £2,704,000 is 0.20.

**4**

It is not sufficient to use the high-low method to obtain an estimate of the cost for 58,200 hours, because that estimate would be made at a single point of cost behaviour. The cost behaviour pattern is different at various levels of output, therefore the expected value should allow for the possibility that actual costs may be incurred at levels of output with different costs behaviour.

58,200 hours is in fact the expected value obtained from the activity data given. Calculation of the expected value of cost is therefore fairly straightforward:

| £ | Probability | £ |
|---|---|---|
| 14,250 | 0.4 | 5,700 |
| 15,000 | 0.5 | 7,500 |
| 15,900 | 0.1 | 1,590 |
| Expected value of maintenance cost | | 14,790 |

219

## Question

### 5

The expected value for each project is calculated by multiplying each profit figure by the probability of its occurrence:

|  |  | Market state |  |  |  | Total expected value |
|---|---|---|---|---|---|---|
|  |  | I | II | III | IV | £000 |
| Probability |  | 0.3 | 0.2 | 0.4 | 0.1 |  |
| North | - profit £000 | 38 | 47 | 42 | 44 |  |
|  | - EV £000 | 11.4 | 9.4 | 16.8 | 4.4 | 42 |
| South | - profit £000 | 40 | 70 | 52 | 62 |  |
|  | - EV £000 | 12 | 14 | 20.8 | 6.2 | 53 |
| East | - profit £000 | 60 | 35 | 48 | 38 |  |
|  | - EV £000 | 18 | 7 | 19.2 | 3.8 | 48 |
| West | - profit £000 | 46 | 60 | 56 | 58 |  |
|  | - EV £000 | 13.8 | 12 | 22.4 | 5.8 | 54 |

The West project offers the highest expected value.

### 6

If June Hipper Limited had perfect advance information about the state of the market, they would select the most profitable project for the market state which the information predicts:

| Market state predicted | Investment selected | Profit £000 | Probability of market state occurring | Expected value £000 |
|---|---|---|---|---|
| I | East | 60 | 0.3 | 18.0 |
| II | South | 70 | 0.2 | 14.0 |
| III | West | 56 | 0.4 | 22.4 |
| IV | South | 62 | 0.1 | 6.2 |
|  | Expected value of profits, with perfect information |  |  | 60.6 |
| less | Highest EV available without perfect information |  |  | 54.0 |
| = | Value of perfect information |  |  | 6.6 |

The value of perfect information is £6,600.

### 7

Relevant cost of using the material on the current contract

|  | Relevant cost £ | Probability | EV £ |
|---|---|---|---|
| If material is needed in 1 month | (15,000) | 0.6 | (9,000) |
| If material is not used | (12,000) | 0.4 | (4,800) |
|  |  |  | (13,800) |
| Less saving in stock holding costs |  |  | 900 |
|  |  |  | (12,900) |

# Question

## 8

If a customer defaults, the actual loss to the company will be the variable cost of the goods sold, which is 60% of the sales value of the order.

Let the sales value of the order be S.

EV of cost of default = 0.15 x 60% of S
= 0.09S

Minimum order size to justify a credit check costing £180 is where
0.09S = £180, S = £2,000

## 9

If average expected sales are 250kg per day, then Roy should decide to purchase either 200kg or 300kg per day:

| Purchase decision | Average sales result | Sales value | Sale of excess stock | Purchases cost | Average daily profit |
|---|---|---|---|---|---|
| kg | kg | £ | £ | £ | £ |
| 200 | 200 | 300 | - | (200 x 0.98) 196 | 104 |
| 300 | 250 | 375 | (50 x 0.20) 10 | (300 x 0.95) 285 | 100 |

Maximum average daily profit is £104, if Roy arranges to purchase 200 kg per day.

## 10

We are asked to determine a purchases policy which will maximise profit over a whole season. Since the purchase process is to be repeated several times, the EV of daily profit is a valid measure of the average daily profit in the long term. We need to calculate which purchase policy will produce the highest expected value of profit.

Looking at each level of purchases in turn, we can deduce the possible sales levels and profits that could arise. Remember to check that for each level of purchases, the sum of the individual probabilities is 1.

| Purchase decision | Possible sales | Sales value | Sale of excess stock | | Purchases cost | | Daily profit | Probability | EV of profit |
|---|---|---|---|---|---|---|---|---|---|
| kg | kg | £ | £ | | £ | | £ | | £ |
| 100 | 100 | 150 | - | | 100 | | 50 | 1.0 | 50 |
| | | | | | | | | | |
| 200 | 100 | 150 | (100 x 0.2) | 20 | (200 x 0.98) | 196 | (26) | 0.25 | (6.5) |
| | 200 | 300 | - | | | 196 | 104 | 0.75 | 78.0 |
| | | | | | | | | 1.00 | 71.5 |
| 300 | 100 | 150 | (200 x 0.2) | 40 | (300 x 0.95) | 285 | (95) | 0.25 | (23.75) |
| | 250 | 375 | (50 x 0.2) | 10 | | 285 | 100 | 0.35 | 35.00 |
| | 300 | 450 | - | | | 285 | 165 | 0.40 | 66.00 |
| | | | | | | | | 1.00 | 77.25 |

Continued...

# COMMENTS

## Question

|     |     |     |              |     |           |       |      |         |
|-----|-----|-----|--------------|-----|-----------|-------|------|---------|
| 400 | 100 | 150 | (300 x x 0.2) | 60 | (400 x 0.92) | 368 | (158) | 0.25 | (39.50) |
|     | 250 | 375 | (150 x 0.2)  | 30  |           | 368   | 37   | 0.35    | 12.95   |
|     | 400 | 600 |              | -   |           | 368   | 232  | 0.40    | 92.80   |
|     |     |     |              |     |           |       |      | 1.00    | 66.25   |

Expected value of profit is maximised when purchases are 300kg per day.

## 11

With no weather information Roy would still order 300 kg per day in order to maximise his long run profit as in the previous question. The best EV of daily profit with no information is therefore £77,250. The value of perfect information can be deduced by calculating the best EV of daily profit that can be achieved with the perfect weather information plus the ability to purchase in varying quantities each day.

| Prediction | Decision kg | Profit £ | Probability | Profit per day £ |
|---|---|---|---|---|
| Sunny | 400 | 232 | 0.40 | 92.80 |
| Fine  | 200 | 104 | 0.35 | 36.40 |
| Rainy | 100 | 50  | 0.25 | 12.50 |
|       |     |     |      | 141.70 |
| *less* Optimum EV without information | | | | 77.25 |
| Value of perfect information | | | | 64.45 per day |

## 12

Since the cost structure changes at different output levels, it is not sufficient to simply calculate the expected sales volume and then work out the contribution for this volume. The probabilities must be used to give sufficient weighting to all of the different cost structures that could arise.

The first step is to calculate the relevant costs:

Direct material: Relevant cost is the opportunity cost of £7 per kg, up to (20,000kg ÷ 5) 4,000 units. Above 4,000 units, relevant cost is £9 per kg (replacement price).

Direct labour: Relevant cost is nil up to 10,000 hours ÷ 2 = 5,000 units. Above 5,000 units, relevant cost is £3 per hour.

Variable overhead is relevant for all production, since it is incurred in active hours only.

*Summary of relevant cost structure*

|  | Up to 4,000 units £/unit | | 4,001 to 5,000 units £/unit | | Above 5,000 units £/unit |
|---|---|---|---|---|---|
| Material (£7 x 5kg) | 35 | (£9 x 5) | 45 | | 45 |
| Labour | - | | - | (£3 x 2) | 6 |
| Variable overhead (£5 x 2) | 10 | | 10 | | 10 |
| *Relevant cost* | 45 | | 55 | | 61 |

Continued...

## Question

The expected value of the contribution can now be calculated:

| Sales volume '000 units | Sales revenue £'000 | Relevant costs £'000 | | Promotion £'000 | Incremental profit £'000 | Probability | E Value £'000 |
|---|---|---|---|---|---|---|---|
| 2 | 130 | (2 x £45) | 90 | 50 | (10) | 0.3 | (3) |
| 5 | 325 | (4 x £45 + 1 x £55) | 235 | 50 | 40 | 0.6 | 24 |
| 10 | 650 | (4 x £45 + 1 x £55 + 5 x £61) | 540 | 50 | 60 | 0.1 | 6 |
| | | | | | | | 27 |

The expected value of incremental profit is £27,000.

**13** The probability of at least breaking even is the probability of sales volume being either 5,000 or 10,000 units = 0.6 + 0.1 = 0.7.

**14** If the sales prediction is 2,000 units, the cancellation cost of £3,000 is preferable to the loss of £10,000 on the venture. If the prediction is 5,000 or 10,000 units, the venture would go ahead.

| Sales prediction '000 units | Action | Resulting cash flow £000 | Probability | Expected value £000 |
|---|---|---|---|---|
| 2 | Cancel | (3) | 0.3 | (0.9) |
| 5 | Continue | 40 | 0.6 | 24.0 |
| 10 | Continue | 60 | 0.1 | 6.0 |
| | | | | 29.1 |
| | Expected value of contribution with no information | | | 27.0 |
| | Maximum amount to pay for information | | | 2.1 |

The information is worth a maximum of £2,100.

**15** The *minimum* achievable profit from each project is as follows:

| Project | If area of demand concentration is | Profit £000 |
|---|---|---|
| E | North | 75 |
| F | South | 90 |
| G | East | 85 |
| H | South | *92 |

*The maximum of these lowest profits is £92,000 therefore select project H.

Continued...

## Question

This decision rule is based on a 'safety first' approach, looking on the pessimistic side of future outcomes and selecting the option that gives the best outcome in the event that the worst happens. (It is more suitable when worst outcomes include serious losses.)

## 16

The highest achievable profit from each project is as follows:

| Project | If area of demand concentration is | Profit £000 |
|---------|-----------------------------------|-------------|
| E | East | 120 |
| F | North | *135 |
| G | South | 120 |
| H | North | 120 |

*The maximum of these highest profits is £135,000 therefore select project F.

The maximax rule is a 'regardless of risk' decision rule, based on selecting the option that offers the greatest possible profits, regardless of what the not-so-good outcomes might be.

## 17

A table of regrets (opportunity costs) can be compiled which shows the amount of profit that might be forgone for each project, depending on the area of demand concentration.

For instance, if project E is selected and demand turns out to be concentrated in the North, then management would wish that they had selected project F. Their 'regret', or opportunity loss, would be the difference between the two profit figures: £135,000 - £75,000 = £60,000. You will see that this is the figure in the top left hand figure of the table of regrets. The other figures are derived in the same way.

*Table of 'regrets'*

| Project | Demand concentrated in: | | | | Maximum regret |
|---------|-------------------------|---|---|---|----------------|
| | North £000 | South £000 | East £000 | West £000 | £000 |
| E | 60 | 22 | 0 | 8 | 60 |
| F | 0 | 30 | 8 | 0 | 30 |
| G | 30 | 0 | 35 | 3 | 35 |
| H | 15 | 28 | 20 | 13 | 28 |

The lowest figure for the maximum regret is £28,000. Project H should therefore be selected, because the possible opportunity loss of selecting H is the lowest.

# Question

**18** One way of approaching the sensitivity analysis is to calculate the NPV taking account of each of the changes in isolation:

|  | Initial forecasts | Initial investment | Variable altered by 10% Expected life | Annual sales volume | Fixed costs |
|---|---|---|---|---|---|
|  | £000 | £000 | £000 | £000 | £000 |
| Annual contribution (35,000 x £8) | 280 |  |  | (x90%) 252 | 280 |
| Fixed costs | 45 |  |  | 45 | (+10%) 49.5 |
| Annual cash flows | 235 |  | 235 | 207 | 230.5 |
| x Annuity at 15% for 10 years | x 5.02 |  | (9 yrs) x4.77 | x 5.02 | x 5.02 |
| Present value of profit | 1,179.7 | 1,179.70 | 1,120.95 | 1,039.14 | 1,157.11 |
| Initial investment | 612.5 | (+10%) 673.75 | 612.50 | 612.50 | 612.50 |
| Net Present Value | 567.2 | 505.95 | 508.45 | 426.64 | 544.61 |

The NPV results show that the project is by far the most sensitive to a 10% adverse change in sales volume.

**19** Annual depreciation = £(612,500 - 12,500) ÷ 10 = £60,000

|  | £ |
|---|---|
| Annual contribution | 280,000 |
| Fixed costs, including depreciation (£45,000 + £60,000) | 105,000 |
| Contribution would fall by | 175,000 |

This is (÷ 35,000 units)                    £5 per unit

The sales price could be reduced from £20 to £15 per unit, and with sales of 35,000 units per annum, the project would still just break even.

**20** This question tests your ability to calculate joint probabilities. Remember that when you calculate probabilities, you should check that they total 1.0.

| Product P Sales | Product Q Sales | Total Sales | Probability of P sales | x Probability of Q sales | = Joint probability | Expected value of sales |
|---|---|---|---|---|---|---|
| £000 | £000 | £000 |  |  |  | £000 |
| 40 | 70 | 110 | 0.3 | 0.2 | *0.06 | 6.6 |
| 40 | 50 | 90 | 0.3 | 0.6 | 0.18 | 16.2 |
| 40 | 40 | 80 | 0.3 | 0.2 | 0.06 | 4.8 |
| 50 | 60 | 110 | 0.5 | 0.4 | *0.20 | 22.0 |
| 50 | 30 | 80 | 0.5 | 0.6 | 0.30 | 24.0 |
| 60 | 60 | 120 | 0.2 | 0.5 | *0.10 | 12.0 |
| 60 | 70 | 130 | 0.2 | 0.5 | *0.10 | 13.0 |
|  |  |  |  |  | 1.00 | 98.6 |

Expected value of annual sales is therefore £98,600.

# COMMENTS

## Question

**21** The probability of achieving sales of at least £100,000 is the sum of all those probabilities marked with an asterisk * in the previous solution.

Probability of annual sales = 0.06 + 0.20 + 0.10 + 0.10 = 0.46
of £100,000 or more

**22**

| Sales units | Probability | Unit variable cost £ | Unit contrib'n £ | Probability | Total contrib'n £000 | Joint probability |
|---|---|---|---|---|---|---|
| 39,000 | 0.15 | 10 | 12.0 | 0.20 | 468.0 | *0.0300 |
| 39,000 | 0.15 | 9.5 | 12.5 | 0.25 | 487.5 | *0.0375 |
| 39,000 | 0.15 | 9 | 13.0 | 0.55 | 507.0 | *0.0825 |
| 37,000 | 0.50 | 10 | 12.0 | 0.20 | 444.0 | 0.1000 |
| 37,000 | 0.50 | 9.5 | 12.5 | 0.25 | 462.5 | *0.1250 |
| 37,000 | 0.50 | 9 | 13.0 | 0.55 | 481.0 | *0.2750 |
| 35,000 | 0.35 | 10 | 12.0 | 0.20 | 420.0 | 0.0700 |
| 35,000 | 0.35 | 9.5 | 12.5 | 0.25 | 437.5 | 0.0875 |
| 35,000 | 0.35 | 9 | 13.0 | 0.55 | 455.0 | *0.1925 |
|  |  |  |  |  |  | 1.0000 |

Probability of contribution exceeding £450,000
= (0.0300 + 0.0375 + 0.0825 + 0.1250 + 0.2750 + 0.1925)
= 0.7425

**23** If an investigation is undertaken, there is a 0.45 probability that it will be uncontrollable; the cost incurred will be £300:

|  | £ | Expected value £ |
|---|---|---|
| (£300) x 0.45 |  | (135) |

If the variance is controllable, the net benefit of
control action will be:

|  |  | £ | £ |
|---|---|---|---|
|  | Saving in cost of unchecked variance | 1,050 |  |
| less | Cost of investigation | (300) |  |
|  | Cost of corrective action | (350) |  |
|  | Net benefit | 400 |  |
|  | x Probability of controllable variance (1 - 0.45) | x 0.55 |  |
|  | = |  | 220 |
|  | Expected value of net benefit of investigation |  | 85 |

# 7: UNCERTAINTY AND DECISION MAKING

## Question

**24** A random number simulation works by allocating random numbers to the various outcomes in proportion to their probabilities:

| £m | *Initial investment* Probability | Random numbers assigned | £000 | *Annual contribution* Probability | Random numbers assigned |
|---|---|---|---|---|---|
| 1.80 | 0.15 | 00 - 14 | 650 | 0.10 | 00 - 09 |
| 1.95 | 0.25 | 15 - 39 | 680 | 0.30 | 10 - 39 |
| 2.00 | 0.40 | 40 - 79 | 700 | 0.55 | 40 - 94 |
| 2.15 | 0.20 | 80 - 99 | 720 | 0.05 | 95 - 99 |

Thus, the higher the probability of an outcome, the more likely the computer is to draw a corresponding random number.

The random numbers drawn are interpreted as follows:

Initial investment - 15 drawn corresponds to £1.95m
Annual contribution - 60 drawn corresponds to £700,000

The net present value can now be calculated:

|  | Present value £000 |
|---|---|
| Initial investment | (1,950) |
| Contribution - £700,000 for 5 years at 16% (700 x 3.27) | 2,289 |
| Net Present Value | 339 |

The net present value produced by this particular simulation run is £339,000.

**25** The expected value of the NPV is the long run NPV that will result if the project is repeated several times, to enable the probabilities to 'work out':

Expected value of initial investment:

| £m | Probability | Expected value £m |
|---|---|---|
| 1.80 | 0.15 | 0.2700 |
| 1.95 | 0.25 | 0.4875 |
| 2.00 | 0.40 | 0.8000 |
| 2.15 | 0.20 | 0.4300 |
|  |  | 1.9875 |

Expected value of annual contribution:

| £000 | Probability | Expected value £000 |
|---|---|---|
| 650 | 0.10 | 65 |
| 680 | 0.30 | 204 |
| 700 | 0.55 | 385 |
| 720 | 0.05 | 36 |
|  |  | 690 |

Continued...

## Question

*The expected NPV can now be calculated:

|  | Expected present value £000 |
|---|---|
| Initial investment | (1,987.5) |
| Annual contribution: £690,000 for 5 years at 16% = (in £000)690 x 3.27 = | 2,256.3 |
| Expected net present value = | 268.8 |

The expected value of the NPV is £268,800.

**26** The probability that *either* of these two independent events will occur is the sum of their probabilities *less*, to avoid double-counting, the joint probability of both events happening together:

Probability = 0.20 + 0.10 - (0.2 x 0.1)
            = 0.28

**27**

*(A) Start South, move North*

|  | Years | Cash flow £000 | Discount factor | Present value £000 |
|---|---|---|---|---|
| Premises | 0 | (200) | 1.00 | (200.00) |
| Net cash inflow (0.7 x 80) + (0.3 x 60) | 1 - 4 | 74 | 2.86 | 211.64 |
| Relocation costs | 4 | (15) | 0.57 | (8.55) |
| Net cash inflow (0.65 x 80) + (0.35 x 60) | 5 - 8 | 73 | 1.63 | 118.99 |
| Net present value |  |  |  | 122.08 |

*(B) Stay South for 8 years*

|  | Years | Cash flow £000 | Discount factor | Present value £000 |
|---|---|---|---|---|
| Premises | 0 | (200) | 1.00 | (200.00) |
| Net cash inflow (0.7 x 80) + (0.3 x 60) | 1 - 4 | 74 | 2.86 | 211.64 |
| Relocation costs | 4 | - | - | - |
| Net cash inflow (0.35 x 80) + (0.65 x 60) | 5 - 8 | 67 | 1.63 | 109.21 |
| Net present value |  |  |  | 120.85 |

Continued...

# Question

**(C) Start North, move South**

| | Years | Cash flow £000 | Discount factor | Present value £000 |
|---|---|---|---|---|
| Premises | 0 | (180) | 1.00 | (180.00) |
| Net cash inflow | 1 - 4 | 66 | 2.86 | 188.76 |
| (0.3 x 80) + (0.7 x 60) | | | | |
| Relocation costs | 4 | 20 | 0.57 | (11.40) |
| Net cash inflow | 5 - 8 | 67 | 1.63 | 109.21 |
| (0.35 x 80) + (0.65 x 60) | | | | |
| Net present value | | | | <u>106.57</u> |

**(D) Stay North for 8 years**

| | Years | Cash flow £000 | Discount factor | Present value £000 |
|---|---|---|---|---|
| Premises | 0 | (180) | 1.00 | (180.00) |
| Net cash inflow | 1 - 4 | 66 | 2.86 | 188.76 |
| (0.3 x 80) + (0.7 x 60) | | | | |
| Relocation costs | 4 | - | - | - |
| Net cash inflow | 5 - 8 | 73 | 1.63 | 118.99 |
| (0.65 x 80) + (0.35 x 60) | | | | |
| Net present value | | | | <u>127.75</u> |

Option D gives the highest NPV.

**28** The workings for the previous question show that the maximum Expected Net Present Value will be about £127,750 or £128,000 to the nearest £000.

**29** If event S is the exceeding of the overdraft limit and event T is the *failure* to negotiate extended credit,

P(S and T) = P(T) x PT(S)

You may recognise this as the conditional probability rule.

∴ Probability    = 0.75 x 0.60
                     = 0.45

In other words, given that the probability of failing to negotiate extended credit is 0.75, there will *then* be a 0.60 probability that the overdraft limit will be exceeded.

## Question

**30** Expected value = $\bar{x}$ = (150 x 0.2) + (200 x 0.5) + (260 x 0.3) = 208

| Net income £000 x | Probability p | $x - \bar{x}$ | $p(x - \bar{x})^2$ |
|---|---|---|---|
| 150 | 0.2 | (150 - 208) - 58 | 672.8 |
| 200 | 0.5 | (200 - 208) - 8 | 32.0 |
| 260 | 0.3 | (260 - 208)  52 | 811.2 |
|  |  | Variance = | 1,516.0 |

Standard deviation = $\sqrt{1,516}$ = 38.936

= £38,940 to the nearest £10

**31** Coefficient of variation = $\dfrac{\text{Standard deviation}}{\text{Expected value}}$ = $\dfrac{£38,940}{£208,000}$ = 0.19

230

# 8: MARKING SCHEDULE

| Question | Correct answer | Marks for correct answer | Question | Correct answer | Marks for correct answer | Question | Correct answer | Marks for correct answer |
|---|---|---|---|---|---|---|---|---|
| 1 | A | 1 | 14 | B | 1 | 27 | C | 1 |
| 2 | A | 1 | 15 | D | 2 | 28 | C | 1 |
| 3 | B | 1 | 16 | B | 1 | 29 | B | 1 |
| 4 | C | 1 | 17 | D | 1 | 30 | B | 1 |
| 5 | B | 1 | 18 | A | 1 | 31 | A | 1 |
| 6 | D | 1 | 19 | C | 1 | 32 | C | 1 |
| 7 | C | 1 | 20 | D | 2 | 33 | A | 1 |
| 8 | C | 1 | 21 | B | 1 | 34 | C | 2 |
| 9 | D | 1 | 22 | B | 1 | 35 | B | 2 |
| 10 | C | 1 | 23 | B | 1 | 36 | C | 1 |
| 11 | A | 1 | 22 | B | 1 | 37 | C | 1 |
| 12 | A | 1 | 25 | A | 1 | 38 | B | 2 |
| 13 | B | 1 | 26 | D | 2 | 39 | B | 1 |

## YOUR MARKS

Total marks available: 45    Your total mark: ☐

---

**GUIDELINES - If your mark was:**

**0 - 14**: You are not sufficiently proficient at manipulating performance data for comparison purposes. Go back and study your text, and then have another go at this chapter.

**15 - 24**: Fair. However, you are still being caught out by some of the tricky data manipulations required. Think carefully about the reasons for your errors and then try the chapter again.

**25 - 37**: Good. You made a few errors, but you are getting there! Try to identify the reasons for your mistakes.

**38 - 45**: Very good. You have a sound understanding of the principles of this important area of management accounting, and you can manipulate the figures well.

# COMMENTS

## Question

### 1

Profit = £85,000 - £20,000 = £65,000

Divisional capital employed = £30,000 + £180,000 = £210,000

∴ Return on investment = $\frac{£65,000}{£210,000}$ × 100% = 31.0%

|  | £ |
|---|---|
| Operating profit = | 65,000 |
| Imputed interest = £210,000 × 25% | 52,500 |
| ∴ Residual income = | 12,500 |

### 2

The new investment will alter the profit and capital employed:

|  |  | Operating profit £ | Capital employed £ |
|---|---|---|---|
|  | Original forecast | 65,000 | 210,000 |
| less | machine sold | (2,500) | (6,000) |
| plus | machine purchased | 5,200 | 15,000 |
|  |  | 67,700 | 219,000 |

∴ Revised return on investment = $\frac{£67,700}{£219,000}$ × 100% = 30.9%

### 3

|  | £ |
|---|---|
| Revised operating profit (see previous solution) | 67,700 |
| Imputed interest - £219,000 × 25% | 54,750 |
| Revised residual income | 12,950 |

### 4

Current ROI = $\frac{360}{1,600}$ = 22.5%

New ROI = $\frac{(360 + 25)}{(1,600 + 130)}$ = $\frac{385}{1,730}$ = 22.25%, which is lower.

Current RI in £000 = 360 - (18% of 1,600) = 72
New RI in £000 = 385 - (18% of 1,730) = 73.6, which is higher.

## Question

**5**  ROI on marginal investment = $\frac{45{,}000}{180{,}000}$ = 25%.

This is lower than the target of 28%.

Change in RI = £45,000 - (20% of £180,000) = +£9,000.

**6**  The divisional manager has control over fixed assets and stocks, but not debtors and not creditors. The interest charge, for calculating controllable RI, should therefore be based on (F + S). The divisional profit before management charges, P, is the controllable pre-interest profit figure, and so the correct answer is D.

**7**  Let the interest rate be R
Residual income,  Division X = 155,000 - 1,000,000R
                   Division Y = 200,000 - 1,250,000R
                   Division Z = 250,000 - 1,500,000R

(1)  For divisional performance based on RI to rank Z over Y, we need

   250,000 - 1,500,000R  >  200,000 - 1,250,000R
              50,000     >  250,000R
                0.20     >  R

(2)  For divisional performance based on RI to rank Y over Z, we need

   200,000 - 1,250,000R  >  155,000 - 1,000,000R
              45,000     >  250,000R
                0.18     >  R

The lower value of R is (1) and (2) must apply, for the RI rankings to be consistent with the ROI rankings. The implied interest rate must not exceed 18%.

**8**  Division Y will buy the 4,000 units available externally at £25, leaving it with only 1,000 units to buy from Division X at £30. Division S profits will be:

|  |  | £000 |
|---|---|---|
| Contribution from: | external sales | 170 |
|  | sales to Y | 12 (1,000 units) |
|  |  | 182 |
| Fixed costs (50 + 120) |  | 170 |
| Profit |  | 12 |

The company as a whole will be paying £(24 - 18) = £7 per unit extra for each unit that Division Y purchases externally, thus reducing the company's profits by 4,000 units x £7 = £28,000.

## COMMENTS

## Question

**9**

|  |  | Division P<br>£000 | Division Q<br>£000 | Division R<br>£000 |
|---|---|---|---|---|
| Profit | Original forecast | 130.0 | 175 | 132.0 |
|  | + Additions | 11.5 | - | 3.5 |
|  | - Reductions | - | (7) | (2.0) |
| *Revised profit* |  | 141.5 | 168 | 133.5 |
| Capital employed |  |  |  |  |
|  | Original forecast | 410 | 620 | 570 |
|  | + Additions | 50 | - | 19 |
|  | - Reductions | - | (45) | (5) |
| *Revised capital employed* |  | 460 | 575 | 584 |

$$\therefore \text{Revised ROCE} = \frac{141.5}{460} \times 100\% \quad \frac{168}{575} \times 100\% \quad \frac{133.5}{584} \times 100\%$$

$$= 30.8\% \quad = 29.2\% \quad = 22.9\%$$

$$\text{Original forecast ROCE} = \frac{130}{410} \times 100\% \quad \frac{175}{620} \times 100\% \quad \frac{132}{570} \times 100\%$$

$$= 31.7\% \quad = 28.2\% \quad = 23.2\%$$

∴ The proposal from division Q is the only one which will earn the manager a higher bonus, if the bonus is based on ROCE.

**10**

|  |  | Division P<br>£000 |  | Division Q<br>£000 |  | Division R<br>£000 |
|---|---|---|---|---|---|---|
| *Original residual income:* |  |  |  |  |  |  |
| Net profit |  | 130.0 |  | 175 |  | 132.0 |
| Imputed interest | (410 × 15%) | 61.5 | (620 × 15%) | 93 | (570 × 15%) | 85.5 |
| Residual income |  | 68.5 |  | 82 |  | 46.2 |
| *Revised residual income:* |  |  |  |  |  |  |
| Net profit (previous solution) |  | 141.5 |  | 168.00 |  | 133.5 |
| Imputed interest | (460 × 15%) | 69.0 | (575 × 15%) | 86.25 | (584 × 15%) | 87.6 |
| Revised residual income |  | 72.5 |  | 81.75 |  | 45.9 |

∴ The proposal from division P is the only one which will earn the manager a higher bonus, if the bonus is based on residual income.

## Question

### 11

The incremental residual income from the division P proposal can be deduced from the workings in the previous solution.

£72,500 - £68,500 = £4,000

*or* The figure can be proved independently as follows:

|  |  | £ |
|---|---|---|
|  | Incremental profit | 11,500 |
| *less* | Incremental imputed interest - 15% x £50,000 | 7,500 |
| = | Incremental residual income | 4,000 |

### 12

|  | Operating profit £000 |  | Capital employed £000 |
|---|---|---|---|
| Original figure | 1,000 | Fixed assets at cost | 7,000 |
| Additional depreciation |  | Accumulated depreciation | 5,000 |
| (200 x 0.70) | 140 | Net book value | 2,000 |
| ∴ Revised profit | 860 |  |  |
|  |  | ∴ Revalued fixed assets (x 1.7) | 3,400 |
|  |  | Net current assets | 180 |
|  |  | Revised capital employed | 3,580 |

$$\therefore \text{Revised ROCE} = \frac{860}{3,580} \times 100\% = 24.0\%$$

### 13

|  | £000 |
|---|---|
| Revised operating profit (see previous solution) | 860 |
| Imputed interest = 3,580 x 15% | 537 |
| = Residual income | 323 |

### 14

For F Limited:

|  | £000 | £000 |
|---|---|---|
| Original operating profit |  | 1,600 |
| Additional depreciation for fixed asset revaluation |  |  |
| (250 x 0.30) |  | (75) |
| Adjustment for computer - add back lease charge | 27 |  |
|                      *less* depreciation as E Ltd | 20 | 7 |
| Adjustment for development costs - charge as per E Ltd | 15 |  |
|                      1/3 charge already in F Ltd accounts | 5 | (10) |
| Adjusted operating profit |  | 1,522 |

# COMMENTS

## Question

### 15

For F Limited:

|  | £000 | £000 |
|---|---:|---:|
| Original cost of fixed assets | 9,400 | |
| Accumulated depreciation | 3,100 | |
| Net book value | 6,300 | |
| Adjustment for development costs - deduct the amount originally shown on F Ltd balance sheet (15 x 2/3) | (10) | |
| | 6,290 | |
| Adjust to replacement cost | (x 1.30) | 8,177 |
| Net current assets | | 230 |
| | | 8,407 |
| Adjustment for computer - F Ltd must include the same amount as shown on E Ltd's balance sheet | | 80 |
| Revised capital employed | | 8,487 |

### 16

Using the adjusted operating profit and capital employed figures from the previous two solutions.

$$ROCE = \frac{1,522}{8,487} \times 100\% = 17.9\%$$

### 17

The new investment will earn a ROCE of $\frac{£70,000}{£350,000} \times 100\% = 20\%$

This is less than the ROCE for E Limited, calculated in the solution to Q12. E Limited will therefore reject the investment.

20% is greater than the ROCE for F Limited, calculated in the previous solution. F Limited will therefore accept the investment.

### 18

The return on new investment is 20%, which exceeds the cost of capital and so will generate extra residual income:

| | £000 |
|---|---:|
| Incremental profit | 70 |
| Incremental imputed interest (350 x 15%) | 52.5 |
| Incremental residual income | 17.5 |

Both companies would therefore accept the investment, if performance is assessed based on residual income.

# Question

## 19

The first thing to calculate is the revised depreciation charge for the year, allowing for the revaluation of fixed assets:

| Purchase year | Purchase cost | Original depreciation in 19X9 (25%) | | Adjust for inflation | | Revised depreciation in 19X9 |
|---|---|---|---|---|---|---|
| | £000 | £000 | | * | | £000 |
| 19X6 | 192 | 48 | x | $\frac{125}{96}$ | = | 62.50 |
| 19X7 | 80 | 20 | x | $\frac{125}{100}$ | = | 25.00 |
| 19X8 | 116 | 29 | x | $\frac{125}{116}$ | = | 31.25 |
| 19X9 | 120 | 30 | x | $\frac{125}{120}$ | = | 31.25 |
| | | $\overline{127}$ | | | | $\overline{150.00}$ |

∴ Increase in depreciation charge = £150,000 - £127,000 = £23,000

\* The inflation adjustment is made by multiplying by the index for the end of 19X9, and dividing by the index at the time of purchase. Since fixed assets were purchased at the *beginning* of each year, it is necessary to take the index at the end of the year *preceding* the purchase. For instance in 19X6, the denominator index is that for the end of 19X5.

The adjusted profit figure can now be calculated:

| | £000 |
|---|---|
| Original profit figure | 240 |
| Increase in depreciation charge | (23) |
| Rented premises are to be capitalised ∴ add back rent | 30 |
| ∴ Adjusted profit figure | $\overline{247}$ |

## 20

You need to carry out the same sort of calculations as in the previous solution, using the indices to adjust the plant and machinery to written down replacement values.

| Year of purchase | Purchase cost | Net book value at end 19X9 | | Adjust for inflation | | Written down replacement value |
|---|---|---|---|---|---|---|
| | £000 | | £000 | | | £000 |
| 19X6 | 192 | (fully depreciated) | - | - | | - |
| 19X7 | 80 | (1/4) | 20 | x | $\frac{125}{100}$ = | 25 |
| 19X8 | 116 | (2/4) | 58 | x | $\frac{125}{116}$ = | 62.5 |
| 19X9 | 120 | (3/4) | 90 | x | $\frac{125}{120}$ = | 93.75 |
| | | | | | | $\overline{181.25}$ |

# Question

The adjusted capital employed figure can now be calculated:

|  | £000 |
|---|---|
| Revalued freehold premises - held for 4 years, increasing in value by 10% per annum = $200 \times (1.10)^4$ = | 292.82 |
| Annual rent, capitalised on the basis that the £30,000 rent represents a 15% return = $30 \div 0.15$ = | 200 |
| Working capital at the end of 19X9 | 150 |
| Written down replacement value of plant and machinery | 181.25 |
| = Adjusted figure for capital employed | 824.07 |

**21** Using the figures calculated above, the fully adjusted ROCE is:

$$\frac{£247,000}{£824,070} \times 100\% = 30.0\%$$

**22** Using the figures calculated above:

|  |  | £000 |
|---|---|---|
|  | Fully adjusted profit | 247 |
| less | Imputed interest (824,070 × 0.20) | 164.814 |
|  | Residual income | 82.186 |

**23** We need to calculate the effect of Investment I on budgeted profit and budgeted capital employed:

|  | £000 |  | £000 | £000 |
|---|---|---|---|---|
| Original budgeted profit | 400 | Original capital employed |  | 1,600 |
| plus reduction in revenue costs | 100 | plus Year-end net book |  |  |
|  | 500 | value of new plant: cost | 300 |  |
| less non-revenue cost: depn = |  | depreciation | 75 |  |
| (300 ÷ 4) | 75 |  |  | 225 |
| Revised operating profit | 425 | Revised capital employed |  | 1,825 |

$$\text{Revised ROCE} = \frac{425}{1,825} \times 100\% = 23.3\%$$

**24** As before, calculate the effect of Investment II on budgeted profit and budgeted capital employed:

|  | £000 | £000 |  | £000 |
|---|---|---|---|---|
| Original budgeted profit |  | 400 | Original capital employed | 1,600 |
| less revenue expenses: |  |  | less |  |
|   system cost | 8 |  | Average stock reduction | 45 |
|   staff cost | 9 | 17 |  | 1,555 |
| Revised operating profit |  | 383 |  |  |

$$\therefore \text{Revised ROCE} = \frac{383}{1,555} \times 100\% = 24.6\%$$

# Question

## 25

As for investments I and II, calculate the effect of Investment III on budgeted profit and budgeted capital employed:

|  | £000 |  | £000 |
|---|---|---|---|
| Original budgeted profit | 400 | Original capital employed | 1,600 |
| Additional contribution | 25 | Average increase in debtors | 35 |
| Revised operating profit | 425 |  | 1,635 |

$$\therefore \text{Revised ROCE} = \frac{425}{1,635} \times 100\% = 26.0\%$$

## 26

Goal congruence will exist for each investment if it meets the group's 18% DCF criterion as well as satisfying Smallparcel Limited's desire to maintain next year's ROCE performance.

We therefore need to assess the DCF return on each investment. We can do this by seeing whether each one generates a positive Net Present Value at an 18% cost of capital, over 4 years.

The changes in stocks and debtors in investments II and III will produce a one-off cash flow in year 1. The discounting process must take account of this.

| Investment | Year | Cash inflow £000 | Cash outflow £000 | Net cash flow £000 | 18% factor | Present value £000 | Decision based on group investment criterion |
|---|---|---|---|---|---|---|---|
| I | 0 |  | (300) | (300) | 1.0 | (300) |  |
|  | 1 - 4 | 100 |  | 100 | 2.69 | 269 |  |
|  |  |  |  | Net present value |  | (31) | Do not invest |
| II | 0 | - | (8) | (8) | 1.0 | (8.0) |  |
|  | 1 | 45 | (9) | 36 | 0.85 | 30.6 |  |
|  | 2 - 4 | - | (9) | (9) | 1.84 | (16.56) |  |
|  |  |  |  | Net present value |  | 6.04 | Invest |
| III | 1 | 25 | (35) | (10) | 0.85 | (8.5) |  |
|  | 2 - 4 | 25 | - | 25 | 1.84 | 46 |  |
|  |  |  |  | Net present value |  | 37.5 | Invest |

Smallparcel Limited will be willing to go ahead with the investments if they improve the ROCE for next year - we are asked to consider goal congruence for next year, therefore we must see whether Smallparcel Limited's decision on each investment would match with the group's decision.

$$\text{ROCE without the investments} = \frac{400}{1,600} \times 100\% = 25\%$$

Continued...

## COMMENTS

## Question

| Investment | ROCE with the investment (see previous solutions) % | ROCE without the investment % | Smallparcel Ltd's decision | Raptin Brown Paper Group plc's decision |
|---|---|---|---|---|
| I | 23.3 | 25.0 | Do not invest | Do not invest |
| II | 24.6 | 25.0 | Do not invest | Invest |
| III | 26.0 | 25.0 | Invest | Invest |

Goal congruence will exist for investments I and III.

### 27

The transfer price between the divisions is:

|  |  | £ |
|---|---|---|
|  | External selling price | 45 |
| less | Variable selling costs | 2 |
|  | Transfer price | 43 |

Since two units of the Division 1 product are required to manufacture one unit of the Division 2 product, the number of units transferred between the divisions will be (Division 2 sales x 2) = 14,000 units.

| Calculation of Division 1 annual profit: | £000 | £000 |
|---|---|---|
| Sales - external = 8,000 x £45 |  | 360 |
|         internal to Division 2 = 14,000 x £43 |  | 602 |
|  |  | 962 |
| Variable cost - external sales = 8,000 x £18 | 144 |  |
|               internal transfers 14,000 x £16 | 224 | 368 |
| Contribution |  | 594 |
| Fixed costs |  | 120 |
| Annual profit |  | 474 |

$$\therefore \text{ROCE} = \frac{474}{1,950} \times 100\% = 24.3\%$$

### 28

|  | £000 |
|---|---|
| Annual profit (see above) | 474 |
| Imputed interest = £1,950,000 x 16% | 312 |
| Annual residual income | 162 |

# Question

## 29

Calculation of Division 2 annual profit:

|  | £000 | £000 |
|---|---:|---:|
| Sales - 7,000 units x £154 |  | 1,078 |
| Costs - variable costs in Division 2 = 7,000 x £33 | 231 |  |
| transfers from Division 1 = 14,000 x £43 | 602 | 833 |
| Contribution |  | 245 |
| Fixed costs |  | 160 |
| Annual profit |  | 85 |

$$\therefore ROCE = \frac{85}{500} \times 100\% = 17.0\%$$

## 30

|  | £000 |
|---|---:|
| Annual profit (see above) | 85 |
| Imputed interest = £500,000 x 16% | 80 |
| Annual residual income | 5 |

## 31

To increase the subsidiary's profits, the transfer price needs to be higher (since it is the subsidiary doing the selling) and the royalty payments by the holding company to the subsidary should also be higher. Both would add to the subsidiary's revenue without affecting its costs.

## 32

If Market State I arises, Division P would have to forgo one unit of external sale of P for every unit of P that is transferred to Division Q.

The opportunity cost would be the contribution forgone = £(27 - 18) per unit
= £9 per unit

| The transfer price would therefore be: | variable cost | £18 |
|---|---|---:|
|  | opportunity cost | £ 9 |
|  | transfer price | £27 |

- which is in fact the external market price for product P.

## 33

With Market State II, the production in Division P will be:

|  | £000 |
|---|---:|
| For external sales of P | 60 |
| For internal sales - 30,000 units of Q x 3 | 90 |
|  | 150 |

Maximum capacity is 215,000 units, therefore there is spare capacity in the division. The opportunity cost of lost contribution from external sales is zero.

∴ Transfer price = Variable cost + £0 = £18

## Question

### 34

There is spare capacity in Division Q with both market states, therefore the manager will accept the special order if the unit price of £70 is higher than Division Q's perceived variable cost per unit.

The perceived variable cost per unit of Product Q in Division Q
 = Variable cost £14 + (3 x Transfer price per unit of product P)

| Situation | Transfer price per unit | * Perceived variable cost per unit | Order price | Division Q decision |
|---|---|---|---|---|
| 1 | £18 | £68 (14 + 54) | £70 | Accept |
| 2 | £27 (see earlier solution) | £95 (14 + 81) | £70 | Reject |
| 3 | £18 + $\frac{£430,000}{215,000}$ = £20 | £74 (14 + 60) | £70 | Reject |
| 4 | £18 | £68 (14 + 54) | £70 | Accept |

From the point of view of the whole company, if Market State I arises the relevant unit cost of the order is:

|  | £/unit of Q |
|---|---|
| Division P variable cost x 3 units | 54 |
| Division Q variable cost | 14 |
| Opportunity cost of sales of P forgone | |
| = contribution £9 per unit x 3 units | 27 |
| Relevant cost per unit | 95 |

The manager of Boxer Trix plc would reject the order if Market State I arises.

For Market State II, there is sufficient capacity in Division P to complete the order without displacing sales, therefore the relevant unit cost of the order is:

|  | £/unit of Q |
|---|---|
| Division P variable cost x 3 units | 54 |
| Division Q variable cost | 14 |
|  | 68 |

The manager of Boxer Trix plc would want to accept the order if Market State II arises, since this relevant cost is less than the £70 price offered.

The decisions of the two managers can now be summarised.

| Situation | Manager of Division Q | Manager of Boxer Trix plc |
|---|---|---|
| 1 | Accept | Reject |
| 2 | Reject | Reject |
| 3 | Reject | Accept |
| 4 | Accept | Accept |

The two managers will make the same decision in situations 2 and 4.

# 8: PERFORMANCE MEASUREMENT AND TRANSFER PRICING

## Question

### 35

| Output | Revenue (1) | Division Q Cost (2) | Net revenue (3)=(1)-(2) | Incremental net revenue | Cost (4) | Division P Incremental cost | Company profit (3)-(4) |
|---|---|---|---|---|---|---|---|
| units | £ | £ | £ | £ | £ | £ | £ |
| 1 | 1,400 | 100 | 1,300 |  | 510 |  | 790 |
| 2 | 2,100 | 150 | 1,950 | +650 | 730 | +220 | 1,220 |
| 3 | 2,550 | 220 | 2,330 | +380 | 960 | +230 | 1,370 |
| 4 | 2,900 | 320 | 2,580 | +250 | 1,200 | +240 | *1,380 |
| 5 | 3,200 | 470 | 2,730 | +150 | 1,480 | +280 | 1,250 |
| 6 | 3,450 | 630 | 2,820 | +90 | 1,800 | +320 | 1,020 |

\* Profit maximising output = 4 units per day.

(a) To persuade Division P's manager to produce up to 4 units per day, the incremental revenue (transfer price) must be at least £240 per unit.

(b) To persuade P's manager *not* to want to produce a 5th unit each day, the transfer price must be less than £280 per unit.

(c) To persuade Q's manager to want to take up to 4 units per day, the transfer price per unit must not exceed £250, which is the incremental net revenue to Q from the fourth unit per day, before deducting transfer price costs.

(d) To persuade Q's manager *not* to want a 5th unit daily, the transfer price must exceed £150 per unit.

Taking (a) - (d), the transfer price range that will satisfy all four conditions is £240 - £250.

### 36

First, check whether there is a limiting factor:

Labour hours required for maximum production =

|  | hours |
|---|---|
| Sales of Long - 1,400 units x 3 hours | 4,200 |
| Sales of Tall - 875 units x 4 hours | 3,500 |
| Sales of Short - 525 units x 2 hours | 1,050 |
| Tall for transfer to Y - 30 units x 4 hours | 120 |
|  | 8,870 |

There is obviously a severe limitation on the number of labour hours in Division X, and the appropriate transfer price rule is 'variable cost plus opportunity cost'.

To calculate the opportunity cost, we need to work out the best allocation of the available labour hours:

# Question

|  | Long | Tall | Short |
|---|---|---|---|
| Contribution per unit | £27 | £40 | £21 |
| Labour hours required | 3 | 4 | 2 |
| ∴ Contribution per hour | £9 | £10 | £10.50 |
| Ranking | 3rd | 2nd | 1st |

The available hours can now be allocated:

| Product | Units | Hours |  |
|---|---|---|---|
| Short | 525 | 1,050 |  |
| Tall | 30 | 120 | (balance) |
|  |  | 1,170 |  |

The 30 units of Tall required for Division Y would therefore displace 30 units which could be sold externally. The opportunity cost is the contribution forgone of £40 per unit.

|  |  | £ per unit |
|---|---|---|
| The appropriate transfer price is therefore: | variable cost | 41 |
|  | opportunity cost | 40 |
|  | transfer price | 81 |

- which is, in fact, the external sales price.

## 37

Using the data calculated in the previous solution, the new total of available hours can be allocated:

| Product | Units | Hours |  |
|---|---|---|---|
| Short | 525 | 1,050 |  |
| Tall | 875 | 3,500 |  |
| Long | 40 | 120 | (balance) |
|  |  | 4,670 |  |

The maximum internal transfer of 30 units of Tall would now displace 40 units of Long, which is achieving a contribution of £9 per hour.

The opportunity cost per unit of Tall transferred is therefore the contribution forgone for each hour that could have been used for Long:

|  | £ per unit |
|---|---|
| Opportunity cost per unit of Tall = 4 hours x £9 contribution forgone = | 36 |
| *plus* Variable cost per unit of Tall | 41 |
| = Transfer price | 77 |

# Question

## 38

The first step is to calculate the profit-maximising output for the company, and then have a think about which transfer prices would encourage the divisional managers to operate at this level.

| Units | | Total Profit £000 |
|---|---|---|
| 100 | (80 - 15 - 25) | 40 |
| 200 | (155 - 32 - 65) | 58 |
| 300 | (230 - 54 - 107) | 69 |
| 400 | (290 - 77 - 139) | 74 |
| 500 | (360 - 110 - 186) | 64 |

The table shows that profit is maximised at an output of 400 units. The transfer price must be set so that the manager of Division K wishes to transfer 400 units to Division L, and the manager of Division L wishes to purchase 400 units from Division K.

Division K will be willing to increase production as long as the incremental costs are less than the transfer price. Division L will be willing to receive transfers so long as the incremental net revenues in the division exceed the transfer price.

| Units | Division L revenue | Division L costs | Division L net revenue (excl transfers) | Division L incremental net revenue (excl transfers) | | Division K incremental cost | |
|---|---|---|---|---|---|---|---|
| | £000 | £000 | £000 | £000 | | £000 | |
| 100 | 80 | 25 | 55 | | | | |
| 200 | 155 | 65 | 90 | (90 - 55) | 35 | (32 - 15) | 17 |
| 300 | 230 | 107 | 123 | (123 - 90) | 33 | (54 - 32) | 22 |
| 400* | 290 | 139 | 151 | (151 - 123) | 28 | (77 - 54) | 23 |
| 500 | 360 | 186 | 174 | (174 - 151) | 23 | (110 - 77) | 33 |

* optimum

Division K will be willing to produce 400 units if the transfer price is higher than £23,000 for 100 units, but lower than £33,000 per 100 units.

Division L will be willing to produce 400 units if the transfer price is lower than £28,000 for 100 units, but higher than £23,000 per 100 units.

The most appropriate narrow range for the transfer price is therefore higher than £23,000 for 100 units and lower than £28,000 for 100 units.

On a unit basis, the transfer price must be in the range £231 to £279 per unit.

# COMMENTS

## Question

**39** Value added shows how much 'wealth' or value the division has created from its own operations, and is measured as sales revenue less 'bought-in' costs of materials, bought-in services (contractors' charges) and other 'bought-in' items such as telephone costs, fuel costs etc. Here we have

|  | £000 | £000 |
|---|---:|---:|
| Sales |  | 570 |
| Direct materials | 120 |  |
| Indirect materials | 15 |  |
| Bought-in services | 50 |  |
|  |  | 185 |
| Value added |  | 385 |

This value added is shared between

|  | £000 |
|---|---:|
| Employees (60 + 150) | 210 |
| Shareholders (40 + 30 + 15 + 90) | 175 |
|  | 385 |

# 9: MARKING SCHEDULE

| Question | Correct answer | Marks for correct answer | Question | Correct answer | Marks for correct answer | Question | Correct answer | Marks for correct answer |
|---|---|---|---|---|---|---|---|---|
| 1 | A | 1 | 11 | B | 2 | 21 | C | 1 |
| 2 | B | 1 | 12 | B | 1 | 22 | A | 1 |
| 3 | C | 2 | 13 | B | 2 | 23 | D | 2 |
| 4 | B | 2 | 14 | C | 3 | 24 | A | 1 |
| 5 | D | 1 | 15 | A | 1 | 25 | B | 2 |
| 6 | D | 1 | 16 | C | 2 | 26 | D | 2 |
| 7 | C | 1 | 17 | C | 1 | 27 | C | 1 |
| 8 | D | 2 | 18 | C | 2 | 28 | C | 1 |
| 9 | C | 2 | 19 | C | 1 | 29 | C | 1 |
| 10 | D | 1 | 20 | B | 1 | | | |

YOUR MARKS

Total marks available  42   Your total mark  ☐

---

**GUIDELINES - If your mark was:**

**0 - 12**  You need to do a thorough revision of the management accounting applications of process costing. Go back to your study text and read the relevant sections carefully.

**13 - 21**  Fair, but you have not yet got properly to grips with the management accounting applications of process costing. Read our solutions carefully and then try this chapter again.

**22 - 32**  Good. There are still a few gaps in your knowledge, but you are well on the way to a good understanding of this difficult topic.

**33 - 42**  Excellent. You have got to grips with the management accounting applications of process costing! Not an easy achievement, so very well done!

# COMMENTS

## Question

**1** One way of approaching this question is to carry out the cost and revenue calculations for, say, 10 kg of input:

|  |  | £ | £ |
|---|---|---|---|
| Sales value: | 3 kg of X at £14 per kg | | 42 |
| | 4.5 kg of Y at £10 per kg | | 45 |
| | 1.5 kg of Z at £4 per kg | | 6 |
| | | | 93 |
| Production costs: | Material M - 4 kg at £5 | 20 | |
| | Material N - 6 kg at £3 | 18 | |
| | Labour - 10 kg at £4 | 40 | 78 |
| Contribution per 10 kg of input | | | 15 |

$$\therefore \text{Breakeven point} = \frac{\text{fixed costs}}{\text{contribution per unit}} = \frac{£45,000}{£15} = 3,000 \times 10 \text{ kg batches per month}$$
$$= 30,000 \text{ kg of input}$$

30,000 kg of input produces 30,000 × 30% = 9,000 kg of product X.

**2**
| | |
|---|---|
| Contribution per 10kg of output (see above) | = £15 |
| Contribution from 75,000kg of input | = £15 ÷ 10 × 75,000 |
| | = £112,500 |
| Profit (subtracting fixed costs of £45,000) | = £67,500 |

**3** The basic data about Wynne Donsomble Limited tells us that in producing an extra 1,500 kg of product X, extra *saleable* output of products Y and Z will result.

1,500 kg of product X will result in the production of 2,250 kg extra of product Y and 750 kg of product Z.

We will assume that fixed costs remain unaffected by the additional volume, except as detailed in the question.

The total material input for 1,500 kg of product X is $\frac{1,500}{0.3}$ = 5,000 kg of material

## Question

|  |  | £ | £ |
|---|---|---:|---:|
| Sales value - | 2,250 kg of Y at £10 per kg | | 22,500 |
| | 750 kg of Z at £4 per kg | | 3,000 |
| | | | 25,500 |
| Production costs: | 5,000 kg x 40% of Material M at £5 per kg | 10,000 | |
| | 5,000 kg x 60% of Material N at £3 per kg | 9,000 | |
| | labour - 5,000 hrs at £4 per hr | 20,000 | |
| | | | 39,000 |
| Excess of cost over sales revenue | | | 13,500 |
| *plus* rental of factory space | | | 500 |
| export and shipping costs | | | 250 |
| = required sales revenue from product X | | | 14,250 |
| | | | ÷ 1,500 kg |
| ∴ Breakeven price per kg = | | | £9.50 per kg |

You could argue that since extra output of product X can be sold in the domestic market for £14, the breakeven sales price is the opportunity cost of diverting output from domestic markets, which is the market price of £14 per kg. This option is not available as a solution, and so is not the appropriate assumption here.

## 4

The budgeted input of material E can be calculated by 'working backwards' from the budgeted output of product P.

Required output of P from process 3 = 95,000 litres.

The loss in process 3 is 5% of liquid *output*, therefore the required input of P to process 3 = 95,000 litres x 1.05 = 99,750 litres.

∴ Required output of product P from process 2 = 99,750 litres.

The loss in process 2 is 30% of input, and product P represents 40% of the output from the process. Therefore, to produce 99,750 litres of P in process 2, the required material input is:

99,750 litres ÷ 0.40 x 100/70
= 356,250 litres

∴ Required output from process 1 = 356,250 litres

The loss in process 1 is 25% of input,
∴ Required material input    = 356,250 litres ÷ 0.75
                             = 475,000 litres
Of this, 50% is material E   = 237,500 litres

## Question

**5**

One of the easiest ways to deal with this type of question is to work with figures on which you can easily calculate the losses and yields. We have selected one litre of each material:

| | £ |
|---|---|
| *Process 1* | |
| 1 litre of material E | 0.20 |
| 1 litre of material F | 0.45 |
| Conversion cost = 2 litres x £0.41 | 0.82 |
| | 1.47 |
| ÷ Output from 2 litres of material input | ÷ 1.50 litres (25% loss) |
| = Cost per litre of output | £0.98 |

**6**

| | £ |
|---|---|
| *Process 2* | |
| 1 litre of process 1 output: cost | 0.98 |
| Conversion cost in process 2 | 0.56 |
| | 1.54 |
| ÷ Output from 1 litre of material input | ÷ 0.70 (30% loss) |
| = Cost per litre of output | £2.20 |

Since joint process costs are apportioned on the basis of output, this cost of £2.20 per litre applies to output of both product P and product Q.

**7**

| | £ |
|---|---|
| *Process 3* | |
| 1 litre of process 2 output: cost | 2.20 |
| Conversion cost in process 3 | 0.20 |
| | 2.40 |

Process loss is 5% of *output*,
∴ Unpacked cost per litre of output = £2.40 x 1.05
= £2.52
*plus* Cost of container £0.30
= Cost per litre of finished product P = £2.82

**8**

We are given the final sales price per litre of completed output for each product. We need to determine the processing cost per litre in processes 2 and 3, and then deduct this cost from the final sales price, to arrive at a notional sales price at the separation point for each product.

The first step, then, is to calculate the processing cost per litre after the separation point. To do this, we need to know the equivalent litres produced in each process.

## Question

|  | Process 2<br>Equivalent litres<br>of process cost |  | Process 3<br>Equivalent litres<br>of process cost |  |
|---|---|---|---|---|
| Closing work in progress | (9,600 x 0.5) | 4,800 | (3,900 x 0.5) | 1,950 |
| Completed output | | 206,400 | | 80,600 |
| | | 211,200 | | 82,550 |
| *less* Opening work in progress | (24,000 x 0.5) | 12,000 | (6,500 x 0.5) | 3,250 |
| Equivalent litres of process cost | | 199,200 | | 79,300 |
| Process cost | | £69,720 | | £39,650 |
| ∴ Processing cost per litre = | | £0.35 | | £0.50 |

We can now calculate the notional sales value at the separation point:

|  | Jay | | Kay | |
|---|---|---|---|---|
| Final sales price per litre | £1.00 | | £0.75 | |
| Further processing cost per litre | £0.35 | | £0.50 | |
| ∴ Notional sales price at separation point | £0.65 | per litre | £0.25 | per litre |
| x Output from process 1 | 192,000 | litres | 78,000 | litres |
| = Notional sales value at separation point | £124,800 | | £19,500 | |

Joint costs in process 1 are to be apportioned according to this notional sales value:

|  | Jay | Kay | Total |
|---|---|---|---|
|  | £ | £ | £ |
| Notional sales value at separation point | 124,800 | 19,500 | 144,300 |
| Process 1 costs apportioned pro rata | £101,189 | £15,811 | £117,000 |

## 9

To allow a notional profit on post-separation point costs, we must first calculate the average rate of profit on all products.

|  | £ | £ |
|---|---|---|
| Final sales value of output from process 1: | | |
|     Jay 192,000 litres x £1.00 | 192,000 | |
|     Kay 78,000 litres x £0.75 | 58,500 | 250,500 |
| Processing costs: | | |
|     Process 1 | 117,000 | |
|     Process 2 - 192,000 x £0.35 (question 8) | 67,200 | |
|     Process 3 - 78,000 x £0.50 (question 8) | 39,000 | 223,200 |
| Profit on all products | | 27,300 |

∴ Average rate of profit mark up places. = $\frac{£27,300}{£223,200}$ x 100% = 12.23% on cost, to two decimal

## COMMENTS

## Question

*Recalculation of notional sales value*

|  | Jay | | Kay | | Total |
|---|---|---|---|---|---|
|  | £ | £ | £ | £ | £ |
| Final sales price per litre |  | 1.00 |  | 0.75 |  |
| Process 2 and 3 costs per litre | 0.35 |  | 0.50 |  |  |
| Profit on these costs (12.23%) | 0.04 | 0.39 | 0.06 | 0.56 |  |
| = Notional sales price at separation point |  | 0.61 |  | 0.19 |  |
| x Output from process 1 (in litres) |  | 192,000 |  | 78,000 |  |
| = Notional sales value at separation point |  | £117,120 |  | £14,820 | £131,940 |
| Process 1 cost pro rata |  | £103,858 |  | £13,142 | £117,000 |

**10** A product is only worth processing further if the incremental costs incurred are less than any increase in sales value. The first thing to calculate is the post-separation cost for each product.

Total output of joint products = 11,000 kg

∴ Joint cost per kg = $\frac{£77,000}{11,000}$ = £7 per kg

|  | Exe £ per kg | | Wye £ per kg | | Zed £ per kg | |
|---|---|---|---|---|---|---|
| Total product costs |  | 11 |  | 10 |  | 16 |
| *less* joint costs apportioned |  | 7 |  | 7 |  | 7 |
| Post separation point costs |  | 4 |  | 3 |  | 9 |
| Increase in sales value through further processing | (15-10) | 5 | (22-17) | 5 | (18-12) | 6 |
| Gain/(loss) through further processing |  | 1 |  | 2 |  | (3) |

∴Product Z should not be subject to further processing, and should be sold at the separation point.

# Question

## 11

We need to calculate the cost per kg of each of processes 2, 3 and 4, and then compare this cost with the increase in sales value which is obtained by processing the products after the separation point.

|  | | Process 2<br>Equivalent kg<br>of process cost | | Process 3<br>Equivalent kg<br>of process cost | | Process 4<br>Equivalent kg<br>of process cost |
|---|---|---|---|---|---|---|
| Closing WIP | (5,000x0.25) | 1,250 | (12,000x0.25) | 3,000 | (1,000x0.25) | 250 |
| Output of refined product | | 243,000 | | 112,000 | | 91,000 |
| | | 244,250 | | 115,000 | | 91,250 |
| *less* | | | | | | |
| Opening WIP | (8,000x0.25) | 2,000 | (4,000x0.25) | 1,000 | (2,000x0.25) | 500 |
| = Equivalent units of processing cost | | 242,250 | | 114,000 | | 90,750 |
| Processing costs | | £72,675 | | £91,200 | | £117,975 |
| ∴ Processing cost per kg | | £0.30 | | £0.80 | | £1.30 |
| Increase in sales price per kg, through processing further | (4.80-4.20) | £0.60 | (7.60-7.10) | £0.50 | (8.30-6.80) | £1.50 |
| Gain/(loss) per kg through processing further | | £0.30 | | (£0.30) | | £0.20 |

Therefore, only products Alpha and Charlie should be processed further, in processes 2 and 4.

## 12

The maximum profit will be earned if products are only subject to further processing if a net gain is made as a result of the enhanced sales value.

|  | S<br>£ per kg | | T<br>£ per kg | | U<br>£ per kg | | V<br>£ per kg | |
|---|---|---|---|---|---|---|---|---|
| Costs of further processing: | | | | | | | | |
| - labour at £5 per hour | | 5 | | 7.5 | | 2.5 | | 10 |
| - other direct costs | | 8 | | 3 | | 7 | | 12 |
| | | 13 | | 10.5 | | 9.5 | | 22 |
| Increase in sales value | (28-12) | 16 | (14-2) | 12 | (18-6) | 12 | (24-3) | 21 |
| Gain/(loss) through further processing | | 3 | | 1.5 | | 2.5 | | (1) |

This analysis indicates that product V should be sold at the separation point and that products S, T and U should be subject to further processing. The resulting profit can now be calculated, given 50,000 kg of input.

# COMMENTS

## Question

|  |  | £000 | £000 |
|---|---|---:|---:|
| Sales revenue - | S  15,000 kg × £28 |  | 420 |
|  | T  10,000 kg × £14 |  | 140 |
|  | U  5,000 kg × £18 |  | 90 |
|  | V  20,000 kg × £3 (sold at separation point) |  | 60 |
|  |  |  | 710 |
| Further processing costs - |  |  |  |
|  | S  15,000 × £13 | 195 |  |
|  | T  10,000 × £10.5 | 105 |  |
|  | U  5,000 × £9.5 | 47.5 |  |
|  |  | 347.5 |  |
| Joint process costs |  | 270.0 | 617.5 |
| Maximum profit |  |  | 92.5 |

Maximum profit achievable is £92,500.

## 13

Labour hours for further processing are now a limiting factor. The company must maximise the gain per labour hour used. Using the workings in the previous solution:

|  | S | T | U |
|---|---:|---:|---:|
| Gain per kg through further processing | £3 | £1.5 | £2.5 |
| Labour hours used | 1 | 1.5 | 0.5 |
| ∴ Gain per labour hour | £3 | £1 | £5 |
| Ranking | 2nd | 3rd | 1st |

The available labour hours can now be allocated:

|  | kg | Hours used |  |
|---|---:|---:|---|
| Process further all of product U | 5,000 | 2,500 |  |
| and 7,500 kg of product S | 7,500 | 7,500 | (balance) |
|  |  | 10,000 |  |

The remaining production must be sold without further processing. The profit can now be calculated:

|  |  | £ | £ |
|---|---|---:|---:|
| Sales revenue - | S  7,500 × £28 (processed further) |  | 210 |
|  | 7,500 × £12 (sold at separation point) |  | 90 |
|  | T  10,000 × £2 (sold at separation point) |  | 20 |
|  | U  5,000 × £18 (processed further) |  | 90 |
|  | V  20,000 × £3 (sold at separation point) |  | 60 |
|  |  |  | 470 |
| Further processing costs - |  |  |  |
|  | S  7,500 × £13 | 97.5 |  |
|  | U  5,000 × £9.5 | 47.5 |  |
|  |  | 145 |  |
| Joint process costs |  | 270 | 415 |
| Maximum profit |  |  | 55 |

Maximum profit achievable is £55,000.

# 9: JOINT PRODUCT COSTING AND PROCESS COSTING

## Question

### 14 - 16

This is a very difficult problem and one that you may well have struggled with. The costing 'rules' are non-standard, and it is important to sort out just what they are.

(1) *Losses.* Losses occur at the *end* of processing, and opening/closing stocks do not include an allowance for scrap. It follows that the cost of any losses in the month should be borne by units of opening stock, other completed units and units of abnormal loss.

(2) To do this, a suitable approach is to begin by giving equivalent units values and a cost to normal loss, and then apportioning this cost between units of finished output and abnormal loss.

(3) The value of *all* scrap will be set off against the cost of materials in the process account, but closing stock values must not 'benefit' from any of this set-off.

See if you can follow these rules in the figures below.

| Item | Total units | Equivalent units Materials costs | Conversion Costs |
|---|---|---|---|
| Opening stock | 6,000 | 0 | 4,500 (75%) |
| Other completed output | 19,000 | 19,000 | 19,000 |
| Completed output | 25,000 | 19,000 | 23,500 |
| Normal loss | 3,000 | 3,000 | 3,000 |
| Abnormal loss | 2,000 | 2,000 | 2,000 |
|  | 30,000 | 24,000 | 28,500 |
| Closing stock | 12,000 | 12,000 | 3,000 (25%) |
| Total (6,000 + 16,000 + 20,000) | 42,000 | 36,000 | 31,500 |

| Costs | (16,000 x 0.75 + 20,000 x 3) £72,000 | £157,500 |
|---|---|---|
| Cost per equivalent unit |  £2 | £5 |

*Next step.* Apportion the cost of normal loss between completed output and abnormal loss.

|  | Materials |  | Conversion cost |  |
|---|---|---|---|---|
| Cost of finished output, normal and abnormal loss | (24,000 x £2) | £48,000 | (28,500 x £5) | £142,500 |
| less value of all scrap | (5,000 x £0.3) | (£1,500) |  |  |
|  |  | £46,500 |  |  |
| Equivalent units of finished output and abnormal loss | (19,000 + 2,000) | 21,000 | (23,500 + 2,000) | 25,500 |
| Cost per unit this month |  | £2.21 |  | £5.59 |

*Final step* Include the brought forward opening stock value to calculate an *average* unit cost for finished output in the month.

Continued...

255

# COMMENTS

## Question

|  |  | Materials cost | Conversion | Total |
|---|---|---|---|---|
|  |  | £ | £ | £ |
| Costs this month | 19,000 × £46,500/21,000 | 42,071 |  | 42,071 |
|  | 23,500 × £142,500/25,500 | - | 131,324 | 131,324 |
| Opening stock b/f |  | 15,000 | 7,600 | 22,600 |
|  |  | 57,071 | 136,129 | 195,995 |

Average cost per completed unit  $\dfrac{£195,995}{25,000 \text{ units}}$ = £7.84  (Question 14)

|  |  |  |  | £ |
|---|---|---|---|---|
| Value of abnormal loss = | Materials | 2,000 × £46,500/21,000 | 4,429 |
|  | Conversion cost | 2,000 × £142,500/25,500 | 11,176 |
|  |  |  | 15,605 | (Question 16) |

|  |  |  | £ |  |
|---|---|---|---|---|
| Closing stock value | Materials | 12,000 × £2 | 24,000 |  |
|  | Conversion cost | 3,000 × £5 | 15,000 |  |
|  |  |  | 39,000 | (Question 15) |

The process account looks as follows.

### Process account

|  | £ |  | £ |
|---|---|---|---|
| Opening stock b/f | 22,600 | Finished goods | 195,995 |
| Material X | 12,000 | Scrap (value of all loss) | 1,500 |
| Material Y | 60,000 | Abnormal loss | 15,605 |
| Conversion cost | 157,500 | Closing stock c/f | 39,000 |
|  | 252,100 |  | 252,100 |

## 17

If joint process costs are apportioned on the basis of weight, then 1 kg of Dot will have the same standard cost as 1 kg of Dash. One way of approaching this question is to calculate the standard cost of 100 kg of input:

|  | £ |
|---|---|
| 70 kg of Material M @ £4 per kg | 280 |
| 30 kg of Material N @ £3 per kg | 90 |
| Processing time - 2 hours @ £27 per hour | 54 |
| *less* value of scrap 20 kg @ £0.60 per kg | (12) |
| Net cost of 100 kg input | 412 |
| Good output from 100 kg input is 80 kg | ÷ 0.80 |
| ∴ Cost per 100 kg of good output = | £515 |

# 9: JOINT PRODUCT COSTING AND PROCESS COSTING

## Question

**18** From the previous solution, the cost of processing 100 kg of input is £412. The resulting good output is 20 kg of Dot and 60 kg of Dash, over which the £412 cost is to be apportioned:

|  | Dot | Dash | Total |
|---|---|---|---|
| Sales price | £20 | £10 | |
| Kg of output from 100 kg input | 20 kg | 60 kg | |
| Sales value of output | £400 | £600 | £1,000 |
| Joint cost to be apportioned pro rata to sales value | £164.80 | £247.20 | £412 |
| ∴ Cost per 100 kg of output | $(\times \frac{100}{20})$ | $(\times \frac{100}{60})$ | |
|  | = £824 | £412 | |

**19** In standard process costing, all stocks and finished outputs are valued at standard cost.

|  | Material cost | Labour and overhead cost | Total |
|---|---|---|---|
|  | Equivalent units | Equivalent units | |
| Closing work in progress | 670 | (× 70%) 469 | |
| × standard cost per unit | £16 | £18 | |
| = closing work in progress value | £10,720 | £8,442 | £19,162 |

**20** The question states that raw material stocks are issued to production at standard price, therefore the correct debit entry is

$$78,000 \text{ litres} \times £2 \text{ per litre} = £156,000$$

**21** The question states that labour hours are charged to production at standard rate, therefore the correct debit entry is

$$21,000 \text{ hours} \times £5 \text{ per hour} = £105,000$$

## Question

**22** In order to calculate the direct material usage variance, we need to know the equivalent units of material produced, so that we can calculate the standard usage.

|  | Direct material equivalent units |  |
|---|---:|---|
| Completed output | 9,500 |  |
| Closing work in progress | 670 |  |
|  | 10,170 |  |
| *less* Opening work in progress | 170 |  |
| Equivalent units produced | 10,000 |  |
|  |  |  |
| Standard material usage for 10,000 equivalent units @ 8 litres = | 80,000 | litres |
| Actual material usage | 78,000 | litres |
| Material usage variance | 2,000 | litres favourable |
| at standard price per litre | £2 |  |
| = Direct material usage variance in £ | £4,000 | favourable |

The correct double entry for this favourable variance is:

| Debit | Process account | £4,000 |
|---|---|---|
| Credit | Material usage variance account | £4,000 |

**23** In order to calculate the direct labour efficiency variance, we need to know the equivalent units of labour produced, so that we can calculate the standard time allowance.

|  | Direct labour equivalent units |  |
|---|---:|---|
| Completed output | 9,500 |  |
| Closing work in progress (670 x 70%) | 469 |  |
|  | 9,969 |  |
| *less* Opening work in progress (170 x 40%) | 68 |  |
| Equivalent units produced | 9,901 |  |
|  |  |  |
| Standard labour hours for 9,901 equivalent units @ 2 hrs = | 19,802 | hours |
| Actual hours | 21,000 | hours |
| Efficiency variance in hours | 1,198 | hours adverse |
| at standard direct labour rate per hour | £5 |  |
| = Direct labour efficiency variance | £5,990 | adverse |

The correct double entry for this adverse variance is:

| Debit | Labour efficiency variance account | £5,990 |
|---|---|---|
| Credit | Process account | £5,990 |

# Question

**24** The efficiency variance in hours has already been calculated in the previous solution.

| | |
|---|---|
| Efficiency variance in hours | 1,198 hours adverse |
| x Standard production overhead per hour | x £4 |
| = Production overhead efficiency variance | £4,792 adverse |

**25** The problem in this question is that losses occur gradually, so that WIP will have suffered some but not all of its loss already. The opening and closing WIP will have lost different amounts, depending on their degree of completion, and the calculation of equivalent units has to take this into consideration.

The calculations are carried out by "reducing" the material content of work in progress down to the eventual output which will result from the units in WIP.

For instance, the closing WIP is 30% complete. This means that 3% of the eventual good output has already been lost in process, and that a loss of 7% of good output is still to be incurred. (Total loss is 10% of good output.) Therefore, for the closing WIP, the stock is 107/100 of the final output which will result from these units.

We can now calculate the equivalent kilograms of production.

|  | Materials equivalent kg | Processing cost equivalent kg |
|---|---|---|
| Completed output | 45,000 | 45,000 |
| Closing WIP 5,350 x $\frac{100}{107}$ | 5,000 | x 30%  1,500 |
|  | 50,000 | 46,500 |
| less Opening WIP 6,300 x $\frac{100}{105}$ | 6,000 | x 50%  3,000 |
| Equivalent production (kg of eventual good output) | 44,000 | 43,500 |

**26** The standard cost data shows that for every 120 kg input, 100 kg of output is produced. Since losses occur evenly, we have to calculate the expected output that will result from WIP stocks.

- Opening stock is 50% complete, and so for every 120 kg input, loss of 10 kg would have occurred already, and another 10 kg loss is still to come. Therefore, opening stock equals 110/100 of expected output.

- Similarly, closing stock is 70% complete, and so for every 120 kg input, loss of (70% of 20 kg =) 14 kg would have occurred already. The closing stock therefore represents 106/100 of expected output.

*Continued...*

# Question

We can now calculate the equivalent kilograms of production:

|  | Materials kg | Labour and overhead kg |
|---|---|---|
| Closing WIP: 4,240 × $\frac{100}{106}$ | 4,000 | × 70%  2,800 |
| Completed production | 50,000 | 50,000 |
|  | 54,000 | 52,800 |
| less opening WIP: 5,500 × $\frac{100}{110}$ | 5,000 | × 50%  2,500 |
| Equivalent production | 49,000 | 50,300 |

**27** Standard material usage for equivalent production = 49,000 kg × $\frac{120}{100}$

|  |  |
|---|---|
|  | = 58,800 kg |
| Actual usage | 62,000 kg |
|  | 3,200 kg adverse |
| at Standard price per kg | × £3 |
| Direct material usage variance | £9,600 adverse |

**28** Standard labour hours for 50,300 kg of equivalent production =

50,300 × $\frac{40}{100}$ hours = 20,120 hours

| Actual labour hours = | 19,000 hours |
|---|---|
| Efficiency variance in hours | 1,120 hours favourable |
| at standard labour rate per hour | × £4 |
| Direct labour efficiency variance | £4,480 favourable |

**29** Efficiency variance in labour hours calculated in the previous solution =

|  | 1,120 hours favourable |
|---|---|
| at standard overhead rate per hour | × £2 |
| Production overhead efficiency variance | £2,240 favourable |

# DCF TABLES

## Present value of £1

The table shows the value of £1 to be received or paid after a given number of years

$V_{nr} = (1 + r)^{-n}$

| At rate *r*<br>After *n* years | 1% | 2% | 3% | 4% | 5% | 6% | 7% | 8% | 9% | 10% | 11% | 12% |
|---|---|---|---|---|---|---|---|---|---|---|---|---|
| 1  | .99 | .98 | .97 | .96 | .95 | .94 | .93 | .93 | .92 | .91 | .90 | .89 |
| 2  | .98 | .96 | .94 | .92 | .91 | .89 | .87 | .86 | .84 | .83 | .81 | .80 |
| 3  | .97 | .94 | .92 | .89 | .86 | .84 | .82 | .79 | .77 | .75 | .73 | .71 |
| 4  | .96 | .92 | .89 | .85 | .82 | .79 | .76 | .74 | .71 | .68 | .66 | .64 |
| 5  | .95 | .91 | .86 | .82 | .78 | .75 | .71 | .68 | .65 | .62 | .59 | .57 |
| 6  | .94 | .89 | .84 | .79 | .75 | .70 | .67 | .63 | .60 | .56 | .53 | .51 |
| 7  | .93 | .87 | .81 | .76 | .71 | .67 | .62 | .58 | .55 | .51 | .48 | .45 |
| 8  | .92 | .85 | .79 | .73 | .68 | .63 | .58 | .54 | .50 | .47 | .43 | .40 |
| 9  | .91 | .84 | .77 | .70 | .64 | .59 | .54 | .50 | .46 | .42 | .39 | .36 |
| 10 | .91 | .82 | .74 | .68 | .61 | .56 | .51 | .46 | .42 | .39 | .35 | .32 |
| 11 | .90 | .80 | .72 | .65 | .58 | .53 | .48 | .43 | .39 | .35 | .32 | .29 |
| 12 | .89 | .79 | .70 | .62 | .56 | .50 | .44 | .40 | .36 | .32 | .29 | .26 |
| 13 | .88 | .77 | .68 | .60 | .53 | .47 | .41 | .37 | .33 | .29 | .26 | .23 |
| 14 | .87 | .76 | .66 | .58 | .51 | .44 | .39 | .34 | .30 | .26 | .23 | .20 |
| 15 | .86 | .74 | .64 | .56 | .48 | .42 | .36 | .32 | .27 | .24 | .21 | .18 |

| At rate *r*<br>After *n* years | 13% | 14% | 15% | 16% | 17% | 18% | 19% | 20% | 30% | 40% | 50% |
|---|---|---|---|---|---|---|---|---|---|---|---|
| 1  | .88 | .88 | .87 | .86 | .85 | .85 | .84 | .83 | .77 | .71 | .67 |
| 2  | .78 | .77 | .76 | .74 | .73 | .72 | .71 | .69 | .59 | .51 | .44 |
| 3  | .69 | .67 | .66 | .64 | .62 | .61 | .59 | .58 | .46 | .36 | .30 |
| 4  | .61 | .59 | .57 | .55 | .53 | .52 | .50 | .48 | .35 | .26 | .20 |
| 5  | .54 | .52 | .50 | .48 | .46 | .44 | .42 | .40 | .27 | .19 | .13 |
| 6  | .48 | .46 | .43 | .41 | .39 | .37 | .35 | .33 | .21 | .13 | .09 |
| 7  | .43 | .40 | .38 | .35 | .33 | .31 | .30 | .28 | .16 | .09 | .06 |
| 8  | .38 | .35 | .33 | .31 | .28 | .27 | .25 | .23 | .12 | .07 | .04 |
| 9  | .33 | .31 | .28 | .26 | .24 | .23 | .21 | .19 | .09 | .05 | .03 |
| 10 | .29 | .27 | .25 | .23 | .21 | .19 | .18 | .16 | .07 | .03 | .02 |
| 11 | .26 | .24 | .21 | .20 | .18 | .16 | .15 | .13 | .06 | .02 | .01 |
| 12 | .23 | .21 | .19 | .17 | .15 | .14 | .12 | .11 | .04 | .02 | .008 |
| 13 | .20 | .18 | .16 | .15 | .13 | .12 | .10 | .09 | .03 | .013 | .005 |
| 14 | .18 | .16 | .14 | .13 | .11 | .10 | .09 | .08 | .03 | .009 | .003 |
| 15 | .16 | .14 | .12 | .11 | .09 | .08 | .07 | .06 | .02 | .006 | .002 |

## Cumulative present value of £1

The table shows the Present Value of £1 per annum, Receivable or Payable at the end of each year for n years.

| Years | Net Rate of Interest Assumed | | | | | | | | | | | |
|---|---|---|---|---|---|---|---|---|---|---|---|---|
| | 1% | 2% | 3% | 4% | 5% | 6% | 7% | 8% | 9% | 10% | 11% | 12% |
| 1 | .99 | .98 | .97 | .96 | .95 | .94 | .94 | .93 | .92 | .91 | .90 | .89 |
| 2 | 1.97 | 1.94 | 1.91 | 1.89 | 1.86 | 1.83 | 1.81 | 1.78 | 1.76 | 1.74 | 1.71 | 1.69 |
| 3 | 2.94 | 2.88 | 2.83 | 2.78 | 2.72 | 2.67 | 2.62 | 2.58 | 2.53 | 2.49 | 2.44 | 2.40 |
| 4 | 3.90 | 3.81 | 3.72 | 3.63 | 3.55 | 3.47 | 3.39 | 3.31 | 3.24 | 3.17 | 3.10 | 3.04 |
| 5 | 4.85 | 4.71 | 4.58 | 4.45 | 4.33 | 4.21 | 4.10 | 3.99 | 3.89 | 3.79 | 3.70 | 3.61 |
| 6 | 5.80 | 5.60 | 5.42 | 5.24 | 5.08 | 4.92 | 4.77 | 4.62 | 4.49 | 4.36 | 4.23 | 4.11 |
| 7 | 6.73 | 6.47 | 6.23 | 6.00 | 5.79 | 5.58 | 5.39 | 5.21 | 5.03 | 4.87 | 4.71 | 4.56 |
| 8 | 7.65 | 7.33 | 7.02 | 6.73 | 6.46 | 6.21 | 5.97 | 5.75 | 5.54 | 5.34 | 5.15 | 4.97 |
| 9 | 8.57 | 8.16 | 7.79 | 7.44 | 7.11 | 6.80 | 6.52 | 6.25 | 6.00 | 5.76 | 5.54 | 5.33 |
| 10 | 9.47 | 8.98 | 8.53 | 8.11 | 7.72 | 7.36 | 7.02 | 6.71 | 6.42 | 6.15 | 5.89 | 5.65 |
| 11 | 10.37 | 9.79 | 9.25 | 8.76 | 8.31 | 7.89 | 7.50 | 7.14 | 6.81 | 6.50 | 6.21 | 5.94 |
| 12 | 11.26 | 10.58 | 9.95 | 9.39 | 8.86 | 8.38 | 7.94 | 7.54 | 7.16 | 6.81 | 6.49 | 6.19 |
| 13 | 12.13 | 11.35 | 10.64 | 9.99 | 9.39 | 8.85 | 8.36 | 7.90 | 7.49 | 7.10 | 6.80 | 6.42 |
| 14 | 13.00 | 12.11 | 11.30 | 10.56 | 9.90 | 9.30 | 8.75 | 8.24 | 7.79 | 7.37 | 6.98 | 6.63 |
| 15 | 13.87 | 12.85 | 11.94 | 11.12 | 10.38 | 9.71 | 9.11 | 8.56 | 8.06 | 7.61 | 7.19 | 6.81 |

| Years | Net Rate of Interest Assumed | | | | | | | | | | |
|---|---|---|---|---|---|---|---|---|---|---|---|
| | 13% | 14% | 15% | 16% | 17% | 18% | 19% | 20% | 30% | 40% | 50% |
| 1 | .89 | .88 | .87 | .86 | .85 | .85 | .84 | .83 | .77 | .71 | .67 |
| 2 | 1.67 | 1.65 | 1.63 | 1.61 | 1.59 | 1.57 | 1.55 | 1.53 | 1.36 | 1.22 | 1.11 |
| 3 | 2.36 | 2.32 | 2.28 | 2.25 | 2.21 | 2.17 | 2.14 | 2.11 | 1.81 | 1.59 | 1.41 |
| 4 | 2.97 | 2.91 | 2.86 | 2.80 | 2.74 | 2.69 | 2.64 | 2.59 | 2.17 | 1.85 | 1.61 |
| 5 | 3.52 | 3.43 | 3.35 | 3.27 | 3.20 | 3.13 | 3.06 | 2.99 | 2.44 | 2.04 | 1.74 |
| 6 | 4.00 | 3.89 | 3.78 | 3.69 | 3.59 | 3.50 | 3.41 | 3.33 | 2.64 | 2.17 | 1.82 |
| 7 | 4.42 | 4.29 | 4.16 | 4.04 | 3.92 | 3.81 | 3.71 | 3.61 | 2.80 | 2.26 | 1.88 |
| 8 | 4.80 | 4.64 | 4.49 | 4.34 | 4.21 | 4.08 | 3.95 | 3.84 | 2.93 | 2.33 | 1.92 |
| 9 | 5.13 | 4.95 | 4.77 | 4.61 | 4.45 | 4.30 | 4.16 | 4.03 | 3.02 | 2.38 | 1.95 |
| 10 | 5.43 | 5.22 | 5.02 | 4.83 | 4.66 | 4.49 | 4.34 | 4.19 | 3.09 | 2.41 | 1.97 |
| 11 | 5.69 | 5.45 | 5.23 | 5.03 | 4.83 | 4.66 | 4.49 | 4.33 | 3.15 | 2.44 | 1.98 |
| 12 | 5.92 | 5.66 | 5.42 | 5.20 | 4.99 | 4.79 | 4.61 | 4.44 | 3.19 | 2.46 | 1.99 |
| 13 | 6.12 | 5.84 | 5.58 | 5.34 | 5.12 | 4.91 | 4.71 | 4.53 | 3.22 | 2.47 | 1.99 |
| 14 | 6.30 | 6.00 | 5.72 | 5.47 | 5.23 | 5.01 | 4.80 | 4.61 | 3.25 | 2.48 | 1.99 |
| 15 | 6.46 | 6.14 | 5.85 | 5.58 | 5.32 | 5.09 | 4.88 | 4.68 | 3.27 | 2.48 | 2.00 |

# LOGARITHM TABLES

| | 0 | 1 | 2 | 3 | 4 | 5 | 6 | 7 | 8 | 9 | 1 | 2 | 3 | 4 | 5 | 6 | 7 | 8 | 9 |
|---|---|---|---|---|---|---|---|---|---|---|---|---|---|---|---|---|---|---|---|
| 10 | 0000 | 0043 | 0086 | 0128 | 0170 | | 0212 | 0253 | 0294 | 0334 | 4 | 9 | 13 | 17 | 21 | 26 | 30 | 34 | 38 |
| | | | | | | | | | | 0374 | 4 | 8 | 12 | 16 | 20 | 24 | 28 | 32 | 37 |
| 11 | 0414 | 0453 | 0492 | 0531 | 0569 | | 0607 | 0645 | 0682 | 0719 | 4 | 8 | 12 | 15 | 19 | 23 | 27 | 31 | 35 |
| | | | | | | | | | | 0755 | 4 | 7 | 11 | 15 | 19 | 22 | 26 | 30 | 33 |
| 12 | 0792 | 0828 | 0864 | 0899 | 0934 | 0969 | | 1004 | 1038 | 1072 | 3 | 7 | 11 | 14 | 18 | 21 | 25 | 28 | 32 |
| | | | | | | | | | | 1106 | 3 | 7 | 10 | 14 | 17 | 20 | 24 | 27 | 31 |
| 13 | 1139 | 1173 | 1206 | 1239 | 1271 | | 1303 | 1335 | 1367 | 1399 | 3 | 7 | 10 | 13 | 16 | 20 | 23 | 26 | 30 |
| | | | | | | | | | | 1430 | 3 | 7 | 10 | 12 | 16 | 19 | 22 | 25 | 29 |
| 14 | 1461 | 1492 | 1523 | 1553 | | 1584 | 1614 | 1644 | 1673 | 1703 | 3 | 6 | 9 | 12 | 15 | 18 | 21 | 24 | 28 |
| | | | | | | | | | | 1732 | 3 | 6 | 9 | 12 | 15 | 17 | 20 | 23 | 26 |
| 15 | 1761 | 1790 | 1818 | 1847 | 1875 | 1903 | | 1931 | 1959 | 1987 | 3 | 6 | 9 | 11 | 14 | 17 | 20 | 23 | 26 |
| | | | | | | | | | | 2014 | 3 | 5 | 8 | 11 | 14 | 16 | 19 | 22 | 25 |
| 16 | 2041 | 2068 | 2095 | 2122 | 2148 | | 2175 | 2201 | 2227 | 2253 | 3 | 5 | 8 | 11 | 14 | 16 | 19 | 22 | 24 |
| | | | | | | | | | | 2279 | 3 | 5 | 8 | 10 | 13 | 15 | 18 | 21 | 23 |
| 17 | 2304 | 2330 | 2355 | 2380 | 2405 | 2430 | | 2455 | 2480 | 2504 | 3 | 5 | 8 | 10 | 13 | 15 | 18 | 20 | 23 |
| | | | | | | | | | | 2529 | 2 | 5 | 7 | 10 | 12 | 15 | 17 | 19 | 22 |
| 18 | 2553 | 2577 | 2601 | 2625 | 2648 | | 2672 | 2695 | 2718 | 2742 | 2 | 5 | 7 | 9 | 12 | 14 | 16 | 19 | 21 |
| | | | | | | | | | | 2765 | 2 | 5 | 7 | 9 | 11 | 14 | 16 | 18 | 21 |
| 19 | 2788 | 2810 | 2833 | 2856 | 2878 | | 2900 | 2923 | 2945 | 2967 | 2 | 4 | 7 | 9 | 11 | 13 | 16 | 18 | 20 |
| | | | | | | | | | | 2989 | 2 | 4 | 6 | 8 | 11 | 13 | 15 | 17 | 19 |
| 20 | 3010 | 3032 | 3054 | 3075 | 3096 | 3118 | 3139 | 3160 | 3181 | 3201 | 2 | 4 | 6 | 8 | 11 | 13 | 15 | 17 | 19 |
| 21 | 3222 | 3243 | 3263 | 3284 | 3304 | 3324 | 3345 | 3365 | 3385 | 3404 | 2 | 4 | 6 | 8 | 10 | 12 | 14 | 16 | 18 |
| 22 | 3424 | 3444 | 3464 | 3483 | 3502 | 3522 | 3541 | 3560 | 3579 | 3598 | 2 | 4 | 6 | 8 | 10 | 12 | 14 | 15 | 17 |
| 23 | 3617 | 3636 | 3655 | 3674 | 3692 | 3711 | 3729 | 3747 | 3766 | 3784 | 2 | 4 | 6 | 7 | 9 | 11 | 13 | 15 | 17 |
| 24 | 3802 | 3820 | 3838 | 3856 | 3874 | 3892 | 3909 | 3927 | 3945 | 3962 | 2 | 4 | 5 | 7 | 9 | 11 | 12 | 14 | 16 |
| 25 | 3979 | 3997 | 4014 | 4031 | 4048 | 4065 | 4082 | 4099 | 4116 | 4133 | 2 | 3 | 5 | 7 | 9 | 10 | 12 | 14 | 15 |
| 26 | 4150 | 4166 | 4183 | 4200 | 4216 | 4232 | 4249 | 4265 | 4281 | 4298 | 2 | 3 | 5 | 7 | 8 | 10 | 11 | 13 | 15 |
| 27 | 4314 | 4330 | 4346 | 4362 | 4378 | 4393 | 4409 | 4425 | 4440 | 4456 | 2 | 3 | 5 | 6 | 8 | 9 | 11 | 13 | 14 |
| 28 | 4472 | 4487 | 4502 | 4518 | 4533 | 4548 | 4564 | 4579 | 4594 | 4609 | 2 | 3 | 5 | 6 | 8 | 9 | 11 | 12 | 14 |
| 29 | 4624 | 4639 | 4654 | 4669 | 4683 | 4698 | 4713 | 4728 | 4742 | 4757 | 1 | 3 | 4 | 6 | 7 | 9 | 10 | 12 | 13 |
| 30 | 4771 | 4786 | 4800 | 4814 | 4829 | 4843 | 4857 | 4871 | 4886 | 4900 | 1 | 3 | 4 | 6 | 7 | 9 | 10 | 11 | 13 |
| 31 | 4914 | 4928 | 4942 | 4955 | 4969 | 4983 | 4997 | 5011 | 5024 | 5038 | 1 | 3 | 4 | 6 | 7 | 8 | 10 | 11 | 12 |
| 32 | 5051 | 5065 | 5079 | 5092 | 5105 | 5119 | 5132 | 5145 | 5159 | 5172 | 1 | 3 | 4 | 5 | 7 | 8 | 9 | 11 | 12 |
| 33 | 5185 | 5198 | 5211 | 5224 | 5237 | 5250 | 5263 | 5276 | 5289 | 5302 | 1 | 3 | 4 | 5 | 6 | 8 | 9 | 10 | 12 |
| 34 | 5315 | 5328 | 5340 | 5353 | 5366 | 5378 | 5391 | 5403 | 5416 | 5428 | 1 | 3 | 4 | 5 | 6 | 8 | 9 | 10 | 11 |
| 35 | 5441 | 5453 | 5465 | 5478 | 5490 | 5502 | 5514 | 5527 | 5539 | 5551 | 1 | 2 | 4 | 5 | 6 | 7 | 9 | 10 | 11 |
| 36 | 5563 | 5575 | 5587 | 5599 | 5611 | 5623 | 5635 | 5647 | 5658 | 5670 | 1 | 2 | 4 | 5 | 6 | 7 | 8 | 10 | 11 |
| 37 | 5682 | 5694 | 5705 | 5717 | 5729 | 5740 | 5752 | 5763 | 5775 | 5786 | 1 | 2 | 3 | 5 | 6 | 7 | 8 | 9 | 10 |
| 38 | 5798 | 5809 | 5821 | 5832 | 5843 | 5855 | 5866 | 5877 | 5888 | 5899 | 1 | 2 | 3 | 5 | 6 | 7 | 8 | 9 | 10 |
| 39 | 5911 | 5922 | 5933 | 5944 | 5955 | 5966 | 5977 | 5988 | 5999 | 6010 | 1 | 2 | 3 | 4 | 5 | 7 | 8 | 9 | 10 |
| 40 | 6021 | 6031 | 6042 | 6053 | 6064 | 6075 | 6085 | 6096 | 6107 | 6117 | 1 | 2 | 3 | 4 | 5 | 6 | 8 | 9 | 10 |
| 41 | 6128 | 6138 | 6149 | 6160 | 6170 | 6180 | 6191 | 6201 | 6212 | 6222 | 1 | 2 | 3 | 4 | 5 | 6 | 7 | 8 | 9 |
| 42 | 6232 | 6243 | 6253 | 6263 | 6274 | 6284 | 6294 | 6304 | 6314 | 6325 | 1 | 2 | 3 | 4 | 5 | 6 | 7 | 8 | 9 |
| 43 | 6335 | 6345 | 6355 | 6365 | 6375 | 6385 | 6395 | 6405 | 6415 | 6425 | 1 | 2 | 3 | 4 | 5 | 6 | 7 | 8 | 9 |
| 44 | 6435 | 6444 | 6454 | 6464 | 6474 | 6484 | 6493 | 6503 | 6513 | 6522 | 1 | 2 | 3 | 4 | 5 | 6 | 7 | 8 | 9 |
| 45 | 6532 | 6542 | 6551 | 6561 | 6571 | 6580 | 6590 | 6599 | 6609 | 6618 | 1 | 2 | 3 | 4 | 5 | 6 | 7 | 8 | 9 |
| 46 | 6628 | 6637 | 6646 | 6656 | 6665 | 6675 | 6684 | 6693 | 6702 | 6712 | 1 | 2 | 3 | 4 | 5 | 6 | 7 | 7 | 8 |
| 47 | 6721 | 6730 | 6739 | 6749 | 6758 | 6767 | 6776 | 6785 | 6794 | 6803 | 1 | 2 | 3 | 4 | 5 | 5 | 6 | 7 | 8 |
| 48 | 6812 | 6821 | 6830 | 6839 | 6848 | 6857 | 6866 | 6875 | 6884 | 6893 | 1 | 2 | 3 | 4 | 4 | 5 | 6 | 7 | 8 |
| 49 | 6902 | 6911 | 6920 | 6928 | 6937 | 6946 | 6955 | 6964 | 6972 | 6981 | 1 | 2 | 3 | 4 | 5 | 6 | 7 | 8 | 8 |

## LOGARITHM TABLES

|    | 0 | 1 | 2 | 3 | 4 | 5 | 6 | 7 | 8 | 9 | 1 | 2 | 3 | 4 | 5 | 6 | 7 | 8 | 9 |
|----|---|---|---|---|---|---|---|---|---|---|---|---|---|---|---|---|---|---|---|
| 50 | 6990 | 6998 | 7007 | 7016 | 7024 | 7033 | 7042 | 7050 | 7059 | 7067 | 1 | 2 | 3 | 3 | 4 | 5 | 6 | 7 | 8 |
| 51 | 7076 | 7084 | 7093 | 7101 | 7110 | 7118 | 7126 | 7135 | 7143 | 7152 | 1 | 2 | 3 | 3 | 4 | 5 | 6 | 7 | 8 |
| 52 | 7160 | 7168 | 7177 | 7185 | 7193 | 7202 | 7210 | 7218 | 7226 | 7235 | 1 | 2 | 2 | 3 | 4 | 5 | 6 | 7 | 7 |
| 53 | 7243 | 7251 | 7259 | 7267 | 7275 | 7284 | 7292 | 7300 | 7308 | 7316 | 1 | 2 | 2 | 3 | 4 | 5 | 6 | 6 | 7 |
| 54 | 7324 | 7332 | 7340 | 7348 | 7356 | 7364 | 7372 | 7380 | 7388 | 7396 | 1 | 2 | 2 | 3 | 4 | 5 | 6 | 6 | 7 |
| 55 | 7404 | 7412 | 7419 | 7427 | 7435 | 7443 | 7451 | 7459 | 7466 | 7474 | 1 | 2 | 2 | 3 | 4 | 5 | 5 | 6 | 7 |
| 56 | 7482 | 7490 | 7497 | 7505 | 7513 | 7520 | 7528 | 7536 | 7543 | 7551 | 1 | 2 | 2 | 3 | 4 | 5 | 5 | 6 | 7 |
| 57 | 7559 | 7566 | 7574 | 7582 | 7589 | 7597 | 7604 | 7612 | 7619 | 7627 | 1 | 2 | 2 | 3 | 4 | 5 | 5 | 6 | 7 |
| 58 | 7634 | 7642 | 7649 | 7657 | 7664 | 7672 | 7679 | 7686 | 7694 | 7701 | 1 | 1 | 2 | 3 | 4 | 4 | 5 | 6 | 7 |
| 59 | 7709 | 7716 | 7723 | 7731 | 7738 | 7745 | 7752 | 7760 | 7767 | 7774 | 1 | 1 | 2 | 3 | 4 | 4 | 5 | 6 | 7 |
| 60 | 7782 | 7789 | 7796 | 7803 | 7810 | 7818 | 7825 | 7832 | 7839 | 7846 | 1 | 1 | 2 | 3 | 4 | 4 | 5 | 6 | 6 |
| 61 | 7853 | 7860 | 7868 | 7875 | 7882 | 7889 | 7896 | 7903 | 7910 | 7917 | 1 | 1 | 2 | 3 | 4 | 4 | 5 | 6 | 6 |
| 62 | 7924 | 7931 | 7938 | 7945 | 7952 | 7959 | 7966 | 7973 | 7980 | 7987 | 1 | 1 | 2 | 3 | 3 | 4 | 5 | 6 | 6 |
| 63 | 7993 | 8000 | 8007 | 8014 | 8021 | 8028 | 8035 | 8041 | 8048 | 8055 | 1 | 1 | 2 | 3 | 3 | 4 | 5 | 5 | 6 |
| 64 | 8062 | 8069 | 8075 | 8082 | 8089 | 8096 | 8102 | 8109 | 8116 | 8122 | 1 | 1 | 2 | 3 | 3 | 4 | 5 | 5 | 6 |
| 65 | 8129 | 8136 | 8142 | 8149 | 8156 | 8162 | 8169 | 8176 | 8182 | 8189 | 1 | 1 | 2 | 3 | 3 | 4 | 5 | 5 | 6 |
| 66 | 8195 | 8202 | 8209 | 8215 | 8222 | 8228 | 8235 | 8241 | 8248 | 8254 | 1 | 1 | 2 | 3 | 3 | 4 | 5 | 5 | 6 |
| 67 | 8261 | 8267 | 8274 | 8280 | 8287 | 8293 | 8299 | 8306 | 8312 | 8319 | 1 | 1 | 2 | 3 | 3 | 4 | 5 | 5 | 6 |
| 68 | 8325 | 8331 | 8338 | 8344 | 8351 | 8357 | 8363 | 8370 | 8376 | 8382 | 1 | 1 | 2 | 3 | 3 | 4 | 4 | 5 | 6 |
| 69 | 8388 | 8395 | 8401 | 8407 | 8414 | 8420 | 8426 | 8432 | 8439 | 8445 | 1 | 1 | 2 | 2 | 3 | 4 | 4 | 5 | 6 |
| 70 | 8451 | 8457 | 8463 | 8470 | 8476 | 8482 | 8488 | 8494 | 8500 | 8506 | 1 | 1 | 2 | 2 | 3 | 4 | 4 | 5 | 6 |
| 71 | 8513 | 8519 | 8525 | 8531 | 8537 | 8543 | 8549 | 8555 | 8561 | 8567 | 1 | 1 | 2 | 2 | 3 | 4 | 4 | 5 | 5 |
| 72 | 8573 | 8579 | 8585 | 8591 | 8597 | 8603 | 8609 | 8615 | 8621 | 8627 | 1 | 1 | 2 | 2 | 3 | 4 | 4 | 5 | 5 |
| 73 | 8633 | 8639 | 8645 | 8651 | 8657 | 8663 | 8669 | 8675 | 8681 | 8686 | 1 | 1 | 2 | 2 | 3 | 4 | 4 | 5 | 5 |
| 74 | 8692 | 8698 | 8704 | 8710 | 8716 | 8722 | 8727 | 8733 | 8739 | 8745 | 1 | 1 | 2 | 2 | 3 | 4 | 4 | 5 | 5 |
| 75 | 8751 | 8756 | 8762 | 8768 | 8774 | 8779 | 8785 | 8791 | 8797 | 8802 | 1 | 1 | 2 | 2 | 3 | 3 | 4 | 5 | 5 |
| 76 | 8808 | 8814 | 8820 | 8825 | 8831 | 8837 | 8842 | 8848 | 8854 | 8859 | 1 | 1 | 2 | 2 | 3 | 3 | 4 | 5 | 5 |
| 77 | 8865 | 8871 | 8876 | 8882 | 8887 | 8893 | 8899 | 8904 | 8910 | 8915 | 1 | 1 | 2 | 2 | 3 | 3 | 4 | 4 | 5 |
| 78 | 8921 | 8927 | 8932 | 8938 | 8943 | 8949 | 8954 | 8960 | 8965 | 8971 | 1 | 1 | 2 | 2 | 3 | 3 | 4 | 4 | 5 |
| 79 | 8976 | 8982 | 8987 | 8993 | 8998 | 9004 | 9009 | 9015 | 9020 | 9025 | 1 | 1 | 2 | 2 | 3 | 3 | 4 | 4 | 5 |
| 80 | 9031 | 9036 | 9042 | 9047 | 9053 | 9058 | 9063 | 9069 | 9074 | 9079 | 1 | 1 | 2 | 2 | 3 | 3 | 4 | 4 | 5 |
| 81 | 9085 | 9090 | 9096 | 9101 | 9106 | 9112 | 9117 | 9122 | 9128 | 9133 | 1 | 1 | 2 | 2 | 3 | 3 | 4 | 4 | 5 |
| 82 | 9138 | 9143 | 9149 | 9154 | 9159 | 9165 | 9170 | 9175 | 9180 | 9186 | 1 | 1 | 2 | 2 | 3 | 3 | 4 | 4 | 5 |
| 83 | 9191 | 9196 | 9201 | 9206 | 9212 | 9217 | 9222 | 9227 | 9232 | 9238 | 1 | 1 | 2 | 2 | 3 | 3 | 4 | 4 | 5 |
| 84 | 9243 | 9248 | 9253 | 9258 | 9263 | 9269 | 9274 | 9279 | 9284 | 9289 | 1 | 1 | 2 | 2 | 3 | 3 | 4 | 4 | 5 |
| 85 | 9294 | 9299 | 9304 | 9309 | 9315 | 9320 | 9325 | 9330 | 9335 | 9340 | 1 | 1 | 2 | 2 | 3 | 3 | 4 | 4 | 5 |
| 86 | 9345 | 9350 | 9355 | 9360 | 9365 | 9370 | 9375 | 9380 | 9385 | 9390 | 1 | 1 | 2 | 2 | 3 | 3 | 4 | 4 | 5 |
| 87 | 9395 | 9400 | 9405 | 9410 | 9415 | 9420 | 9425 | 9430 | 9435 | 9440 | 0 | 1 | 1 | 2 | 2 | 3 | 3 | 4 | 4 |
| 88 | 9445 | 9450 | 9455 | 9460 | 9465 | 9469 | 9474 | 9479 | 9484 | 9489 | 0 | 1 | 1 | 2 | 2 | 3 | 3 | 4 | 4 |
| 89 | 9494 | 9499 | 9504 | 9509 | 9513 | 9518 | 9523 | 9528 | 9533 | 9538 | 0 | 1 | 1 | 2 | 2 | 3 | 3 | 4 | 4 |
| 90 | 9542 | 9547 | 9552 | 9557 | 9562 | 9566 | 9571 | 9576 | 9581 | 9586 | 0 | 1 | 1 | 2 | 2 | 3 | 3 | 4 | 4 |
| 91 | 9590 | 9595 | 9600 | 9605 | 9609 | 9614 | 9619 | 9624 | 9628 | 9633 | 0 | 1 | 1 | 2 | 2 | 3 | 3 | 4 | 4 |
| 92 | 9638 | 9643 | 9647 | 9652 | 9657 | 9661 | 9666 | 9671 | 9675 | 9680 | 0 | 1 | 1 | 2 | 2 | 3 | 3 | 4 | 4 |
| 93 | 9685 | 9689 | 9694 | 9699 | 9703 | 9708 | 9713 | 9717 | 9722 | 9727 | 0 | 1 | 1 | 2 | 2 | 3 | 3 | 4 | 4 |
| 94 | 9731 | 9736 | 9741 | 9745 | 9750 | 9754 | 9759 | 9763 | 9768 | 9773 | 0 | 1 | 1 | 2 | 2 | 3 | 3 | 4 | 4 |
| 95 | 9777 | 9782 | 9786 | 9791 | 9795 | 9800 | 9805 | 9809 | 9814 | 9818 | 0 | 1 | 1 | 2 | 2 | 3 | 3 | 4 | 4 |
| 96 | 9823 | 9827 | 9832 | 9836 | 9841 | 9845 | 9850 | 9854 | 9859 | 9863 | 0 | 1 | 1 | 2 | 2 | 3 | 3 | 4 | 4 |
| 97 | 9868 | 9872 | 9877 | 9881 | 9886 | 9890 | 9894 | 9899 | 9903 | 9908 | 0 | 1 | 1 | 2 | 2 | 3 | 3 | 4 | 4 |
| 98 | 9912 | 9917 | 9921 | 9926 | 9930 | 9934 | 9939 | 9943 | 9948 | 9952 | 0 | 1 | 1 | 2 | 2 | 3 | 3 | 4 | 4 |
| 99 | 9956 | 9961 | 9965 | 9969 | 9974 | 9978 | 9983 | 9987 | 9991 | 9996 | 0 | 1 | 1 | 2 | 2 | 3 | 3 | 3 | 4 |

**Further information**

The Password series includes the following titles:

*Order code*

| | | |
|---|---|---|
| Economics | P01X | EC |
| Basic accounting | P028 | BA |
| Financial accounting | P036 | FA |
| Costing | P044 | CO |
| Foundation business mathematics | P052 | FB |
| Business law | P060 | BL |
| Auditing | P079 | AU |
| Organisation and management | P087 | OM |
| Advanced business mathematics | P095 | AB |
| Taxation | P109 | TX |
| Management accounting | P117 | MA |
| Interpretation of accounts | P125 | IA |
| Financial management | P133 | FM |
| Company law | P141 | CL |
| Information technology | P15X | IT |

Password is available from most major bookshops. If you have any difficulty obtaining them, please contact BPP directly, quoting the above order codes.

BPP Publishing Limited
Aldine Place
142/144 Uxbridge Road
London W12 8AA

Tel:  01-740 1111
Fax:  01-740 1184
Telex: 265871 (MONREF G) - quoting '76:SJJ098'